Born in Texas in 1917, William Ash worked his way through school and college during the Great Depression, graduating from the University of Texas, Austin. At the outbreak of war in Europe he rode the rails to Canada and enlisted in the Royal Canadian Air Force. A Spitfire pilot, he saw action with 411 Squadron. Shot down over France in March 1942, he was eventually captured and sent to a succession of POW camps, from which he escaped or attempted to escape on a regular basis. At war's end, he was awarded an MBE for his escaping activities. After gaining a further degree at Balliol College, Oxford, Bill worked for the BBC in India, then as a producer for BBC Radio Drama. A writer and journalist, he is also past president of the Writers' Guild. Married to the academic Ranjana Ash, he lives in London.

Brendan Foley grew up in Belfast and now divides his time between London and Santa Monica. An award-winning features journalist, he ran a successful communications consultancy and now writes full-time, including fiction, biography and screenplays. His first feature film is currently in pre-production with Affinity Films International.

Brendan first met Bill Ash in the 1980s. Inspired by the former pilot's life, he wrote a screenplay of his wartime adventures, then encouraged Bill to tell his story to a wider audience, through *Under the Wire*.

Praise for *Under the Wire*

'An astonishing tale – totally spellbinding . . . Perhaps his greatest achievement was to emerge from the horrors of the war with his faith in ordinary people enhanced. That's the real heroism of the man, and of the book'
Alan Plater

'A story of bravery in the face of brutality, of comradeship, of a never-say-die attitude; and running through it is a sense of humour that cheers up the grimmest situation' *The Times*

'A great read – a powerful and moving wartime story of adventure, humour, heroism and hardship' Jim Corrigal

www.**booksattransworld**.co.uk

'Bill Ash has led a life of adventure that will inspire, astonish, and sometimes even amuse . . . readers who like stories of wild and magnificent adventure are going to love this book!'
Homer Hickam, author of *Rocket Boys*

'His exploits may well have provided the inspiration for Steve McQueen's iconic role in *The Great Escape* . . . Sixty years on, that inspiration is still undimmed' *Yorkshire Evening Post*

'A remarkable story of one man's refusal to give in to his captors, brilliantly told and with all the authentic sights, sounds and smells of the World War II prison camp' Tony Rennell, co-author of *The Last Escape*

'A real page-turner . . . this is not just an autobiography for those interested in Second World War memoirs, but for anyone who is interested in adventure and the human spirit . . . A wonderful story, wonderfully told'
Julia Strong

'Well-written and exciting . . . packed with incident and vividly recreates the oft-neglected early days of Stalag Luft III . . . It also makes a refreshing change to read a memoir by someone who is politically literate and knew exactly what he was fighting against and what he was fighting for. There are passages in this book . . . that make the reader want to stand up and cheer'
Charles Rollings, author of *Wire and Walls*

'One of the greatest escapers of all time . . . An extraordinary adventure, full of humour and daring, one man's war against the Nazis, and a book well worth waiting sixty years for' *Oxford Times*

'Everything I would expect from a memoir by Bill Ash – fast-paced, exciting and moving, but also coloured by his mischievous sense of humour. He has a real gift as a storyteller . . . He endured a lot, but never lost his essential humanity and zest for life, something that comes through very strongly in his book . . . a joy to read' Jonathan Vance, author of *A Gallant Company*

'An amazing story' *Yorkshire Post*

'Thoughtful, deep and poignant . . . Ash has a humour and insightfulness that adds to the history. His book is a testament to man's deep-seated yearning to be free' Robert Wilcox, author of *Scream of Eagles*

'He tells his story with humour and lightness of touch' *Wales on Sunday*

UNDER THE WIRE

The wartime memoir of a
Spitfire pilot, legendary escape artist
and 'cooler king'

WILLIAM ASH
with Brendan Foley

BANTAM BOOKS

LONDON • TORONTO • SYDNEY • AUCKLAND • JOHANNESBURG

UNDER THE WIRE
A BANTAM BOOK : 9780553817119

Originally published in Great Britain by Bantam Press,
a division of Transworld Publishers

PRINTING HISTORY
Bantam Press edition published 2005
Bantam edition published 2006

5 7 9 10 8 6

Set in 12/15pt Times by
Falcon Oast Graphic Art Ltd.

Bantam Books are published by Transworld Publishers,
61–63 Uxbridge Road, London W5 5SA,
a division of The Random House Group Ltd.

Addresses for Random House Group Ltd companies outside the UK
can be found at: www.randomhouse.co.uk
The Random House Group Ltd Reg. No. 954009.

Printed and bound in Great Britain by
Cox & Wyman Ltd, Reading, Berkshire.

The Random House Group Limited makes every effort to ensure that the
papers used in its books are made from trees that have been legally
sourced from well-managed and credibly certified forests. Our paper
procurement policy can be found at: www.randomhouse.co.uk/paper.htm.

Mixed Sources
Product group from well-managed
forests and other controlled sources
www.fsc.org Cert no. TT-COC-2139
© 1996 Forest Stewardship Council
FSC

From Bill to Ranjana
and Brendan to Shelly

all mary

Feb 2008

Contents

Foreword

In a modern world in which heroes are generally either non-existent or else two-dimensional media fabrications, there is an understandable search for something or someone better. In many years of covering feature stories on subjects ranging from banking to bomb disposal, I have only ever met one genuine hero, and that is Bill Ash.

Bill would laugh at such an idea, but then he is one of those rare individuals who can find something funny in any situation. He even managed a smile through broken teeth when he was being beaten by the Gestapo in Paris, answering their demand to betray 'just one name' of those who had helped him by offering up the name of his French teacher back in Austin, Texas.

His ability to laugh at himself in the middle of wartime life-or-death situations runs through all his adventures like a watermark of honesty. Yet Bill is not just the master of seeing the funny side. His humour in the face of the carnage and cruelty of the Second World War is simply the most obvious and constant reminder of something bigger – the sense of shared humanity that brought him into the war while his country was still neutral.

Bill's instinct to defend those less capable of defending themselves seems to have been present almost from birth, just like his fascination for escaping. What started with battles against playground bullies in Depression-hit Texas ended in his volunteering to fight possibly the greatest bully of all time – Adolf Hitler. He is a modern Huck Finn, transplanted from the Mississippi to occupied Europe, his raft replaced by a Spitfire.

In wartime Britain, Bill stood out among the fearless but mainly upper-class young Englishmen who risked their lives as fighter pilots. By contrast, he was a constantly hungry, resourceful American son of the Great Depression, fighting on his own terms, even though doing so cost him his citizenship. His position as an outsider gave him a unique perspective. He witnessed the bravery of French Resistance members first hand as they tried to keep him from capture, but when the Gestapo finally seized him, he had a chance to see the darker side of humanity. Bill claims he organized his war badly: if he had started off in the hands of the Gestapo, he would have been a bit clearer about why he was there in the first place.

His mix of grit, humour and humanity make his story unique, illuminating world events through small, person-sized adventures. Through his eyes, we share the feelings of 1930s America as it teetered on the brink of war, and understand in a far more profound way than we would through any dry history book how the Nazis were stopped, and just who defeated them.

While most prisoners of war would assist others' escape attempts, only a minority risked death as active escapees. Fewer still became serial escapologists like Bill. Most did not live to tell their stories, and those who did paid a high price. The fictional American pilot played by Steve McQueen in the film *The Great Escape* captured the imagination of millions. Bill Ash is one of the few real-life 'Cooler Kings' of the war, fact rather than fiction. Each time he was released from solitary confinement, he would restart his escape activity within days, sometimes within hours, burrowing under the wire in a tunnel, through it with cutters or vaulting over it to freedom like some ungainly flightless bird.

Bill's one-man war touched the lives of hundreds, from Depression-hit America to flight training in Canada to Blitz-hit London, the skies over occupied Europe and the streets of Paris. As an escapee he moved through France, Germany, Poland and Lithuania like a roadrunner with an unknown destination. As his incredible wartime journey evolved, he realized that his own instinct for freedom was simply an articulation of a desire felt by millions; and his own unique war, whether in the air or on the run, was a microcosm of the world's most terrible conflict.

His last challenge was an attempt to escape from a raging battlefield just weeks before the fall of the Third Reich. To have survived so much and yet be willing to risk his life in the dying days of the war, partly to save sick and injured comrades and partly just for the hell of it, says something special about Bill. To me, it says he is that rarest of things, a good friend and a genuine hero.

Brendan Foley
London, 2005

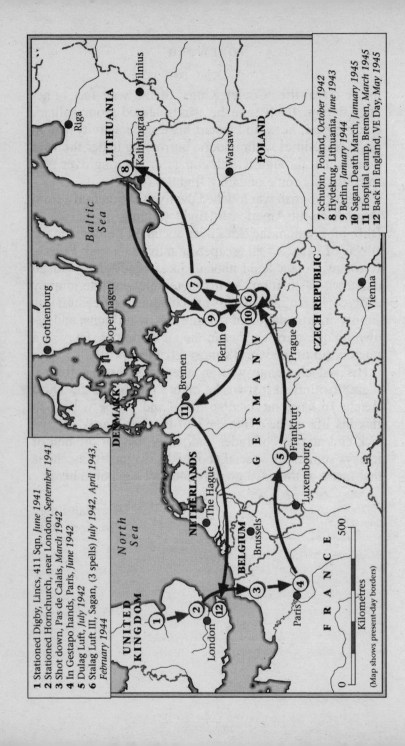

1 Stationed Digby, Lincs, 411 Sqn, *June 1941*
2 Stationed Hornchurch, near London, *September 1941*
3 Shot down, Pas de Calais, *March 1942*
4 In Gestapo hands, Paris, *June 1942*
5 Dulag Luft, *July 1942*
6 Stalag Luft III, Sagan, (3 spells) *July 1942, April 1943, February 1944*

7 Schubin, Poland, *October 1942*
8 Hydekrug, Lithuania, *June 1943*
9 Berlin, *January 1944*
10 Sagan Death March, *January 1945*
11 Hospital camp, Bremen, *March 1945*
12 Back in England, VE Day, *May 1945*

(Map shows present-day borders)

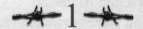

An Apprenticeship in Escapology

More than sixty years ago in March 1942, I was a young warrior – a rare creature in the form of an American Spitfire pilot, flying a magnificent, gleaming machine in the skies over occupied France. I had joined up to fight the Nazis while America was still neutral. That action had cost me my citizenship and in an ill-considered burst of gratitude, the British had put me in charge of a Spitfire.

A Spitfire cockpit is small. It smells of metal and leather, of raw horsepower and excitement. Once in the sky a Spitfire pilot is alone, a hunter, an acrobat and a king. The only trouble in my case was that the king was about to be beheaded.

I looked down at a small French village, looming closer by the second. Then I looked up at half-a-dozen enemy aircraft, Focke-Wulf 190s and ME 109s, circling and taking leisurely turns in trying to blow me out of the sky. For the first time, I began to wonder if the British were about to regret entrusting me with their splendid flying machine. My plane was shot up. My gun button was jammed and useless. I had just switched off my coughing engine, which was full of cannon holes and threatening to burst into flames.

As the Luftwaffe planes roared in for the kill I turned to face them, minimizing myself as a target, and stared directly into their cannon fire. I knew that it was time to end one career, as a Spitfire pilot, and to start a new one. My career choices were limited – I could become a prisoner, an escape artist or a corpse. How, I asked myself as I looked for a field in which to crash-land, did an American, flying for the Canadians, fighting for the British, come to be blown out of the sky by a German, somewhere over France?

People seeking an answer to that question, or those who know a bit about my first wartime career as a Spitfire pilot and my second rather longer stint as a prisoner of war and escape artist, sometimes ask me about my early life. They are apparently looking for clues as to why a young American would go halfway across the world to fight for the British against the Nazis while the United States was still staunchly neutral. Sometimes they also ask me if there was anything in my childhood in Depression-hit Texas that pointed me towards a career as an unlikely escapologist on what turned out to be a some-what bumpy unauthorized tour of occupied Europe. To them, and to you, all I can say is that from my earliest memories I have always disliked bullies and, from just as early, I have always loved running away.

I was born in 1917, at about the same time as the Russian Revolution, but into the slightly less tempestuous world of Dallas, Texas. My father was into ladies' hats. Not that he wore them himself: rather he was a travelling hat salesman, though for all the hats he sold he might as well have worn them himself. He was the quietest, gentlest soul you could imagine in the toughest, most brutal of professions. He had a great baritone voice and used to sing while my mother accompanied him on the piano, until several stern-faced men turned up at our house one day and repossessed it. My father was also a very talented artist who would spend his evenings quietly sketching or with his head buried in a newspaper, but the 1920s and '30s were tough times in which people made their living in any way they could, rather than thinking much about what they would like to do. In another time and place my father's creativity would have taken him far, but as it was it took every bit of his fortitude and optimism to face a world of flinty-faced shop owners who would greet him or any salesman clutching his cherished samples with a cheery 'Whadda you bringing that crap in here for?'

My formative years were a succession of ups and downs dictated by the precarious fortunes of my father's work. We moved from place to place, usually to a smaller cheaper apartment as times got tough, not so much white collar as frayed collar. Our family car – upon which my father's job and our ability to eat depended – was just as changeable. He was always having it carted away when he could not keep up with the payments, like a cavalry-man having his horse shot from under him during a rout. Just as changeable as my address and my father's mode of transport was the school I attended, as we moved about to stay one step ahead of the rent collector.

I attended numerous grammar schools, mostly in the poorer, rougher parts of Dallas, and being a newcomer on a regular basis led to what seemed like an endless string of fights and schoolyard battles. I've never liked fighting, but despite my passion for running away from places, I've always been stubborn about not running away from battles.

At James Bowie School, when I was about six, I remember that the local kids had found a better amuse-ment than beating each other up. They would force two smaller kids to fight and bet on the outcome. A gang of boys, so big and sophisticated that they must have been all of eight years old, had captured my friend George and were holding him like a victim destined for human sacrifice. Two other big boys grabbed me and told me that I could easily beat my friend. Even then I was quite a tough little soul, with a wiry build that later enabled me to be quite a handy boxer. I had a tuft of hair that stood up as if it was looking for a fight even if I wasn't. To impress on me the point that my victory was assured, they said that if I lost the fight they would batter me as well. As a crowd formed, the boys held us from behind like fighting cocks, urging us to hammer each other while they placed massive wagers of pennies and bubble gum on the outcome.

Then something strange happened. George looked over at me and burst into tears. A red mist came down on me at the thought of those bigger boys bullying my friend and when we were released like reluctant gladiators, instead of charging at George I made a beeline for one of his bigger tormentors and belted him on the jaw. George turned around and started in on another of them. I'd like to say that we polished off the lot of them, but life, as I was to rediscover during the war, is not like that. Still, we did shut down the tote for the day.

My mother regarded such events as occupational hazards of boyhood, and was determined that her son would rise to become President of the United States at the very least. She was a handsome, determined woman who diverted all her exasperation at her easy-going husband's lack of success into an attempt to propel her only son into the financial stratosphere.

Perhaps that's why I can never remember a time after I was old enough to walk that I did not have at least one job. When I was hardly past the toddling stage and certainly could not read, I was selling magazine sub-scriptions door to door, egged on by free gifts for the best salesperson such as tiny paper-tissue model airships, which were in vogue in the 1920s, just like the real thing. Unfortunately, like their larger counterparts, when the toys were filled with hot air, they had a propensity to burst into flames, a fact that crept back into my mind many years later as I was being shot from the sky in my sputtering Spitfire over northern France.

Dallas in the 1920s and '30s was a tough, boisterous town with one foot already heading for its oily boom-town future, but the other one stuck firmly in its Western past. Just down the road, Fort Worth was even more of a cattle town and I grew up in the noisy cross-roads between an ever-changing city landscape and the changeless scenes of the old West.

Not that Dallas would have thanked you for reminding it of the Wild West. It was hurrying into the future for better or worse. A few years before I was born there was a huge flood that killed several people and destroyed millions of dollars' worth of property in the town, and the good burghers of Dallas decided it was a good excuse for a new town plan. The following decades saw new build-ings, parks and hundreds of small companies emerging, many of them linked to the oil business that was just start-ing to take off in the surrounding areas of Texas. Things were so speeded up that living there felt a little like being in one of the silent Buster Keaton movies of the time. Other businesses were turning from local stores into national institutions, such as Nieman Marcus, whose first store was doing booming business in downtown Dallas, or the 7–11 chain that started life in the city in 1922. I added the role of shelf-stacker to my childhood résumé.

Perhaps it was to escape the endless array of jobs and

chores, sandwiched between our precarious domestic existence and the non-stop battles in ever-changing school yards, that somewhere along the way I developed a taste for running away from home in search of adventure. I had been inclined to wander off from the earliest time I can remember, but by the age of seven or eight this had evolved into fully fledged escapes.

At about that age I was walking to school one day when I decided to just keep walking, past the school and all the way out of town to the road that led to Fort Worth. Once on the road, I flagged down a passing model T Ford and explained that I had to reach my parents who were gravely ill in Fort Worth. The driver peered at me and asked me which parent was ill. I told him both of them, and confided that I suspected food poisoning. Just as he was getting justifiably suspicious, I produced an envelope addressed to a hat factory in Fort Worth and ordered him to make haste to their place of employment. It seemed good enough for the driver and we zoomed out of town. The envelope was one of hundreds my father would send looking for work, but in those tough times he might as well have saved the stamp, and as it turned out he did, for his young son thoughtfully delivered it by hand.

When we reached the Fort Worth hat factory, I thanked the driver, walked in the front door, deposited my father's letter and walked out the back door. I spent the day seeing the sights, then exchanged my lunch money for a trip to the movies and by the evening decided it was probably

19

time to head home. I turned myself in to the local police and enquired whether there were any reports of search parties looking for small boys from Dallas. They said there were not, but were kind enough to drive me home, where as always my mother administered a stern punishment. Later, she would dine out on an ever-growing store of anecdotes about her little boy's adventurous streak.

It may seem strange in these much more dangerous times that a child could survive such escapades unscathed, but there was still something of a sense of innocence in the air in the 1920s. There was also a sense of adventure. The freewheeling history of the Wild West was recent enough for some of the old timers from that era still to be walking around, capable of inspiring young minds with a thirst for excitement. I remember befriending one old codger during a childhood vacation in New Mexico. As I sat beside him on the warm red earth, he told me stories of gunfights and galloping, of jail breaks and burning barns. He turned out to be George Coe, who rode with Billy the Kid during the Lincoln County War. George had his trigger finger shot off in the Battle of Sawyers Mill in 1878, yet even without it, he seemed to be able to beckon me into a world with more adventure than there was in the one I was forced to inhabit. I became so enamoured with the world of cowboys and gunslingers that, at school, I became known as Billy the Kid. George filled me with such a love of tales of the old West that, years later, when I was a pilot, I used to hurry home from aerial battles over France in order to find out what happened in some Western potboiler novel I had left unfinished at the base.

In the 1920s, Dallas still pined for a long-dead dream that it might somehow become a river port and the centre of life in the Midwest, but the Trinity River proved hard to navigate and it was only when the army made Camp Dick in Dallas a hub for its newfangled flying machines during the First World War, at about the time I was born, that a different possible future presented itself. The same ambitious eyes that oversaw the local business world saw new alternatives in the form of motor cars and aviation. Both got into full swing just as I was growing up. 'Let the automobile be our wagon and the air be our Ocean,' the city fathers declared, sincerely, if slightly pompously, and set about building a big commercial airfield at Love Field that was bought by the city in 1927.

My memory of these great business and architectural changes is clouded by the fact that a young boy with a sense of adventure has much more important things to think about. Our proximity to so much flying may have given me my first yearnings to become a pilot, but in the meantime there was always something crashing or burning down or someone being shot that seemed much more interesting. But I remember feeling that we were hurtling into the future when at the age of six I stared in wonderment at Dallas's latest claim to fame – the city's first electric traffic light, which attracted crowds of spectators outside the vaudeville theatres and new movie palaces springing up along Elm Street. It was invented by a quirky old Dallasite called Henry Dad Garrett, who ran the local fire station. There cannot have been too many fires, since he also had time to invent the first car radio and install the first police and fire emergency radio system in the country at about the same time. He could also be said to have invented public radio in America, for when there were no fire or police signals to send out he used to play his own classical record collection for anyone with a crystal radio set who happened to be listening in.

The feeling of growth, change and possibilities continued throughout the 1920s. When I was ten in 1927, I and 40,000 other kids rejoiced in escaping from school when we were given the day off to go see Charles Lindbergh, the celebrated aviator, who was flying into Dallas in his plane *The Spirit of St Louis* on his victory tour following his solo flight across the Atlantic that year. The day was a cold one in September and it rained constantly, but every one of us children and about another 60,000 grown-ups formed the largest, soggiest crowd in the city's history, lining the streets of his parade route through downtown Dallas. People climbed trees, clung to lamp-posts, crowded onto balconies and wriggled dangerously along rooftops for a better view. When Lindbergh arrived, the city went wild, cheering and waving as he passed by in an open-top automobile. This must have been his 101st victory parade, and he seemed a bit less excited than the rest of us. The local newspaper reported that 'A glassy stare and a mechanical lifting of his hand to his bare head were his only reactions to the cheering of his admirers.' Still, once again that thought crept into my head: it must be great to be able to fly.

Ironically, while I later became one of the first Americans in the air war, Lindbergh became a cheerleader for isolationism.

Even in the supposed boom-times of the Roaring Twenties, things were quite tight for me and my family, so my range of part-time jobs proliferated. In a few years my door-to-door efforts to sell magazine subscriptions and shelf stacking at local stores had been joined by paper rounds, and by the time I was about ten I had amassed the considerable fortune of two hundred dollars as the only possible route to bankrolling my future education. But in 1929, a family friend who worked for General Electric pointed out to my parents that it was a crime not to have that money working for my future in the form of stocks and shares. He even gave them a stock tip for American Commonwealth Power. No sooner had my personal fortune gone in to their coffers than the entire American stock market collapsed in the crash of October 1929 that heralded the start of the Great Depression. I found myself a ruined tycoon, just in time for my twelfth birthday. The family friend took me to one side and warmly explained that the financial lesson this event taught me would stand me in good stead for the rest of my life and was worth far more than a paltry two hundred dollars. Speaking personally, I still miss the two hundred dollars.

By late 1929 my father's business was in real trouble,

and after many adventures of moving home and running away from home, home finally ran away from me. When I was twelve my mother decided that she should join my father on the road, believing that the hatchet-faced hat-shop owners would have a harder time pushing her around than my gentle, amiable father. My sister Adele was sent to live with relatives in Ohio and I took a room close to my high school. Adele was beautiful, kind and very smart. In another time and with more opportunities she would have had an amazing career. Instead, in those early years she sometimes had to make do with very little. I remember that when she was out with a date who tried to impress her with a flashy tip to the waiter, she would forget her hat or bag accidentally-on-purpose so that she could scoot back to the restaurant and re-distribute the wealth between the undeserving waiter and herself in order to fund future breakfasts for her ever-hungry brother. I'm proud to say that Adele and I were not just siblings but became best friends. In comparison to many Americans in the newly born 'Hungry Thirties', we were not badly off, but they were certainly tough times and more about survival than lofty aspirations. It makes me smile when I read in history books that 'Dallas was not affected by the Depression.'

As the hard times bit deeper, employers instituted wage cuts in many industries from department stores to clothing manufacturers. Not everyone took such treat-ment meekly. At the time one of my many occupations was chasing copy and advertising for the *Dallas Morning*

News, so I frequently found myself somewhere close to the action. Sometimes it was just a bent fender after a car collision on Elm Street but I also stared silently at the bullet-riddled bodies of Bonnie and Clyde, our home-grown Dallas bank robbers, when the law had finally caught up with them in 1934. No-one seemed to have told them that the economy was not so bad locally, and their attempts to shoot their way out of the Depression ended badly.

Not everyone who protested against the poverty of the times used tommy guns. At about the same time there was a strike among the skilled lady dress-cutters of Dallas, whose pay was chiselled down to less than ten dollars a week when cutters were getting up to forty dollars elsewhere in the country. When some of them joined a union they were sacked and victimized, but the strike quickly spread to fifteen factories in the town. The police were ordered to escort scab labour into the factories, but the striking ladies descended on them, scratching, biting and bashing both the police and their charges. The strikers entered two of the factories and ejected the women who had been brought in to do their jobs, having first removed all the strike-breakers' clothing. This proved very popular with us local office boys and made headlines all over the world, the insurgents being dubbed 'the stripping strikers'. Within two years the strikers had quietly been given their pay increase and union rights, and the weapon of clothes removal disappeared once more from the staid streets of Dallas.

To support myself as I worked my way through Highland Park high school, the number of my part-time jobs continued to rise and by the time I reached Texas University in the state capital of Austin, I was working half a dozen of them. Not that they were all conventional jobs – at one stage while being a gas pump attendant and full-time student, I was also publishing an ersatz version of *Who's Who* for the more egotistical students on the campus, charging them five dollars each to be in this exclusive tome, with the only entry requirement of course being the ability to give me five dollars. Simultaneously I was running a scam writing essays on behalf of the richer, lazier students for a small fee, working as an assistant librarian, operating a small dance hall in downtown Austin and chasing advertising copy. Somewhere along the line I managed to read enough books and write enough essays of my own to get a reasonably decent degree – the first in my family.

At about that time in the later 1930s I was reunited with my wonderful sister Adele and in my last year at the university we rented a little place together. The Depression still had us eternally searching for our next meal, no matter how many jobs we worked or scams we attempted, but we developed some creative ways of making our money go further.

No matter how carefully we tried to make our meagre money last all week, we knew we would be utterly broke and hungry before the next payday, so we devised a way to make sure that we did not spend it all at once. Every week when we got our pay cheques, we would instantly cash in two dollars for twenty dimes. Standing in the centre of the room we would hurl the dimes in all directions. Over the week we would pick up and use the ones that were easiest to spot, and at the end of the week when we were starving and had run out of money we would turn the room inside out and usually find a thin dime hiding under a piece of furniture or lodged in a crack in a floorboard. At that time a dime was the difference between breakfast and coffee for two and going hungry. The searching took our minds off our rumbling stomachs and the jubilation at finding a dime and heading for the diner was about the same as if we had won the lottery.

Despite our lack of funds, we embraced every form of culture and entertainment we could find. I remember one particular night, when returning to my digs from one of the half-dozen jobs that barely kept me fed and housed, so tired that I was almost sleepwalking, I heard the strains of music coming from a church hall. It was Beethoven's Fifth Symphony, and it was the first classical music I can recall hearing. The magnificent sound floated out of the church into the Texas night, stopping me in my tracks. I stood and listened until the very last notes had died away. It was a love affair with music that was to run like a silver thread through the rest of my life. Music, playing on the gramophone, on the radio or just inside my head, helped to keep me sane despite the myriad dull jobs and the ever-present twin anxieties of completing the next essay assignment and finding next week's food and rent money.

One other thing also helped to keep me on track during the Great Depression, which most of us thought might never end, and that was my ability to escape normality. By the late 1930s my runaway childhood had given way to occasional bouts of youthful madness that would see me abandon my work and studies and disappear into the wilderness, paddling a canoe up a wild river or riding a borrowed horse through unspoiled Western territory.

I remember summer days when I pondered what I might do with my future as I lazed with a fishing pole beside a remote riverbank. I looked up on one such occasion and saw groups of Texan robins, much bigger than normal ones, as are most things in Texas, gorging themselves on wild berries. The summer was ending and the wild fruit had started to ferment on the branch, so there were scores of drunken robins, wheeling and flapping in wobbly arcs in the sky, trying not to collide with each other. It made me think, once again, how great it would be to fly. In my head I was still listening to Beethoven's music and from that moment on I realized that music, flying and successful escapes were three of the great loves of my life. All three could allow me to soar away from gravity, from hard times and from imprisonment of the body, or worse still imprisonment of the mind.

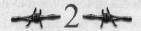

Discovering America

By early 1939 I had left Austin, a young, restless Texan with an urge for adventure and not much hope of getting a real job in the depths of the Great Depression, when ten million people were unemployed. I drifted from place to place all over the Midwest for the best part of a year, mostly hitching rides in battered cars, but sometimes riding the rails and avoiding the railway 'bulls' who were employed to knock non-paying passengers off the freight wagons to which they were clinging. In truth though, by the end of that tumultuous decade, the bulls had almost given up. The volume of men 'hobo-ing' from one place to another looking for work was so great, usually matched by an equal number coming in the opposite direction for the same reason, that the train bullies lowered their expectations. Instead of attempting to eradicate the entire species, they concentrated on keeping the hobos out of stations and cracking a few heads when they thought they could get away with it.

The most common place to hop a train, free from the threat of the bulls, was always on what was called a 'blind'. This was usually a place on the outskirts of town, sometimes on an upward gradient which slowed the train, and not far enough out of town for it to have picked up too much speed or for it to be too hard for us non-paying passengers to reach. Where these conditions coincided with a curve, there was often a blind spot towards the rear of the train where the driver and guard could not see what was going on, and that was the perfect spot for jumping on.

Years later, trapped behind the multiple layers of wire in prisoner-of-war camps, I was to find this early training in blind spots very handy. Sometimes prison machine-gun posts were built along the wire in such a way that there was a small blind spot between the guard posts where the searchlights or lines of sight could not reach, and these were perfect places for a tunnel to emerge or for an attempt to chop through the wire with home-made cutters.

The art of 'chasing a train' must now be largely for-gotten. I would race alongside a freight train that seemed to go on for ever in either direction, and did not seem to be moving all that slowly compared to me, with my worldly possessions slung in a bindle or blanket-bundle around my neck. I was often one of a small army of people, all trying to get on the same train at the same time. I would look for a freight door that had been left open a crack and try to prise it open enough to hurl myself on board, sprawling in the dust or the straw on the floor. At times there were already hobos and travellers on board and sometimes helping hands would be extended, hauling the newcomers up. This was partly an act of humanity, but it also had a certain logic: hobos tended to share what little they had, and sooner or later each of us would be the one trying to get on, looking for a hand-up from a new friend.

As I sat in the open doorway and the train picked up speed I would meet other voyagers from a remarkable variety of places and backgrounds, all reduced to riding the rails and living rough in search of work. My childhood may have been precarious and I may have worked jobs to help pay the bills since I was old enough to toddle, but at no stage in my strange, wandering boyhood had I ever gone to sleep really hungry or without a roof over my head until now. The Depression had created a vast tide of humanity that swept back and forth, breaking like waves on the outskirts of each city. The desire for fairness and justice that I was born with started to grow keener, aimed not just at people and places on the newsreels in faraway Europe, but also at the complacent politicians at home who could regard this vast waste of human hope and potential as a price worth paying for their own cosy lives.

Looking around one straw-strewn cattle car in which I landed, I saw all too much evidence of its previous four-legged inhabitants, but now it was occupied by a small band of those united by the search for non-existent jobs and – in the shorter term – for their next meal. They ranged from morose loners to small groups optimistically exchanging leads for work with each other.

In another corner, there was a lean man picking out a tune on a battered guitar. Hobos respected musicians for their skill and their ability to raise the spirits of people with little hope of a job, or at least temporarily make them forget their hunger. A musician could often make enough for a meal by playing on a street corner for a few pennies and nickels.

Most hobos never found the mythical job they were searching for, but got by on a day's work here or there, often odd jobs, from pushing a broom to a little bit of gardening in return for a meal. In short, the only thing that kept them alive was small amounts of work provided by other people not too different from themselves. I never felt much of a sense of stigma as I rode the rails, partly because I was one among so many, but mostly because a quick look around me told me that wherever the blame lay for our tough, rather hopeless conditions, it did not belong to these decent people, swaying in the perpetual twilight of a rolling boxcar, just trying to get by.

Most of the travellers were single men of all ages, but there were women and children too, particularly travelling by the roads and living in the jungle camps that sprang up on the edges of most towns. Some estimates put the number of women and children riding the rails in the 1930s as high as a quarter of a million.

Over in another corner of the boxcar was a whiskery older man, who had obviously been riding the rails for some time. Indeed he was part of a hobo tradition that stretched back to the days of the Civil War, and which grew along with the hobos' unwilling hosts, the railroads themselves. While the old guy in the corner was no doubt tough as an old boot, I remember feeling sorry for him, since jumping on or off a moving train was not easy, even for a young man, and it must have become more and more of a struggle for some of the older hobos who had been riding the rails for decades. Suddenly, in recent years their world had become full of newcomers, many of whom were like me, following in the footsteps of Jack London, unsure of the rules and still finding novelty where the old timers only saw yet another day on the iron road.

After my time at university, this experience gave me a very different but equally valid education in the ways of the world. It also introduced me to a world that had its own unique language and symbols, now largely forgotten. Hobos were called many things, few of them polite, ranging from Bindle Stiff, from the blanket rolls many of them carried, to Bum, Bumper or Boxcar Jockey – and that was just the Bs. Everything was a euphemism, from 'California blankets' – newspapers used to keep warm at night – to 'hitting the grit', which meant being forced to jump from a train unexpectedly.

Alongside the spoken language was one of symbols or 'glyphs' that some of the old timers used to help fellow hobos know where to go or what to look out for. These were symbols, much like present-day Internet chat icons, usually hastily chalked on a road or wall. There were simple cartoons or squiggles with meanings for those who understood such as 'Bone polisher [fierce dog] lives here' or 'Take care – cops around' and good ones too, like 'Nice lady lives here' and 'Safe place to sleep'.

In the boxcar, the old man jumped up, almost as if a sixth sense had told him where to get off, but in reality probably because he had grown to understand the sounds of the train itself, like a second language, and he could hear it slowing down at a favourite jumping-off point. Just as it was advisable to avoid the bulls at the starting station, it was also smart to get off before the train reached its final destination. Waking up in a station, a dozy hobo could expect a night in jail for vagrancy or perhaps a beating from an over-zealous bull who didn't yet know that the war with the hobos was over and that the bulls had lost to our sheer weight of numbers.

Swinging the doors open, the old man led the charge as one by one the inhabitants of the boxcar jumped like paratroopers from the open door at a point when the train was going relatively slowly.

Struggling to keep up with my aged companion, I headed for the nearby hobo jungle. These encampments ranged from a huddle of ramshackle tents to small metropolises made of shacks and junk. Some sprang up and disappeared like mushrooms, while others lasted for years. They were inhabited not only by single men looking for work but by destitute families, drifters, grifters and shifters. Some were farmers or farm workers pushed off their land after generations when the banks used the Depression as an excuse to foreclose on an entire generation, so as to move the land from small farms to larger tracts owned by conglomerates. Others were factory workers, pushed out of work when the mills and steel works closed as the slump began to bite. A few were trade union organizers, blacklisted for trying to organize workplaces in the teeth of the Depression, when there were always ten men willing to take the job of anyone who objected to low wages or dangerous conditions. But mostly they were just ordinary young men in need of a good meal, a roof and job to wake up to.

As with all societies, from native tribes to prisoner-of-war camps, the hobo jungle had its own set of rules. It was usually positioned on the sunny side of a hill, where possible near an easy source of clean water. Most importantly, it was rarely far from roads or a 'catching out' spot on the railroad line, from which a hobo in a hurry could leave town. In some cases, small groups gathered inside towns, often in derelict or burnt-out buildings. The outlying jungle camps tended to be bigger and friendlier.

The camp rules were unwritten and enforced by collective willpower rather than a police force. They included always leaving pots and pans clean, never stealing from other hobos in the camp and not committing crimes such as burglary that would lead to trouble for the whole camp. The hobos were generally tough men in search of honest work, and while it would be foolish to say that there was not a certain amount of law-breaking, hobo life was remarkably civilized, given what these people went through on a daily basis just to survive. Crime such as it was tended to consist of the odd piece of food snatched from outside a store, or maybe an item of clothing filched from a clothes line.

At nights the camps glowed with a collection of camp fires large and small. Some families kept to themselves, but others shared what little food they had, and each person showing up was expected to do the same. After we had eaten whatever we had managed to acquire during the day, there were often discussions as the camp fires died down. There was no electricity, and radios and television were just a rumour, but there were often musicians who would play the music of the fields or the streets as the darkness crept in.

Sometimes we had discussions about the world we lived in and what we would like to see happen, though most people were too busy surviving to care very much. I remember one young man asking me about the Spanish Civil War. I told him about the heroic loyalists' battle against Franco and his fascist army and said I had wanted to go and fight with the American international brigade, but that the war had ended already. He asked me who had won. I told him that my guys had lost to the fascists and he looked at me as if I was slightly touched. 'Why would you want to go over there and fight for the losers?' Years later, when I was holed up in a prison camp and the outcome of the war looked far from certain, I often thought what a good question that was. Luckily, sometimes even the losers can win.

My brief immersion into this twilight world prepared me for a lot of my wartime activities – being an unwelcome non-paying passenger, avoiding the unwanted attentions of guard dogs or the authorities, sharing food and political discussions with men just as badly off as myself, and sometimes just laughing in the face of everything the world can throw at you. As I dozed off that night in the hobo jungle someone was playing an old tune on the harmonica, singing about hobo heaven, a world in which 'the guard dogs all have rubber teeth and the hens lay hard-boiled eggs.'

Next morning I was up early as usual. I've never been able to laze in bed, as I always have the feeling I may be missing out on something exciting. The Nazis were later to attempt to cure this by locking me in solitary confinement, but even then I would jump up to hang from the bars over my cell's one tiny window in the hope of glimpsing whatever it was I was missing. But in the Depression, most of the excitement had to be self-generated and usually related to procuring the next meal or day's work.

Among my activities at that time was my habit, on arrival in a new town, of signing up as a door-to-door salesman, getting my suitcase of samples, and then selling the contents at a flea market for enough food for one good meal. Some people may tut-tut at such activity, but

I suggest they try not eating for a day or two and then see if it does not seem like an excellent idea. In a strange way, it also felt like divine justice for all the times hard-nosed men had slammed doors in my quiet and polite salesman father's face.

Then there was my spell as a shop assistant at a clothing store in Kansas City. My efforts to sell men's fashions were hampered by my own wardrobe, which at the time consisted of a pair of second-hand tomato-coloured lady's slacks, a purple shirt and a large scout knife that was useful in a hobo jungle encampment but intimidated the more nervous customers. Even though the store fired me, when I was shot down over France and declared missing presumed dead the store bosses put up a plaque in my honour. I heard later that it mournfully recorded me as a loyal employee who had fallen fighting for freedom. I always meant to go back after the war and put them to the trouble of taking it down, but never quite got around to it.

One other job I remember was a brief spell working in a bank. When my counting skills were found lacking, they deployed me as an elevator operator, a job whose ups and downs seemed very appropriate for my career at that point. While I was working there I bumped into someone who recognized me from my precarious days at Texas University. They enquired whether my employers knew I had a summa cum laude arts degree. 'Yes,' I replied, 'but they've agreed to overlook it.'

This was about the time of the declaration of war

between Britain and Germany. To most Americans the war was a distant event until their own country was finally galvanized into battle by the bombing of Pearl Harbor some two years later. During my travels, I got into a few rather vigorous exchanges of views and blows with some of those early enthusiastic American Bund supporters of Hitler, who felt that we should be doing the same sort of thing as he was to whoever took their fancy – usually the lefties, the Jews or the unemployed. In an extension of some of my earlier playground battles, I had become quite a useful boxer. In one such altercation a helpful bystander pointed out that if I wanted to fight so much, perhaps I should pay Hitler a personal visit.

And so after a year of hobo-ing from job to job and place to place all over the country, in early 1940 I arrived, slightly ragged and fresh off a freight train, at the Hungry Man diner in Detroit. It was a rough 'one-arm joint' where you leant on the counter with one arm and shovelled stew with the other. You could have all the stew you could get on a plate for fifteen cents, but you were fined a dime if you left any on your plate. This was the unlikely jumping-off point for my war against Hitler. I remember some of the locals having a laugh at my expense as I set off walking over the border bridge to Windsor, Ontario, where I attempted to enlist in the Royal Canadian Air Force.

In Canada, a dour British recruiting sergeant gave me a physical exam and pronounced me too malnourished to be any use. I complained that since I wanted to join the air force it was in their interest for me to be as light as possible. Think of all the fuel they would save! Despite my seamless logic, I was sent packing and limped my way back to the Hungry Man diner to be scoffed at by my detractors for having won the war so quickly.

I persuaded one of the doubting locals to lend me twenty dollars, which he reluctantly did at 20 per cent interest, compounded monthly 'just to teach me the value of money'. I handed over my new riches to the short-order cook at the diner and took up residence at one of the tables. Every day, like a desperate man in an eating contest, I consumed everything they could shovel into me. I even became something of a local landmark as people checked in to the diner to see my progress. The cook wanted me to stay on, since business boomed thanks to this new tourist attraction, but two weeks to the day of my rejection, I waddled back to Canada.

As I walked across the bridge that morning I stopped and looked down at the swirling waters, wondering where they might carry me. I was leaving a country at peace, still becalmed in the Depression, and going to one at war, fighting for its survival. I was more excited than frightened. Most of my family and friends were baffled. My own government was still in the sway of those who wanted to turn a blind eye to Hitler. It was not our war. It was not my fight. I had heard it all, but I kept on walking.

For a moment when I re-entered the RCAF recruiting station, my thoughts became more mundane. Would they throw me out again, for being too thin, or too fat, as if I was in some mad version of Goldilocks and the Three Bears? This time, however, when I stepped onto the air force weighing scales like a prize-fighter, the entire office cheered. I was in.

But there was a price to pay. Like every American who joined up in Canada, years before America entered the war, I immediately had my citizenship and passport revoked for the crime of fighting for the King. The fact that so many of us Americans who volunteered in the Second World War before the United States entered it lost our citizenship for the privilege of getting shot at in the interests of freedom remains to this day one of the least reported and least glorious chapters in the history of our early neutrality in the conflict. The US government attitude was simple: to fight for Britain you have to swear allegiance to the King and to do that you lose your American citizenship. I thought about it for a moment, my pen poised above the enlistment papers that would change my life. Then I went ahead and signed up. There are some things that are more important than bits of paper.

If I had thought it would have done any good, I would have pointed out to the President of the United States that I was not so much for the King of England as against Hitler. Maybe, I reasoned, the President would feel differently when Pilot Officer Ash returned, having sorted out the Third Reich.

My basic training in Kingston, Canada, during 1940 at

last revealed something I was better at than being an elevator operator or seller of hats. It seemed I had a natural aptitude for flying. I made new friends among the Canadians and a handful of equally mad Americans who had joined up at about the same time as me. The instructors were mostly British former RAF pilots, this being before the introduction of the Empire Training Scheme, the Canadian pilot training regime that was to mass-produce Allied flyers for the war effort that led up to D-Day.

At first I was a little dismayed to find that the British connection even extended to the food. Amid a sea of Canadian plenty, the RCAF base was a little desert island of English rationing. Luckily one of my first friends there, Paul Burden, was from New Brunswick, where his parents ran a chicken farm, so we were never short of supplies. To make sure of not being hungry we took the precaution of making our unofficial headquarters in the local Chinese restaurant. Each payday we turned over our air force pay cheques to the proprietor and he fed us all month and even doled out pocket money.

The reality was that there was little time to spend it. We were woken at six for a particularly gruelling series of exercises and then it was straight into flying practice. We did our service training on Fairey Battles. The Fairey Battle was a rather underpowered fighter bomber that had been retired after the aerial skirmishes over France during the blitzkrieg a few months earlier. It was a sluggish beast and I could just imagine the thoughts of the British pilots who had to face roaring Messerschmitts in them. They must have felt as if they were riding a turtle.

The defeat in France in 1940, when the British troops were practically driven into the sea at Dunkirk and hundreds of thousands were rescued in a heroic evacuation operation involving thousands of tiny boats, was fresh in our minds. We had huddled around radios, listening to stories of horror and heroism, feeling very far away and unable to help. The disaster had opened the immediate possibility of Hitler's invasion of Britain, which now stood alone as the last bastion of opposition to fascism in the west. The only thing that had delayed the invasion, code named Operation Sealion, was the battle for air supremacy which raged over the skies of southern England between the Luftwaffe and the RAF as my volunteer friends and I were frantically training in Canada.

The Battle of Britain, as that era has come to be called, was a period of the war, rather than a one-off conflict, at its most intense in the second half of 1940. Reports of both the heroism and the losses in Britain made us itch to get into the fight to even up the odds. A few pessimists wondered if there would be any Britain left for us to defend, but most of us burned with a desire to be out of training and into action. We studied and practised as if our lives depended on it, which of course they did.

I remember the final seconds before my very first solo flight. We had studied the theory of flying: thrust by a propeller creates a vacuum over a curved surface such as a wing, and that vacuum lifts the object skywards. Staring at this hulking great machine on the runway, I was utterly unconvinced that anything other than a stick of dynamite could cause it to move upwards. But once I was airborne, all my doubts evaporated.

Suddenly I was soaring. I had left the ground, the Depression and the land-locked expectations of others far below, where people looked like ants and even the huge air-craft hangars looked like toys. My destiny was in my own hands and I felt like an eagle looking down, master of all I surveyed. I knew that my new power and liberty was a fragile thing and that I could be brought crashing down in flames – like Icarus flying too close to the sun – by a single mistake, but I also knew I was alive, that flying was a form of music and that the song in my head was the one I had been born to sing.

The only other experience I can compare that first flight to is swimming underwater, where the rules of gravity are suddenly changed and you can do all sorts of things that would be impossible on the ground. I didn't dwell on the science too much, since I figured that if I did, I might plummet to earth in a burst of logic. Maybe that's why I loved flying so much – for the sense of basic incredulity and delight that I was actually up in the air, which never left me, at least not until I was shot down. That certainly put a crimp in my sense of wonderment.

After lunch each day there was on-the-ground training in navigation, tactics and Morse code, which we had to comprehend at fifteen words a minute. We learned to read the instrument panels, then practised air navigation over the still vastness of rural Canada, where I remember a thousand ribbons of silver lakes winking up at me. They looked almost identical to a young, slightly lost pilot who has been told to fly a triangular journey of a hundred miles and end up exactly over the training airfield he started from. Somehow we all made it back.

Some of the early training took place in a Link Trainer – a very primitive sort of on-ground flight simulator – but most of it was up in the air. As the weeks turned into months, we flew for three or four hours a day, and much to my surprise I found myself becoming a real pilot.

Paul Burden was also progressing very well. In the air we both encouraged each other and when we were back on terra firma we discussed what we had learned. Together, we bought an old car and used it to venture out of the training station. Paul was a big, amiable handsome man and the local girls gravitated to dashing men in uniform, so he was a great accomplice. More importantly, the car allowed us to get to his parents' farm in Fredrickton, where we were treated like royalty and allowed to bring back all manner of food including tinned chicken and fresh eggs to the ration-hit station.

The days were long and tough, crammed with both theory and practice, but the novelty of being fed regularly and paid to do something I loved made me strive for ever better performances in the air. I particularly took to aerobatics, even squeezing creditable loops and rolls out of the bumbling Fairey Battles. As our confidence increased, we were given 'height tests' in them, in which we were required to take them up with a full bomb load to 18,000 feet without oxygen, then make three perfect landings in a row.

The best thing about this experience with the lumbering Battles was that later in Britain when it came to flying sleek, responsive planes such as Spitfires, I felt like that man who runs marathons while wearing a deep-sea diving suit, suddenly released and allowed to run free, feeling almost weightless.

I started to get something of a reputation when my desire to experiment led me to a phase of flying upside down for as long as possible, working out how to use the controls while inverted, like someone learning to write while looking in the mirror. I liked the sense of precision and knowing the limits of responsiveness. Perhaps that is what prompted me to fly under my first bridge. The feeling of dread you get when approaching a bridge flying low above a great expanse of water is surpassed only by the feeling of exhilaration when you emerge unscathed, having somehow squeezed a hurtling metal machine below a concrete span between two arches and a few feet above a raging river. Soon under-bridge flying became a significant part of my unofficial training curriculum.

While it would be fair to say that the authorities were less than keen on my aerobatics, they recognized that soon the mad young men they were training would be facing experienced Luftwaffe pilots in sophisticated planes. We would be fighting not just to conquer our own fear but for our lives, and potentially for the fate of soldiers and civilians far below.

When it came to firepower, they wisely started us with camera guns that took pictures of the targets we were meant to have shot and just as often of empty spaces and interesting clouds when we missed. But soon we were playing for real, with Browning machine guns, churning out .303 ammunition, with the wiser instructors staying well behind us as we learned.

After a few more months and 150 hours in the air, the powers that be decided I was safe to unleash on Hitler and awarded me my wings. Better still, they recommended me as a fighter pilot. As I emerged with my wings, I felt ten feet tall. There would be plenty of time to ponder on the dangers that came with the wings later. For that one moment I had left the Depression behind and felt a sense of elevation I could never have known, no matter how many times I went up and down in the elevator of a Texas bank.

Paul Burden also passed with flying colours and he was asked to stay on as an instructor. It was typical of him that while I galloped off in search of adventure, he agreed to stay on, probably making a bigger contribution to the war effort by helping to train a whole new generation of pilots than either of us flying alone. Later in the war, he saw active service too, piloting a Lancaster bomber and winning a Distinguished Flying Cross before he returned to Canada.

By then it was early 1941 and still a very bleak point in the war. Hitler's armies and air force were dominating both eastern and western Europe, with the small island of Britain at one end and a still-neutral Russia at the other offering the only hope of a future other than fascism. Opinion in America, particularly that of the Establishment, was still staunchly neutral, but among working people sympathy for the British was on the rise. This was countered by business tycoons and many newspaper proprietors who were determined to keep America out of the war at all costs, either because they quite liked Hitler or because they feared the derailment of their own gravy train.

Not every newspaper was against intervention and when I left for Britain, my home-town papers the *Dallas Journal* and the *Dallas Morning News* ran front-page stories of how a local boy was going off to sort out the Luftwaffe. When a group of Texan newspapermen visited the Canadian training field shortly after I had left for England, they crowded round Paul Burden as he told them tall tales of life in the skies, in a convincing Texas drawl. When they eventually found out he was Canadian he told them that I had left my accent with him in Canada for safekeeping, along with my half share in our ancient automobile. He claimed he was just looking after them while I was away, but I took slightly longer to get back than I had planned.

The Texas newspapers gave me a rousing send-off. Their reporting was exciting and sympathetic, if not very accurate. They announced that while everyone in Dallas was having their dinner, I would be 'winging my way across the ocean, flying a bomber', and within a week would be 'spitting death at German Stukas'. At the time I was rolling around below decks on a troop ship destined for England, hoping that neither seasickness nor the U-boats would end my career before the Luftwaffe even had a chance.

My journey from Canada in a 28,000-ton troop ship called the *Georgic* was a tense few days. The ship had just been converted in a Belfast shipyard from being the last luxury liner of the White Star line, which had produced that other memorable vessel the *Titanic*. Despite that fact, our ship felt as big and sturdy as an island, even if the original guests would not have recognized it once 3,000 seasick troops had been on it for more than a week.

On deck, looking about at the vastness of the grey Atlantic, it was hard not to think about the U-boats circling the convoys, waiting their chance. The rules of war were harsh. If one ship in a convoy was hit, the others often had orders to steam ahead rather than themselves becoming victims of another torpedo. Our nervousness was increased by a cheery sailor who informed me that one of our main cargoes was 'aviation fuel for you flyboys'. He assured me that if the ship was hit, it was more likely to go up in the air in tiny pieces than down.

Despite the nervous days and the seasick nights we made it to England's shores in one piece. I promised myself that if I ever got the opportunity to guard a convoy I would look after it with every ounce of energy I had, and in the coming months I was to get a chance to do so. I also had cause to remember the words of the cheery sailor when just a few months later I read that the same ship had been bombed while on transport duty carrying nearly 1,000 Italian prisoners of war and internees near Suez. Her fuel oil caught fire, then her massive ammunition magazines exploded, leaving the once mighty ship half-submerged and burnt out. Amazingly, she was salvaged, returned for repairs in Belfast and was back in the war by 1944. I was just glad to be back on dry land.

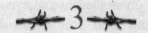

411 Squadron

I arrived in England in early 1941, a country in flames from the Blitz and under siege from the all-conquering Nazi army just a few miles across the English Channel. I was sent to the operational manning unit – a sort of mustering and orientation station at Hawarden, in Clwyd, north Wales. That is where I caught my first close look at a Spitfire and it was love at first sight.

I had had a mental picture of a Spitfire, but in real life it was much smaller than I expected. There it sat, a compact, finely engineered bundle of power and grace, like a Platonic ideal of a perfect aeroplane. From the elegant curve of its wings to the in-line engine tucked away behind its elongated nose, the whole structure had style. Long noses, whether on British gentry, borzoi dogs or Spitfires have always seemed very aristocratic to me.

Of all the planes I flew, Spitfires were the only ones that had no discernible bad habits. While other planes were sluggish just when you needed power most, or tightened up when you were in a spin, Spitfires always seemed to know what to do and when to do it. Even throttled back to just 40 mph, a Spitfire would simply glide downwards on an elegant and even keel.

But if the plane itself seemed heroic, some of the instructor pilots I started to meet seemed more like legendary figures from mythology. This period was the immediate aftermath of the Battle of Britain, and the instructors were mainly outstanding pilots, such as Joe Pegge, taking a well-deserved break after a year of intense aerial combat – though the idea of playing nurse-maid to a bunch of nervous rookies flying close formation in brand-new Spitfires might have made these veterans yearn for the simpler dangers of facing the Luftwaffe at odds of five-to-one against.

Like most rookie pilots, I was desperate to get into action, though I was to discover in the coming years and months that there were still plenty of invaders to go around. So, while at the time some of these preparations and training seemed like an obstacle to doing my job, in reality they were saving my life.

As I sat in the cockpit of my brand-new Spitfire, waiting to take off on my first solo flight in it, under the stern eye of the instructor who was there to grade my flight, my hands fluttered around the unfamiliar controls. Since a Spitfire is a single-seater aircraft, there is no-one around to tell you what buttons to press, and which knobs and levers you should definitely leave alone. I was in awe of this complex, elegant piece of machinery, with its purring Merlin engine and such firepower – two cannons and four machine guns – waiting only for the gentlest touch on the control-column gun button. Suddenly it did not seem so small after all. As I raced down the runway the knot in my stomach hardened.

But as soon as I was airborne, all fear left me. I was too busy trying to make sure that everything went well for the watching eyes below. In a Spitfire, making everything go well meant applying the gentlest, most subtle of guidance and letting the magnificent plane do the rest. Unlike the ponderous old Fairey Battles I had trained on, which had to be pushed and pulled to do what you wanted, the Spitfire needed only the slightest of hints.

Soon I was diving and climbing and then, probably far too soon, I tried a full roll. It worked beautifully. I landed and as I walked past the instructor, still writing notes on his clipboard, I saw that he had a half-smile on his otherwise stern face. He looked up and gave the tiniest possible nod of approval, though whether it was for me, or out of respect for the remarkable aeroplane, I will never know.

Next we learned about shooting an aerial target. We were sent to shoot down a barrage balloon – a sort of airborne obstacle for enemy aircraft – that had escaped its moorings and was drifting about somewhere near Liverpool. I remember being very pleased when we blasted it from the skies, but as one of our battle-hardened instructors warned us, balloons are easier than enemy planes – they don't shoot back.

Back at Hawarden, I had become friendly with another new pilot at the training unit and one day I watched as he taxied along the runway. A workman was crossing the strip at the same time and my friend pulled up too sharply to avoid him. His plane flipped over and, full of fuel, it burst into flames. Several of us ran over. We charged desperately into the smoke and tried to get him out as machine-gun bullets from his magazines started to crackle and explode all around us as the fire took hold. We could not reach him and were driven back, only able to watch helplessly as he died, engulfed in flames.

From then on I understood that while the turbulence of wartime forges some of the closest possible bonds between strangers, few pilots liked to get too friendly with their fellow airmen. Behind the laughter and the camaraderie was often a reserve, caused not by any coldness but really the opposite – knowing that any day any one of us might simply be dead and gone, and that the others would have to keep going, that day and the next, and the next, until the war was over or we too were memories.

Within a few weeks of completing training I was posted to an RAF squadron in Eleven Group, which meant I would be in the thick of things immediately, but somewhere along the line my orders were changed. The plan was to build a new squadron with all the Canadian pilots. Since I was one of very few Americans, they seemed reluctant to make me a squadron on my own. As I was from somewhere in the general direction of Canada and had trained there, they decided I would fit in best among my New World cousins and therefore transferred me to the newly formed 411 Squadron at Digby in Lincolnshire as part of Twelve Group.

I remember being impatient at this move, as I knew that the new squadron would take weeks to get in shape, but arriving at Digby in June 1941, I soon recognized that there was a great deal to do on the ground as well as in the air. Many of the Canadians I had met at initial training were being funnelled into this new outfit, and they were a great bunch.

Our new abode was stunning: a magnificent old stately home called Ashby Hall, built on the edge of a tranquil lake. It was quite a culture shock for the young man from downtown Dallas who only a few months earlier had been sharing a can of beans over an open fire in a hobo jungle encampment.

My new comrades sent me out to buy gramophone records for the officers' mess in the nearest metropolis, sleepy Lincoln, but were horrified when I came back with Bach, Mozart, Brahms and Beethoven; it wasn't quite what they had in mind. Even my protestations that I had got them some pop music fell on deaf ears when they discovered I was referring to a selection of Strauss waltzes. My plan worked. The records were banished, as I knew they would be, and I got to listen to Beethoven's Fifth again in my own room, a long way from Texas. As Spitfire engines droned in the background, I wondered where I might find myself listening to it next. As it turned out, I'm glad I did not know the answer.

Life in the air was even more exhilarating. Flying a Spitfire is at once an intensely individual experience and a completely collective one. When you were in the air, it quickly became obvious that you were relying for your life not just on the colleagues whom you could see on either wing but on a small army of ground crew, from those elegant young women monitoring enemy aircraft on giant plotting maps to the oil-smeared mechanics who worked long and hard overnight to repair the damage of the previous day's battle and to nurse the Merlin engines back to health after they had been put through the punishment of aerobatics in a dogfight.

A Spitfire cockpit is tiny, barely big enough for a young man to squeeze into. During combat, you might suffer from a dry mouth, but there would usually be no time to be afraid. That came before or after. In the air, as a pilot climbed at dawn he would sometimes get the amazing sight of two sunrises, one at 30,000 feet and a second one after he landed as the sun came over the ground-level horizon. Each time it made you glad to still be alive.

In the air, as the pilot of a fast single-seater aircraft, you were the king of all you surveyed. At high altitude the air was thin and no matter how warmly one was dressed it was still freezing. Some of what today are regarded as affectations such as fleece-lined flying jackets and silk scarves were as vital to survival as the machine guns and landing gear. The scarf was silk so that a pilot could crane around to check for enemy planes from all angles without wrenching his neck against leather. As for the fleece and leather, warmth was a matter of life and death too. If a pilot's brain slowed down for even a split second because of the altitude and cold, and his reflexes to evade or to fire kicked in a second too late, it could cost him his life.

The drone of the Merlin engine and the popping of your own machine guns would mix with the crackle of the radio, with pilots calling warnings or a leader calling short, sharp orders over the R/T, as we called the receiver/transmitter radio. Suddenly, the icy cold would seem very hot indeed.

The feeling as you lined up an enemy in your sights and a thumb pressed the firing button was very different from how it might seem in the movies. A Spitfire at that time had a maximum of fifteen seconds' worth of ammunition. Every single burst had to be calculated. Would you waste it on a half-lined-up shot and risk being left defenceless for the rest of the battle and the flight home? Or would you end up going home with unspent ammo and a regret that you had let the enemy get away? You might have half a second to make the decision, while flying at high altitude in the cold, thin air, and often that half-second of thinking time would be interrupted by an enemy pilot or flak crew on the ground firing at you.

There was rarely any time to feel sorry for your foes during the battle, and afterwards it was too late.

Not long after we arrived at Digby, we got news that Hitler had launched Operation Barbarossa, his massive invasion of Russia. From then until the end of the year, news from the eastern front was universally bad. The Nazi blitzkrieg rolled all the way to the gates of Moscow, scooping up millions of Russian prisoners, while the country scrambled to relocate its industry far to the east while leaving nothing for the invaders but scorched earth. The reality behind this for us was that if we had continued to face the entire might of the Luftwaffe over the following years, rather than only a part of it, with the rest being kept busy on the Ostfront, fewer of us new arrivals would have survived.

Most of the pilots were even younger than I was, still in their teens; at twenty-four I was older than many. One very fine pilot whom I was to meet later in the war was a good example of the breed. Paddy Barthropp was an amiable, slightly wild young man from an upper-class Anglo-Irish family. He had flown in the Battle of Britain while only nineteen. He lived wartime life to the full, as most of us did, for we never knew what was coming next. He had one almost miraculous escape after his plane was badly shot up in a dogfight over the Channel, when he seemed to make it home fuelled by sheer willpower, defying the laws of engineering and gravity. He explained this feat away by saying that he had been out for a somewhat lively evening of drinking and dancing with some of the apparently infinite supply of beautiful young women drawn to a pilot's uniform and he was determined to make it home because, being Catholic, he did not want to crash before he had a chance to go to confession.

While most of us were young, I remember being deeply impressed when I met and learned from older men such as Harry Broadhurst or Victor Beamish. It seemed remarkable to me that these 'old men' of about forty were still flying and shooting down enemy planes on a regular basis. To my young eyes it was as if the managing directors of some huge companies still regularly left the boardroom to go out selling door-to-door.

Harry Broadhurst had a square, pugnacious face, eyes that flashed electricity beneath bushy eyebrows, and was universally known as Broady. He had started out in the RAF in the 1920s and must have quickly built up an immunity to fear of crashing. He originally failed his medical to get in, because of low blood pressure, but a kindly doctor told him to run twice around the block, then re-apply. This time he was accepted.

On his way to his first day of service he came off his motorbike at high speed and spent his first month of duty in hospital. Then, after six weeks of training, mostly on planes left over from the First World War, he was sent to complete an exam at another airbase, hitching a ride in a bomber. When the bomber crashed, killing the pilot, Broady woke up three days later, back in hospital.

From these unpromising starts, he became one of the

most skilled pre-war pilots in the RAF, and the leader of an aerobatic display team. In the 1930s he was sent on a fact-finding mission to Germany, where he was grilled by an overly friendly Hermann Goering about the capabilities of the new British planes such as the Spitfire and Hurricane. Broady could see that war was looming and gave little away while trying to learn as much as possible about the enemy air strength.

He was soon able to test his knowledge at the start of the Battle of Britain in 1940 as he was put in charge of the Hornchurch Wing. He was hugely popular with his pilots, partly because he was a great pilot himself who flew alongside them and partly because he was a good leader on the ground too, spending time talking to his men, both teaching them how to survive and listening to their grumbles. His own exploits in the air during the pivotal battle for air superiority over southern England earned him the first of two Distinguished Service Order medals. By the time I got to know him, he was something of an institution, and meeting him along with Victor Beamish gave me a sense that I would ultimately be on the winning side.

Knowing that my life would soon depend on it, I tried to learn from experienced pilots and started to get in as much flying in my new Spitfire as possible. My practice flights took me all over the south of England. One of my most enduring memories is climbing up above the cloud to see the sun bursting through and then diving down again to find myself flying above the ancient stone circle at Stonehenge as the sun gradually illuminated the stones. Still in the West Country, I added the Clifton Bridge to the list of those I had enjoyed flying under. On my way back from these forays I became fairly proficient at navigation and always looked out for the three great Gothic towers of Lincoln Cathedral, soaring above the vast, flat fenlands, as a sign that I was nearly home.

For a Texan used to wide blue skies, the variations in the cloud formations I flew through in England were amazing. One day, flying over the cathedral, I pushed through what felt like great celestial draperies of cloud and rain, streaming in the wind, and when they opened, there below me was the cathedral and around me a sight you can only see from the air – a perfect complete circle of rainbow, with my small, sleek Spitfire flying apparently through the middle. It was magical.

My flying was improving with practice and in the brief lull while the squadron was formed we got in a good deal of practice on the station Magister or Maggie – a two-seater with dual controls often used for training or for ferrying people from one airfield to another.

On one occasion I was at the controls, flying back to Digby with Buck McNair, a great, larger-than-life friend from the west of Canada who had enlisted at about the same time as I had. Buck had his eye on one of the rare 'golden caterpillar' pins that were awarded to anyone whose life was saved by a parachute. He was also curious as to just how well our parachutes might work, so he decided to jump rather than wait for me to land. I was less than keen on this plan, since I thought some unkind soul might take it as an unfavourable comment on my flying, so I ruddered down and started losing altitude for the landing. Meanwhile, at the controls behind me, Buck was attempting to stage a coup, hauling back so that we started to gain altitude for his jump. As we went up and down, wrestling for the controls, he clearly decided we were high enough and out he jumped. Luckily, his parachute worked.

In the inevitable disciplinary inquiry that followed, there was some wild speculation that he had fallen out by accident during one of my admittedly frequent un-authorized aerobatic displays, but Buck stuck to his claim for a golden caterpillar, arguing that a landing with me at the controls represented a grave danger to passengers, so his jump should be classified as a life-saving action.

Buck went on to a remarkable career as one of Canada's top pilots in the war and beyond, becoming a wing commander and winning the Distinguished Flying Cross. Just a few months after his unofficial parachute training Buck shot down an ME 109 and then was shot down himself. As he was losing altitude with his plane belching smoke, the second ME 109 which had shot him down came down to gloat in a flyover. Buck managed to shoot him down too as he whizzed by. A few seconds later, Buck parachuted safely as his Spitfire plunged into the sea. He landed in the chilly waters near the French coast. He was lucky not to be captured and made a prisoner of war. Instead he was saved in some style by the brave men of the Air Sea Rescue service and was back with the squadron almost before he had been reported lost. Along the way he not only picked up a golden caterpillar badge for a legitimate parachute jump but also got a 'golden goldfish' to add to his collection, a badge produced by the inappropriately named Messrs P. B. Cow and Sons, purveyors of air/sea rescue equipment to the services.

Many of the new pilots were very young, some still in their teens. One was John Gillespie Magee, a fellow American who had enlisted in the RCAF at about the same time as I had and had trained with us in Canada. He was with 412 Squadron, also at Digby, but was a great friend of one of our small band of 411 Squadron pilots, Jack Coleman.

As the squadrons started to shape up at Digby, Magee – a slim boy with a sparse moustache and intense eyes – flew a test flight in a newer version of the Spitfire Mark V, soaring and twisting at 30,000 feet. When he came down he wrote to his parents in America, saying, 'Am enclosing a verse I wrote the other day. It started at 30,000 feet, and was finished soon after I landed.' On the back of the letter he had scribbled what was to become the most famous aviation poem of the war, 'High Flight':

> Oh! I have slipped the surly bonds of Earth
> And danced the skies on laughter-silvered wings;
> Sunward I've climbed, and joined the tumbling mirth
> Of sun-split clouds, – and done a hundred things
> You have not dreamed of – wheeled and soared and swung

High in the sunlit silence. Hov'ring there,
I've chased the shouting wind along, and flung
My eager craft through footless halls of air.
Up, up the long, delirious burning blue
I've topped the wind-swept heights with easy grace
Where never lark, or ever eagle flew –
And, while with silent, lifting mind I've trod
The high untrespassed sanctity of space,
Put out my hand, and touched the face of God.

A few months later Magee was killed in a mid-air collision with an Oxford trainer out of Cranwell airfield, not far from Digby. Both planes were in thick cloud cover and must never have seen each other. He was buried nearby at Scopwick. His friend Jack Coleman lasted only another few months, shot down and killed while flying escort for bombers over France.

In the early months of building the new squadron, such losses were all too common. Bringing together so many new pilots and new machines under the pressures of a war that was already in full swing was never going to be easy.

Another one of the small, tragic events from which all wars are built still sticks in my mind. The nice old man who served in our officers' mess would go out at first light hunting for mushrooms on the airfield perimeter, because, he said, 'My boys love them so much with their breakfast.' One day a Spitfire scrambling in the half-light of the early morning failed to see him. It took his head off with its propeller.

Luckily, most of the accidents had less tragic consequences. Our squadron adjutant, Flying Officer Whalley, whose job it was to keep us airborne, had a wry sense of humour that rings out across the years in his entries in our operations record book, a sort of military day book. His less-than-formal observations from that period include the suggestion that our squadron motto be changed from *Inimicus inimico*, meaning 'Hostile to the enemy', to 'Hostile to ourselves' because of the frequency of accidents. A few weeks later he added, 'The squadron appears to be up to form – at least in the way of accidents.' So frequent were the accidents that he wrote about them when there was a week without any, commenting simply, 'Most gratifying, no prangs.'

In desperation to slow down our ability to demolish both ourselves and His Majesty's property, Wing Commander Ernie McNab proposed a punishment, threatening to redeploy accident-prone pilots to tow targets at gunnery schools. Since the trainee gunners were just as accident-prone as ourselves when shooting at moving targets, it was not a very popular option.

The accident rate, high in all the new squadrons, was a by-product of the huge expansion the RAF was under-going at that time, both in men and new machines, following the high casualty rate among experienced pilots in the Battle of Britain fought in the previous year. Our squadron was fairly typical in managing, during our establishing period of June to October 1941, to chalk up sixteen major accidents in just 2,601 hours' flying. Yet while the services are always good at identifying problems, the solutions are not always so speedy. When our new-version Spitfires, the Mark VBs, arrived, we were given all of two days to get used to them before testing them in combat.

When we were not causing problems for ourselves, the Luftwaffe was doing its best to give us new ones. I remember a group of us walking around the perimeter of an airfield on the east coast around that time. Suddenly our stroll was interrupted by the drone of enemy engines. Two ME 109s howled out of the sky, intent on shooting up the airfield. They zeroed in on us as easy targets, out in the open. We ran like ants in all directions as bullets started to chew up the airstrip. I dived for cover and made it into a bunker as the world seemed to be ending a few feet above my head. One of my colleagues was less prudent. He dashed past a dispersal bay and into a rickety wooden shed that would not have kept out a stiff breeze, never mind enemy cannon fire. When the smoke cleared and we emerged, we found him unscathed. His first action on getting inside the flimsy hut had been to lock the door behind him, though quite what good that was meant to do we never found out. People do funny things in wartime.

On one occasion, returning from a successful September sortie over France, with nothing much more than dinner on my mind, I was surprised to see a reception committee. As I taxied to a halt, a clutch of people hurried towards the plane. There were important-looking officials and top brass along with a photographer and a portly, balding gentleman in a tweedy suit. As I opened the cockpit and stood up to get out, the man was helped up on to the wing. He shook my hand as flashbulbs popped and he introduced himself as Mackenzie King, the Prime Minister of Canada.

King was over on a morale-boosting visit to see how the first squadron of Canadian pilots in England was shaping up. I remember thinking it was odd that he should be perched on my Spitfire wing, shaking hands with an American, when there were so many Canadians about, but part of the war effort was to convince the rest of the United States that they might as well join me. There were actually several thousand Americans, mostly in the army and navy, who like me had lost their citizenship in order to fight the Nazis before the country as a whole decided it was a good idea, but in 1941 American Spitfire pilots were still something of a rarity.

One thing that my time at Digby started to teach me was just how different this conflict was from the Great War that had shaped my and my parents' generations. In that war, the men had gone off to fight somewhere else, while life at home continued, apparently little changed. The Great War produced a lot of great poets, but unlike young Magee they mostly wrote of despair and disillusion. In our war, everyone was at the battlefield. We pilots got recognition because our fight was plain to see in the skies above Britain and France, but there were just as many acts of heroism that were carried out without much fanfare, and with much less recognition, by the ordinary men and women who worked around us and shared the risks.

One typical unsung hero was a jolly, red-faced farmer in Lincolnshire whom I often saw enjoying a pint in one of the wonderful local pubs. When he was not propping up the bar, he was quietly carrying out his own private war with the Luftwaffe. Each night, presumably after a full day on the farm, he would get on his tractor and head for a local Q-site. This was effectively a dummy airstrip, designed to lure the attackers into bombing nondescript countryside while thinking they had hit an RAF base.

Q-sites consisted of mock landing strips, up to a mile or more in length with a V-shaped approach funnel and rigged-up runway lights. They sometimes had makeshift structures designed to look like aircraft taxiing on the ground. As you can imagine, a Q-site was not somewhere you wanted to be in the middle of a German bombing raid. But the farmer headed straight for it on a regular basis. He rigged up his tractor with two long planks in the position of wings, with a red lamp on the left wing and a green one on the right. Each night, as the Luftwaffe bombers came over, hunting for the local RAF base but wary of dummy sites, the lights would go on at the imitation base, and the farmer would start up his tractor engine and rumble up and down the length of the field – a finishing touch which frequently convinced the enemy to drop their bombs on the site and head for home. The fact that for the farmer success meant being on a tractor with wooden wings in the middle of a bombing raid seemed simply to add to his satisfaction. Back in the pub, rubbing shoulders with the pilots, he would smile and tell us: 'Got the bastards to drop three sticks on me last night.' Then he would go back to sipping his beer.

Despite all the disasters, tragedies and comedies of the time, we somehow shaped up into a real fighter squadron. As we were located so near the east coast, our first duty was to fly guard duty on the shipping convoys that were Britain's life blood, and which were under constant danger of air attack as well as the invisible menace of the U-boat 'sea wolves' beneath the chilly surface of the North Sea. Looking down on the convoys, either nervous because they were so close to home after a perilous transatlantic journey from America, or perhaps just setting out on an even more dangerous voyage through ice floes to Murmansk with supplies for Russia, I hoped that the sight of us would give the sailors heart. At the same time, flying over British escort ships was always a bit nerve-racking, as we had to make sure that they knew we were friendly aircraft and not hostile ones. There is nothing quite like the feeling of having to trust people you have never met as you fly low and close around a ship, watching the huge guns on the deck swivel around to follow your progress.

At about that time, I became involved in one of the most remarkable deceptions of the war. Several of us were sent to fly guard duty over an aircraft carrier in the

English Channel, only it was not what it seemed. In reality, it was an old tramp freighter with a huge false wooden deck, painted to look like an aircraft carrier. It was designed to lure the enemy bombers out to attack it and very obligingly, they did just that.

For some days the enemy planes returned, wasting ammunition and energy on a wooden dummy boat. Then, on one particularly dark night, a lone Stuka dive-bomber risked oblivion to swoop down over the ship. Before it veered away, it dropped a single bomb which clattered onto the deck but did not explode. A bomb disposal expert inched up to examine it. It was a wooden bomb, dropped on a wooden boat, the Luftwaffe's way of saying the game was up.

Not all our coastal duty was so successful. Germany's most famous battleship, the *Scharnhorst*, was cornered alongside a good chunk of the German fleet in the French port of Brest, together with the formidable pocket battleships *Gneisenau* and *Prinz Eugen*. Together, these ships had wreaked havoc on the convoys in the north Atlantic, sinking more than twenty vessels and sending over 100,000 tons of shipping to the bottom – with the cost of thousands of Allied lives.

By now the tide of the sea war had changed. The enemy U-boats continued to wreak havoc, but the Royal Navy controlled at least the surface of the English Channel and the RAF could support it from the air. The British command knew that at some point the enemy ships might make a break for it, either south into the

Atlantic to attack convoys, or north through the Channel to the safer German ports.

In April 1941 the Air Ministry started issuing edicts telling the Fighter, Bomber and Coastal Commands to prepare to meet the foe as the ships left port. Coastal Command was told to keep an eye on the vessels, but neither the fighters nor bombers that would be needed once the ships were on the open sea were to be kept on standby: we were ordered to go about normal operations, as there would be plenty of time once the warning came that the battleships were leaving port. In the meantime Bomber Command with fighter escorts would try to sink the ships in Brest harbour.

My colleagues and I started going on joint training exercises with a squadron of Beaufort bombers, flying from Manston on the English east coast. Although officially called Operation Fuller, among us mere participants the drills went by the ingenious code name of 'What to do if the boats come out'. The Beauforts were sophisticated torpedo bombers, and it was almost possible to feel sorry for the huge, lumbering *Scharnhorst*, like a floating island waiting to be sent to the bottom. But a few seconds' thought of the lives of the brave merchant seamen who were keeping Britain going on the US convoy runs and braving the atrocious arctic run to keep the Russian war effort supplied, ensured that none of us would have any hesitation in sinking the pride of the German navy.

While our drills of fighter escorts and torpedo bombers

went on, there was a war of hide-and-seek between Bomber Command and the German navy, centred on the ships at rest in Brest. Attempts to bomb them while they were under repair in the harbour started at the end of March 1941 and continued over the summer months, with up to a hundred aircraft in each raid. The bombing took up more than three squadrons, about a tenth of British bomber capacity, but given the tremendous threat to Britain's maritime supply routes that the ships posed, the Air Ministry and Churchill himself were determined not to let them get back into the war. Most of the raids were at night-time, which kept the casualty rate among the air crews relatively low but had the drawback that it was virtually impossible to hit the targets, despite repeated attempts. Although failing to dent the *Scharnhorst* or its sister ships, the raids had the effect of prompting the enemy fleet not to hang around in Brest waiting for one of Bomber Command's five-hundred-pound armour-piercing missile bombs to strike lucky.

The bombing was bad news for the people of Brest. In an echo of the British dummy aircraft carrier, the Germans dressed a French cruiser, the *Jean d'Arc*, with planks and canvas to look like the *Scharnhorst* from the air, while the real ship was disguised with a small dummy town of mocked-up 'buildings' on parts of her deck. As a result many of the Allied bombs fell on the town of Brest, while the *Scharnhorst* remained relatively unscathed.

By December 1941 the *Scharnhorst* had been hit several times, but the damage was relatively minor, and over the months the RAF had lost more than a hundred aircraft. The Air Command was growing impatient and the Royal Navy, although increasingly stretched by the war against the Japanese in the Pacific, was reluctant to send larger elements of its fleet to that theatre of war only to find the *Scharnhorst* causing havoc closer to home.

Air Commodore Durston, the senior link-man between the air force and navy, grumbled that we 'continue ad infinitum to waste our bomber effort on these ships . . . or allow a large part of our bomber force to be held idle at the mere whisper of the departure of one of them'. All the services then agreed on a plan. There would be one huge attack, involving more than three hundred aircraft dropping vast amounts of explosives, with bombers going over in waves every half an hour for several hours. In the words of the Air Ministry, the objective was to leave the destroyers and battleships 'as twisted masses of metal or very seriously damaged in the shortest amount of time'.

Meanwhile, my unit and other fighters, as part of Operation Fuller, were ready to escort the Beaufort torpedo bombers should the ships try to make a run for it before they could be flattened in the harbour. Another Air Ministry letter contained the immortal phrase, 'It is considered unlikely that the enemy would attempt the passage of the Straits in daylight.' Unfortunately no-one told the German navy, and that is exactly what they did.

At this point Group Captain Victor Beamish, a friend of mine, and one of the most remarkable leaders of fighter aircraft in the war, became more involved than he expected. While most men of his rank concentrated on 'flying a desk', Victor's philosophy was never to ask a pilot to do something he would not do himself. Unfortunately for the rest of us, he was a superb pilot and utterly fearless, so there was not much that he would not ask of his men. He made up for this by always being there, often flying alongside the formations under his command and increasingly getting into hot water with his superiors for risking life and limb as a common-or-garden fighter pilot.

Victor inspired me and other young pilots like me, and he was also a source of excellent tactical advice. He was fearless in close-quarters dogfights, and also a superb aerobatic pilot, having led the British national aerobatic squad in 1930s peacetime before he had to leave the service because of a bout of tuberculosis. It was characteristic of Victor that he battled his way back to fitness and rejoined a few years before the start of the war.

He came into his own during the Battle of Britain. Surrounded by fresh-faced youngsters, this square-jawed northern Irishman, then in his late thirties, flew an astonishing 126 sorties. By the time I met him, he was an almost legendary figure. He could be dogmatic and stubborn, but there was no man who could raise the morale of tired, frightened fighter pilots more, either by appearing from nowhere in the sky to join a fighter sweep, or on the ground as he shambled around the many airfields under his command in tatty overalls with no indication of his rank.

Most infuriating to his commanders was his habit of flying off on his own 'looking for luckless Huns' in his Hawker Hurricane, painted with a large trademark letter B. He found them more often than not as he roved over the North Sea and English Channel, and in the course of his career he shot down at least eight enemy aircraft with another dozen 'probables'. Frequently he would run into large enemy fighter formations and more than once was lucky to make it back from the Channel, chased by what must have felt like half the Luftwaffe, his plane and on one occasion his posterior full of shrapnel.

It was on one such freelance shopping trip over the sea, when he was busy at his favourite pastime of shooting up E-boats along with Robert Finlay-Boyd, a small pugnacious Scot who was Wing Leader at Kenley, that Victor looked down through a break in the cloud on a rather remarkable sight. The German ships were indeed coming out. In broad daylight at ten o'clock in the morning, the ships were happily steaming up the middle of the English Channel in a little armada, flags waving, with a flotilla of smaller support ships and a swarm of German fighters giving them cover. For some reason the early warning system had failed.

Visibility was good at that point in the day, with some cloud cover at about 3,000 feet, and the two pilots nosed down to get an amazing view. The *Scharnhorst*, *Gneisenau* and *Prinz Eugen* were surrounded by destroyers, mine-sweepers and E-boats in a grand naval formation, sailing north gracefully in the general direction of Germany.

After the war it emerged that most of the German navy commanders had not been at all keen on heading up the Channel at any time of day or night, but Hitler, no doubt in consultation with one of his court astrologers, had decided that the war would be won or lost in Norway, and wanted his ships where they could do the most good, fearlessly defending the fjords. To get there, they first had to reach safer German waters. The German Fleet Commander, Otto Cilliax, came up with the plan to use surprise, leaving at night but sailing in broad daylight with support from 250 Luftwaffe planes. So while we were busy practising for Operation Fuller, the German navy was busy sailing off in Operation Cerberus.

Victor Beamish and Robert Finlay-Boyd stared saucer-eyed at the armada below and went down for an even closer look. Suddenly the sky erupted in a wall of blue and red anti-aircraft fire coming up from the heavily armed ships, which had been expecting a full-scale battle but were so far faced by just two British planes. The fire was so intense partly because the ships had added to their already formidable arsenal by placing 20mm quadruple-mounted guns from the local onshore coastal defence batteries on board as an extra layer of anti-aircraft defence.

Beamish, never a man greatly dismayed by long odds, peeled down almost to sea level and both planes attacked an E-boat, which they left listing and engulfed in smoke. By this time their presence had been noted by a dozen ME 109s flying cover above the flotilla and the German planes started to peel down to take on the raiders.

Beamish realized that he had to get back with the news. All pilots were under strict orders not to use their radios for highly confidential messages, so he and Finlay-Boyd made a dash for home. Luckily for them the enemy planes were slowed down in their pursuit by the wall of flak from their own ships, and once Beamish and Finlay-Boyd had out-turned them, the German pilots decided to stay with the convoy rather than engage in a probably fruitless chase which would end over Britain, with them low on fuel and having to worry about British flak instead of their own.

Beamish landed at Kenley aerodrome and charged to the nearest dispersal phone. He told me later that his first response from baffled officialdom was something like 'No, no, old boy, the exercise is later on, get off the line.' They assumed he was still playing the popular game of 'What to do if the boats come out'. Gradually he convinced the person on the other end of the phone that he was serious and was passed up the chain of command, who still seemed reluctant to believe him. Was he sure? Might it not just have been a smaller ship that looked bigger at the time? Victor hit the roof. 'Now see here! I know a bloody battleship when I see one!' he bellowed.

The astonishment in officialdom may simply have been based on the certainty that a daytime escape by such a flotilla up the Channel was virtual suicide, but it may also have been based on well-intentioned intelligence reports from in and around Brest. A brilliant German deception intended to show that the ships would eventually be heading south included oil drums marked 'For use in the tropics' being loaded at the Brest docks, along with white hot-weather uniforms. The German Admiralty even sent bogus invitations to all their key naval officers for an onshore party on 12 February – the day the fleet sailed north. Some or all of this may have got back to the British, as was intended, and reinforced their faith that the ships would probably sail south.

In reality, the *Scharnhorst*'s gamble, though risky, was well calculated. The Germans knew that a large chunk of the British fleet was anchored off Iceland and that other elements, including several ships armed with torpedoes, were on exercise in the far North Sea, unable to be recalled in time. Most of all, they knew that if their warships stayed in Brest they were sure to be sunk. Both sides were playing for high stakes.

When Churchill heard that the ships had made their daytime break, he was enraged and ordered, 'At all costs the ships must be intercepted and made to pay dearly for their audacity.' My own squadron, with no advance warning, was only at an hour's readiness when we were ordered to scramble, with me leading eight planes because the squadron leader and other more senior pilots could not be recalled in time. Our few planes headed for Manston, joining up with a greater number from

72 Squadron. I assumed we would rendezvous with the Beauforts as we had on previous drills, but we did not. What exactly happened is unknown, but one theory is that some Beauforts had just returned from an exercise and had been disarmed while others were away on another exercise. Also the Beauforts were normally stationed at Britain's extremities in Scotland, Cornwall and Portsmouth and the plan relied on their having enough notice to get to the right place for a concerted attack.

For whatever reason, a confused group of Spitfires from several squadrons found ourselves escorting just six Fairey Swordfish aircraft from Manston. The Swordfish was no doubt a mighty weapon of naval warfare in its time. This was not its time. The biplanes, their two wings held together by struts and string, looked as if they had just flown in from a previous war. Their top speed was under a hundred miles an hour, and that was downhill.

The half-dozen Swordfish were led by Lieutenant Commander Eugene Esmonde, already a hero from his part in torpedoing the *Bismarck*. He must have known that the task was hopeless, but he and the six planes under his command pressed on as ordered. On the way out over the Channel, our biggest problem as a fighter escort was flying slowly enough for the Swordfish to keep up. The weather, from a sunnier start, was turning vile, with cloud cover down to a few hundred feet, and there were more than a hundred German fighters far above, waiting for us to show up. We still looked in vain for the Beauforts, some of whom were looking in vain for Spitfires some-where else.

The Swordfish were piloted by incredibly brave men, and despite the fact that most of the planned attack force, most of their fighter cover and virtually all the logic of the attack had been left behind in the garble of mis-communication and surprise, the Swordfish did what they had come for and attacked anyway, like tiny, fearless mosquitoes hurtling towards an elephant.

The Spitfires guarded them as best we could, but the wall of German aircraft was keeping us busy from above and the waves of anti-aircraft fire blazing up from below added to our sense of being trapped between a hammer and an anvil. Each of us was twisting and turning, trying to stay out of the thick of the red and green flak surging up, while also engaging with the ME 109s, which were out in incredible force and had the advantage of altitude. At best we could shelter the Swordfish from annihilation by the fighters from above, though the main thing keep-ing many of the German planes from coming down to engage was fear of their own ships' flak rather than terror of us and a handful of Swordfish. Through all this, Commander Esmonde led his own crew and those of his followers into low-level torpedo runs one at a time on an ironclad armada that was steaming ahead at twenty-seven knots.

I learned later that the German Captain Hoffman on the bridge of the *Scharnhorst* followed their progress, then put down his binoculars, shook his head and said, 'Poor

fellows. They are so very slow. It is nothing but suicide.'
A terrible wall of anti-aircraft fire filled the sky. One by
one the Swordfish went down, Esmonde first. Sometimes
they managed to get an ineffectual torpedo off before
they crashed in flames. Sub-Lieutenant Brian Rose in
another Swordfish managed to fire off a torpedo despite
being shot in the back, while crashing into the water with
his gunner already dead behind him. Of the six crews, all
were shot down. A few crew members including Rose
survived and were picked up by small British boats, but
most were dead even before they hit the icy water. It
was heroic and tragic at the same time. Even our foes
were impressed yet horrified. Fleet Commander Cilliax
described the action later as 'a mothball attack by a
handful of ancient planes, piloted by men whose bravery
surpassed any other action by either side that day'.

Eventually, when we had run out of Swordfish, but
there still seemed to be no shortage of Germans both
above and below, we unhappy few of the fighter escort
went home, had a few pints and tried to work out what it
was all about. The German fleet made it to their home
waters, though their days of terrorizing the shipping lanes
were over: the *Scharnhorst* was damaged by two sea
mines and the ships were to play little active part in the
rest of the war.

Back on land, I attended some of the military post-
mortems on the fiasco, at which a litany of reasons were
put forward, from faulty equipment to messages being
sent in Morse for people listening for voices on radios. As

I sat at a highly polished table in Whitehall for one inquiry, the most junior foreigner among all those senior officers with wide white hat bands and gold 'scrambled egg' uniform decoration much in evidence, I was dismayed that the best they seemed to come up with was a rather fatalistic 'You win some, you lose some.' But that was the real war – heroism and stupidity, tragedy and farce, usually side by side.

Victor Beamish, who also gave evidence at the inquiry, was as enraged as the rest of us. A few pen-pushers even quietly tried to blame him for not sending a radio message instead of maintaining radio silence and bringing the news of the German fleet leaving Brest back in person some twenty minutes later. The reality was that without Beamish being on one of his freelance hunting trips the first Winston Churchill might have heard of the fleet would have been the news of their safe arrival in German waters, which probably would have made him swallow his cigar. The inquiry was as feeble a whitewash as most modern government inquiries, where senior officers and politicians play Pass the Parcel with blame.

In those dangerous days there was little time to dwell on the past, and soon we were back in action. Beamish certainly did not have the time or character to brood on political parlour games.

A few days later heavy snowfall clogged many of the runways in the south-east, including Kenley. Beamish not only ordered them to be cleared ready for action by every man capable of holding a shovel but turned up himself to help. He rounded up a few more 'volunteers' from the station kitchen staff and joined the surge towards the non-commissioned officer (NCO) who was giving out brooms and shovels as if they were going out of fashion. In his haste to get going, Victor charged to the front of the line. He was as usual wearing his battered old flying overalls, with no trace of rank or insignia. The NCO failed to recognize him and barked 'Oi, you! Get to the back of the queue!' Beamish, a man who would tell it as it was to anyone up to and including Churchill, and who would calmly face odds of twenty to one in the skies, smiled and meekly went to the back of the line. Less than a year later he was killed in action, plunging into the same icy waters over which he had soared like an eagle.

✳ 4 ✳

London's Burning

Towards the end of 1941, 411 Squadron relocated south to Hornchurch in Essex and started to take the air war to the enemy. Tactics had changed, partly because of the success of new theories about massive force strategically applied in the form of wings by dozens or even hundreds of fighters, as well as new observations about the importance of altitude supremacy. Essentially, if you hit them hard enough and from high enough, you tended to win.

Hornchurch was a long-established fighter base and arriving there gave me the feeling that I was joining part of a well-oiled machine that had been running for a while. The first time I tiptoed into the plotting room and watched the elegant female ballet of officers from the Women's Auxiliary Air Force (WAAF) listening to positions from radar and radio, then charting movements on a huge map, I felt that here were not just a few brave or foolish souls throwing themselves around in the air but a real war effort.

But Hornchurch had three other appealing aspects to me – location, location and location. Since it was based just nine miles from central London, it took about the same amount of time – under an hour – to be in the air war over France or listening to a concert at Piccadilly in the heart of that remarkable, vibrant city. It would be hard to overstate just what an amazing time it was to be a young American in London, never mind a young American Spitfire pilot.

The Dallas of my youth had not been exactly a haven for good music or theatre, and on days when the weather closed in on Hornchurch, making operations impossible, I would hurry into London on the tube, often passing the devastation of previous Blitz attacks. By midday I would be sitting in the National Gallery, coffee and sandwich in hand, listening to the lunchtime classical music recital by a chamber orchestra. The music seemed to sound all the better for the fact that not very far away on the French coast there was a huge force determined to stamp out everything beautiful and good. I remember being in love with the girl who played the cello. I never actually spoke to her, but one day, before hurrying back to Hornchurch to resume operations, I bought her a huge bouquet of flowers.

As I explored London in the midst of wartime turmoil and destruction, I seemed to see ghosts from much older times. It was Shakespeare's London of narrow alleys with ancient names, or Dickens' London with the fog rolling in over the Thames, wrapping grey water and silent ships in its embrace.

Walking the streets of London in pilot's uniform, I soon realized that I was benefiting from the affection felt by the population for the fly-boys who had fought for the previous eighteen months to save the country from invasion, and more recently to reduce the threat posed by the nightly bombing raids on cities such as London and Coventry. But being a restless young man, I aspired for even more. Looking around me, I could not help but notice how well the Londoners took to volunteers from overseas, whose presence seemed to affirm Britain's role as the centre of opposition to Hitler, and perhaps in some odd wishful way to promise ultimate victory. Many of the overseas volunteers had shoulder-flashes on their uniforms proclaiming 'Free France' or 'Free Norway'. I rustled up my own label and sewed it on my sleeve. It read: 'Free USA'.

Whether it was because of the uniform, the label or the accent, 1941 in London represented a very pleasant war for me. If I went to the cinema and bought a ticket for the cheap seats for the princely sum of one shilling and threepence, I was immediately herded to the best, more expensive seats, the 'two-and-nines', by some patriotic usherette. Londoners particularly loved their fighter pilots, wherever they were from. They knew, without ever saying so, that for some of the young men enjoying themselves in London that night, depending on their fortunes in the air war the next morning, this might be their last visit.

Probably in an effort to curtail the worst excesses of marauding amorous pilots, the Powers That Be attempted to regulate our social life by staging tea dances at Grosvenor House, where well-brought-up young ladies would risk life and limb dancing with foreign pilots. In order to get on the social register, we pilots had to turn up at an imposing house near Cadogan Square for a sort of upper-class interview. I think we were given points for polite chit-chat and not slurping our tea. The winners were invited to dances or to weekends in stately country mansions that looked like the setting for Agatha Christie murders. I seem to remember that the person in charge of such things was called Lady Frances Haggard. She was probably even more haggard because of the behaviour of some of her adopted pilots.

After my tea-time interview, I was curious to know how I had scored. I got to know one of the girls who worked there and persuaded her – probably at the risk of a firing squad for supplying information to the enemy – to retrieve my notes from the files. The report read 'Nice American manners . . . can go most places'. I felt as if I had been mentioned in dispatches.

At about the same time, I got to know Sir Walter Elliot, a former government minister and adviser to the royal family, who was now devoting his time as a sort of PR man, in particular attempting to encourage America to join the war effort, rather than just sending me as a delegate. One day, when I was looking spectacularly dishevelled after some especially good party the night before, he dragged me off to a reception somewhere in the centre of town, where I found myself slightly sheepishly being introduced to the Queen by this latter-day Sir Walter as 'a somewhat disreputable friend from the other side of the Atlantic'. If she had her doubts about the unkempt colonial, she kept them to herself, probably in the hope that a few million more just like me would be persuaded to join in. I tried to look as if I had not personally kicked George III out of the colonies.

I decided not to tell her that my only other experiences of the royal family had not gone very well. One of these was lining up in the rain on the most miserable day imaginable in Lincolnshire when George VI came out to inspect the new squadron. Royalty, then as now, has developed a skilful line of small talk about the weather, but when he reached me, obviously interested to find out what made this strange American stray tick, he asked me why I had come over all the way from Texas. As rain trickled off the end of my nose and the Lincolnshire dampness soaked into my uniform, I told him I had been attracted by the weather. He smiled and moved along swiftly.

By now I was on a roll in terms of dealing with royalty. A few months later, when the Duchess of Kent visited a fighter station I happened to be at, some bright PR man decided that the resultant photo opportunity would look more heroic if the Duchess were waving off some valiant Spitfire pilots who were about to take off on the runway behind her. My plane was closest to her, and as I took off across wind on our simulated scramble the slipstream from my plane blew her skirt over her head, rather like that later famous picture of Marilyn Monroe. After that, I was not asked to participate in too many photo opportunities with royalty.

Whether king or commoner, in the services or civilian, it was a dangerous, exciting time to be around London. I remember sitting on a park bench, late one night in St James's Park, stuck during the Blitz, watching as the bombs fell, arc lights searched the sky and fires from burning buildings glowed on the skyline. The rumble of exploding bombs was counterpointed by the chatter of ack-ack guns, like a vast demented symphony and firework display all rolled into one for which I had a free ringside seat. Meanwhile, the theatre shows played on and the concerts continued. In the course of the Blitz some 100,000 civilians were killed or wounded and more than 130,000 houses destroyed, yet the more the enemy bombed, the more determined the Londoners seemed to be to resist.

This characteristic was particularly impressive to a young American. In general Americans are demonstrative people, not known for their stoicism. I remembered the reaction about four years earlier in America to the broadcast of *The War of the Worlds*, Orson Welles' radio drama about the Martians invading earth. Those who thought it was a real news bulletin drove off in all directions in a panic, crashing into each other, taking up arms and generally causing mayhem. In London, in the middle of a Blitz firestorm, I watched as the locals calmly queued up to get into an air-raid shelter – 'After you,' 'No, please – after you.'

Unlike the First World War, this was a battle that involved everyone in the country. People knew what they were fighting for and they did so in whatever way they could. Despite that difference, one of my Hornchurch colleagues, Hankin, an intelligence officer and veteran of the Royal Flying Corps from the Great War, used to get his world wars mixed up, particularly after he had too much to drink. He would drag a group of us around the back streets of London, often in the middle of a blackout or blitz, looking for some wonderful little bar that had disappeared twenty years earlier from the real world but still existed inside his fuddled mind.

When, at the end of such evenings, we would weave our way back to the tube station to catch the last underground train back to Hornchurch, the Londoners would already be settling down with blankets on the platforms, for the stations were being used as ready-made air-raid shelters. Sometimes they would call to us as we staggered onto the train – 'Give 'em hell, boys.' With their homes under threat or in ruins and their capital city under nightly attack, the thoughts of us taking the war to the fascists seemed to cheer them up. On the other hand the sight of a handful of merry, weaving pilots propping each other up as they barely managed to catch the last tube train might not have inspired them with much confidence. I and my fellow pilots lost count of the times we fell into a hazy slumber on that last train of the night and woke up at the terminus in Upminster, for a long late-night walk or hitchhike back to the base.

Back at our quarters at Hornchurch there would often be further festivities in the officers' mess, usually into the wee small hours. For those like me, not always used to getting enough to eat, this place was heaven. Spitfire pilots, even in the midst of severe rationing, were fed like prize geese, in order to ensure that we could function under the pressures of aerial combat, where a fast mind and quick reflexes at high altitude made the difference between a fighter ace and a dead pilot. The rest of the population, faced with endless rationing of even the most basic foods, did not seem to begrudge us fighter pilots the extra bacon and eggs. The person in charge of catering at Hornchurch was no less a figure in peacetime than the chef of the Dorchester Hotel. As I crammed in some great meal before or after a sortie, I would sometimes smile at the thought of me having to eat my way into the war in Detroit because I was too light. At this rate, I might end up too heavy to get out again.

But combat was always good for burning off calories, and if that failed, an average night in the officers' mess would often do the same. One of the most impressively wild parties I have ever been to must have been around that time. Someone fairly high up the RAF food chain decided it would be much more efficient to administer all the air force station mess funds centrally. Previously each location had operated its own fund and some of these had built up quite impressive surpluses. All of us recognized that this was a sensible move, but we felt we should at least see all that cash off by using a little of the surplus to throw it a farewell party or two. The best one was at Biggin Hill, where there were pilots from all twelve group stations who arrived by air and parked their Spitfires and Hurricanes like stylish limos outside the Oscars. It was quite a night, and as I watched the wobbly take-offs and several dozen pilots weaving around in the sky the next morning, I remembered sitting by that riverbank in Texas, watching a bunch of drunken Texan robins doing much the same. If Hitler had chosen that moment for his big offensive, we would have been in some difficulty.

Such parties usually resulted in mayhem and the destruction of His Majesty's property, but few fatalities. I have slightly hazy memories of a fine party at our satellite aerodrome in Southend, at which I was riding a motorbike around inside the house that was serving as our mess – and it certainly was a mess. I had a lovely young WAAF officer riding on the pillion as we raced from room to room before finally roaring out of the front door and taking off down some steps. I can't remember landing, but I found out that she got engaged to one of the Czech pilots a week later.

Many of us were very keen on motorbikes and sports

cars at the time, particularly if they were filled with high-octane aviation fuel, which made them go like rockets. The aviation fuel was dyed bright green to prevent such wicked misuse, but our youthful wartime perspective on life and death meant that we were not overly bothered by such regulations. Some of our cars and bikes had dummy fuel tanks with just enough of the legal fuel to pass the spot checks by the stern men from the Special Investigations Branch, who sometimes paid us unexpected visits waving their dipsticks menacingly.

When not attempting to break speed records, we were avid players of demented communal games, which were usually somewhere between a team sport and a riot. Near the heart of virtually every such venture was a superb flyer called Wilfred Duncan Smith, known to one and all as Drunken Duncan. When he was not leading the inebriated festivities, he was one of the most skilled and deadly fighter pilots I ever met. He taught me tactics for surviving and winning a dogfight that were not to be found in any training manual and almost certainly saved my life. When he was in party mood he was just as unstoppable.

One of his performances that was in greatest demand was his impersonation of a Heinkel 111 German bomber on a daring daylight raid over London. With no props but a few chairs and a very bad Hitler impression, he would launch his bombing raid, using anything that was handy as projectiles, and would stop only when the rest of us had shot him down and sent him crashing to the floor.

Other games were based on the losers buying the winners drinks, which inevitably led to more games in which the winners had to reciprocate, until no-one could remember if they had won or lost. A favourite one was Prisoners, with no discernible rules, other than the objective to capture as many of the other team as possible and sit on them at your side of the room until eventually everyone was on the same side of the room, either being sat on or perched on top of a heap of prisoners. While it was funny at the time, my later experiences in prisoner-of-war camps across Europe made me realize what it was like to be sat on for several years in a row.

Best of all was the game Shipwreck. Anything that was floor space was regarded as sea water, to be avoided at all costs. Survivors would clamber on furniture rafts, or use curtains and light fittings as Tarzan ropes to swing from one island to the next, knocking their foes into the deep blue sea of a wooden floor. A lifetime later, I was reminded of Duncan Smith's heroic attempts to hold together his raft of tables and chairs, which was drifting perilously apart as he valiantly tried to repel boarders until he finally capsized to the floor. The memory sprang back to life as I watched his offspring on television, sixty years later. His son Iain Duncan Smith, erstwhile leader of the Conservative Party in Britain, had the same look on his face when he was trying to hold that unruly bunch together until he too ended up in the soup.

When we could take no more, we would crash into bed for a few hours' sleep before the air war began again in earnest, often at dawn. I had started out being billeted in the officers' mess, which was convenient in that it was not very far to stagger to bed after our celebrations, but not a great place to get any privacy or sleep. Eventually, I managed to get a room all to myself in the married quarters, with my own bath. I used to lie in a bubble-filled tub listening to wonderful classical music on a battered old wind-up gramophone, thinking it was not such a bad war after all.

For Intelligence Officer Hankin, still feeling the effects of his night on the town, the line between work and play, and between waking and sleeping, would sometimes become blurred in much the same way as he got his wars mixed up. He shared a room with a pilot who, like most of us, would sometimes have nightmares in which the moments of tension and fear from previous dogfights would resurface. As the young pilot called out in his sleep, deep in a dream battle, Hankin would blearily roll out of bed, grope for paper and pencil, and start to fill out a combat report in the dark. 'Not so fast, old lad, let me get it down,' he would mumble, before shambling back to bed. The next morning, on his bedside table, there would be a garbled, barely decipherable combat report of a nightmare dogfight that neither of them could quite remember.

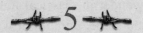

5

Fierce Fiery Warriors

Somehow, the next morning, we would be up early and in our cockpits, taking off with first light in one of the great fighter formation sweeps which were then becoming a favourite tactic. As the war progressed, these sweeps, known by odd code names such as Rhubarb or Circus, had one drawback. Sometimes, when flying over enemy-held territory, we would have half-a-dozen bombers flying out front as bait, then scores of fighters stepped all the way up to 30,000 feet. The Luftwaffe decided to avoid such confrontations and fight on their own terms, employing methods that included low-level hit-and-run raids by small groups of FW 190s, which at the time were outpacing even the current Spitfire Mark Vs. In fact a captured 190 helped in the development of the more powerful Spitfire Mark IX, the first of which were based at Hornchurch.

Below: My sister Adele and I prepare for a quick getaway, Dallas, Texas, 1925.

Right: My childhood friend George Coe (who rode with Billy the Kid) pictured in 1926.

Below: I was given a day off school to watch Charles Lindbergh's parade through Dallas following his first transatlantic flight, 1927.

Above: Our early training in Canada in 1940 was mostly in the lumbering Fairey Battles.

In the cockpit of a Battle, 1940.

Above: The converted liner troopship *Georgic* brought me to England in early 1941. She was bombed at Suez later that year.

Left: The formal portrait that I sent home to my family in 1941.

Below left: 411 Squadron CO Stan Turner would light his pipe in the cockpit after a successful engagement.

Below right: Cowboy Blatchford, a great pilot and friend, killed in 1943.

The dual-control Magister which I flew and from which Buck McNair jumped.

Waiting to scramble outside the dispersal hut, Digby, 1941. I am on the right looking up.

Buck McNair spins me another tall tale. He went on to become one of Canada's fighter aces.

Don Blakeslee, later a USAAF fighter ace, me, and Gordie Chamberlain in 1941. Gordie was killed in action two weeks after this photograph was taken.

An unexpected handshake from Canadian
Prime Minister Mackenzie King, 1941.

Top: The German battle cruiser *Scharnhorst* was the target of the ill-fated 'Channel Dash' attack in early 1942.

Above: Victor Beamish was the first to spot the *Scharnhorst*. He was killed in action in March 1942.

Left: My friend and mentor Wilfred Duncan Smith, father of politician Iain Duncan Smith.

In the cockpit of my beloved Spitfire DBF, late 1941.

Returning from one of many eventless circus sorties, I remember thinking that if I was a German pilot and I knew that the equivalent of a flying sledgehammer was coaxing me out to play, the invitation would be one I could definitely decline. In fact it would not be a prospect that would lure me out of a burning hangar, even with the juicy prospect of half-a-dozen bombers beckoning like bait on a celestial hook. On one such sweep I remember a group of German planes, apparently as oblivious of us as we had been of them, coming out of the sun and flying straight through our formation, both sides intent on going somewhere else. I found myself passing so close to an ME 109F that I could see the pilot clearly. I gave him a good hard glare, no doubt with devastating effect, but perhaps at this stage in the war I was not aggressive enough, for I struggled to equate some of the enemy pilots with the monstrous actions being inflicted on the people of Europe, even though the two were inextricably linked.

During that first year of combat flying, I had a few close shaves. I helped improve the aim of several enemy ack-ack crews along the French coast when I was on my way home from beating up targets in northern France or shooting up flak ships. On more than one occasion I came back with a neat line of holes made by Bofors guns, which usually ended somewhere near the cockpit. Each time I thought about it, I reached out for a piece of wood to touch for continued good luck.

Perhaps that's why, like most of my colleagues, I

became a bit superstitious. I always believed in the scientific efficacy of knocking on wood, but the cockpit of my beloved Spit, though brilliantly designed, was a bit short on mahogany. I solved this small design oversight by fixing a little wooden matchbox under the reflector sight of my gun. As the war progressed I found that I only had to think a half-optimistic thought of the 'I'm still here' variety and I would be reaching for my matchbox, like an additional instrument on my dashboard.

For much the same reason, I had an apple painted on the nose of my Spitfire. When asked why, my answer would depend on what mood I was in. Sometimes I blathered about the Bible and the apple in the Garden of Eden that brought about the Fall of Man. If I was in a classical mood, I rambled about Homer and the golden apple that Paris gave to the wrong girl in the world's first beauty contest, leading to the Fall of Troy. But mostly I stuck with a third explanation, of the apple that struck Newton on the head, making him realize a few things about gravity and the eternal truth that 'What goes up must come down,' though not necessarily all in one piece.

To save me from such thoughts, I looked to older, more experienced pilots such as Wilfred Duncan Smith or Victor Beamish. They gave off an aura of affable but deadly capability, as did some of the newer recruits such as Buck McNair, who was as ambitious and competitive as he was talented.

Another great comfort was our commanding officer at the time – Stan Turner, a Canadian who had flown with

Douglas Bader's squadron. When we were on the way home from some tough sortie, at last heading in the right direction for survival, he had the endearing habit of lighting up his pipe. The rest of us would glance over at his cockpit as it filled with pipe smoke and imagine that somewhere in there he was warming his hands on an open coal fire and probably wearing carpet slippers. Little things like that were incredibly important to us. In a world turned upside down, anything that had even the vaguest whiff of stability and security was something to be cherished. The next day always brought more danger, or sometimes unexpected news.

Which brings me to one otherwise uneventful scramble from Hornchurch in December of that year. One of my colleagues came haring out of the hangars and ran over to the plane where I was preparing with others for take-off. He ran alongside and shouted. With all the noise and commotion it took a few seconds for the news to sink in: the Japanese had bombed Pearl Harbor and the United States was at war with all the Axis forces.

I reached out and patted my lucky matchbox before I took off. My mind was full of emotions, some of which were at war with each other. My main feeling was a shiver of relief. At last the huge productive power of America would be turned on Hitler. The massive population of the United States, many of whom had hated the policy of neutrality when they could see the suffering in Europe, would now be employed in building a war machine that would sweep the fascists back, all the way to Berlin.

Britain in the west and Russia in the east were no longer alone.

Yet a tiny part of me also marked the end of a very special time. I was no longer going to be the only US kid on the block with a Spitfire. Soon the United States would be turning out phalanxes of new pilots in new fighters and new bombers. I rubbed the home-made sign on my shoulder – 'Free USA'. Maybe I should go into mass production? But if a tiny part of me mourned the passing of my status as a rare creature, like a Texan robin who had thrown in his lot with a flock of English sparrows, most of me rejoiced. The Yanks were coming.

While that juggernaut of the American economy finally snapped itself out of the Depression and started picking up speed, like an express train getting up steam, life for me and my fellow flyers in 411 squadron went on as before, though my contacts with the enemy seemed to become ever more frequent and ever more fierce.

One such day in January 1942 started much like the rest. A gentle but insistent prodding woke me from what seemed like about five minutes' sleep. There had been one of the frequent parties the night before and the thought of getting up before the sun held little appeal. The prodding continued. As on every morning, it was an orderly bringing me a cup of coffee. Having spent so much of my life fending for myself, I was always quietly impressed at how well the RAF looked after me, but there always came a point when the service felt it was time for me to pay back all the cups of coffee and concerts, and it was usually about this time in the morning.

I wriggled into my gear and walked into the icy morning towards the dispersal hut. Already the roar of Spitfire engines being tested or warmed up gave the day a sense of anticipation. The first sortie was pretty routine. We roared off over the English Channel to guard convoys, and one of our group spotted a JU 88 heading for home at 5,000 feet, but we lost it in the clouds and returned to base. Our second sortie was more lively. Four of us took off again from Hornchurch at about three o'clock in the afternoon. We made a quick stop at Manston and set off again with full tanks, flying fast and low across the Channel. The sea looked a cold slate grey, but as always there was a rush of exhilaration when France loomed up in front of us and we crossed the coast near Dunkirk.

It was only a year and a half since the waters below had been filled with dead or desperate British troops in the chaotic evacuation that marked Germany's triumph in mainland Europe. Then, the sea was covered with small boats as anything that could float came to help with the mass evacuation. The rescuers came in fishing boats and coal barges, in lifeboats from liners and brightly painted holiday yachts.

My friend Douglas Bader had been in the skies over Dunkirk that day and once described the scene. Planes milled about, both British and German, with no apparent order or plan on either side. He said that the scene at sea level during the evacuation looked like a coastal road in

England on a bank holiday. There were so many boats that it seemed as if a person could walk from Britain to France without getting his feet wet. Oil tanks in Dunkirk harbour had been set ablaze and the British pilots were able to follow the smoke, which rose in a huge funnel, straight up in a windless sky. It could be seen all the way from the English coast, like a pillar at the end of a long, floating arrow made up of tiny vessels. Soon, every British plane was engaged in desperate actions trying to fight off vastly superior numbers of German aircraft which were bombing the rescue ships and strafing the men huddled on the chaotic beaches below.

Another of my friends from later prison-camp days, Bob Tuck, had flown back and forth over the heads of the hapless British soldiers below, trying to protect them from air attack. He shot down five enemy planes in one day.

Today there were no heroes, nor any signs of life below. The sea was flat and empty as we roared low across the coast. This was a Rhubarb sortie, in which we were to fly low in small numbers, identify military or economic targets of opportunity, move in fast, shoot them up and get home, preferably unscathed. Our first target loomed below, a group of barges on a canal, loaded with supplies. It was like being back in Canada, flying low above the rivers with my own plane's shadow racing along the ground beside me. I was right behind Flight Lieutenant Boomer and we both flew directly over the barges at virtually zero height, raking them with fire as the men on board dived for the safety of the water.

Making our way back to the coast, we came across a beach swarming with German troops laying barbed wire and sea defences to repel any thoughts of an Allied invasion. Boomer roared down and strafed them. Part of me felt sorry for the poor ant-like creatures running and diving for cover that was not there, maybe because I had been thinking of the other floundering and dying British soldiers who had lost their lives on the same beaches around Dunkirk two years earlier. But another part of me knew that this was what the war was about and that if these men were allowed to continue with their barbed wire and tank traps, there would be young American and British bodies entangled on that same wire if ever we managed to launch a counter-invasion.

Suddenly, the air around us exploded as if we were in a fireworks display. We were being pounded by a German anti-aircraft ship that was moored just offshore. A line of flak fragments thudded into the root of my port wing, but it held fast. I tried to remember everything I had been taught. One lesson from Duncan Smith came back to me. As he weaved about during one of our endless drunken party games back at the officers' mess, he had stared at me wisely and said, 'Never stay on the same vector longer than you have to!'

As the flak explosions crackled around me, I took Duncan Smith's advice and peeled off, diving down almost to sea level before changing direction again and vectoring on to the flak ship. It was still blazing away at me, but I was changing direction and moving fast, coming up at it from the stern. I started firing the cannons just as I reached the ship and I could see the results thudding home in impressive fiery lines that led directly to the wheel house. I sustained the fire as long as I could and then peeled away, changing direction again as I gained altitude. Looking down, I could see smoke coming from the wheel house. Our ammunition and fuel were getting low, so we headed for home.

The sense of relief at getting back home after a successful mission was almost palpable, and I was always anxious to get out of the plane and back into normal life for a few hours at least, to a world of good food, a wild social life and some quiet evenings in listening to Mozart while reading a cowboy novel.

Despite the illusions of normality though, one by one I saw friends and comrades with whom I had flown since the formation of the squadron take off and never return. Jack Coleman and Sergeant Donald Court set off on a fairly routine mission flying top cover for a formation of Hurri-bombers – Hurricanes specially converted for dive-bombing techniques learned from the Stukas. They were jumped by a large formation of enemy aircraft and both were shot down and killed over the sea.

A week later one of my closest friends of the time, Gordie Chamberlain, along with Tom Holden, were protecting a convoy not far from Calais when they were attacked by five ME 109s. Both were killed in the dog-fight that followed. I came to understand what I had started to learn when my fellow trainee had burned to death in front of my eyes some months earlier. The death of my closest comrades resulted in my developing some of the reserve I had originally found so strange among the veteran pilots I most admired. Like Duncan-Smith, they would be the soul of the party and ready for anything, but they kept something in reserve for themselves and the lonely battles ahead.

On one dusk patrol off the east coast, my wing man and I were vectored on to a couple of JU 88s, heading back out to sea after pulverizing some unfortunate factory or street. By this point in the war, such daylight raids were increasingly rare, with the Luftwaffe sticking more to night-time operations. We zeroed in on the 88s and I was still shooting holes in one when it disappeared into cloud. That is where the plotting charts stopped and it was assumed to have been shot down – my first air victory, though like most things in life, not quite the way I had imagined it.

On another occasion, I was flying over occupied Holland with Cowboy Blatchford, when we ran into a wartime moral conundrum. We found ourselves peering down at a Luftwaffe formation flying below us and were about to scream down on them when we noticed that they were light trainer aircraft with no armaments. Now, if I had been back in London, catching the last tube to Hornchurch, and had conducted a poll among the Londoners huddled under blankets along the platforms, their homes in danger or already flattened, there would have been little doubt of the majority view: every

German trainer aircraft and every trainee enemy pilot blasted out of the sky was one less to cause destruction later. But for me, looking down on a bunch of kids who could not fire back, the issue did not seem so clear cut at the time.

We were still pondering this moral maze like a couple of medieval theologians when we ourselves were jumped by six ME 109s who had been flying even higher than we were, keeping an eye on the trainees below. We made a desperate bid to get back to England, with all six of the enemy constantly trying to blow us out of the sky. We survived because we watched each other's tail, and when things got really hairy we turned back into them and gave them a taste of their own medicine, before returning to our long retreat. They finally gave up on us about halfway across the Channel, no doubt reluctant to continue this adult version of kids in a fight getting their big brother to fight your big brother.

If anyone was going to be watching your tail, Cowboy Blatchford from Edmonton in the Canadian west was a great choice. Cowboy and I had earlier tried to introduce some songs of the Old West to our reluctant Anglo-Saxon colleagues. Our duet rendition of the cowboy classic 'Blood on the Saddle' became something of a milestone in tuneless musical history, and an unofficial anthem for our section. Cowboy, a great friend of our commander Harry Broadhurst, was the first Canadian to shoot down an enemy plane during the war, in the chaos of 1939 over France. Later, he led an attack that accounted for eight destroyed and five damaged enemy aircraft in a single action. Badly shot up and out of ammunition, Cowboy had turned back into the enemy and started attempting to ram them, chopping bits out of his foes with his propeller – an action that won him a Distinguished Flying Cross. I was proud to be flying beside him that day. Cowboy was killed in action a year later in 1943.

And so I reached a day towards the end of March 1942, when I was heading home for Hornchurch from a sweep that had taken us all the way to Commines in Belgium. We were on our way back and I was glancing over to our commanding officer Stan Turner's plane on my wing, to see if he had lit his pipe yet. He hadn't. A garbled crackle over the radio from someone in the squadron called urgently for my section to break formation. I did a tight 180-degree turn, thanking my lucky stars that I had done so much aerobatic flying in my training just for the hell of it.

I was just in time to see a Focke-Wulf 190 banked over on one side as it pulled away to the right some distance below me. If I simply pushed the nose of my Spitfire down in hot pursuit, the fuel injection system that we were using at the time would have caused my engine to cough and splutter, and I would have lost a lot of speed. Instead, I did a great whooshing three-quarters roll to my left, losing a great deal of height by doing so.

Much to my delight, and no doubt to the luckless Luftwaffe pilot's dismay, I came out neatly directly behind him at the same height at a range of just 200 yards. I pressed the gun trigger and as I closed in, I could see I was hitting home. Bright cannon shells crackled and exploded in a deadly line along one of his wing roots. Bits of the Focke-Wulf's engine cowling disintegrated into the air and then the whole thing went down in a cloud of smoke.

Jubilant, I pulled up and looked for my formation. By now they were specks in the distance. To my left another straggler Spitfire, probably from my own section, was also trying to catch up, but he was in big trouble: an ME 109 was right on his tail. I shouted a warning over the radio and pushed the throttle through the gate as I changed course and headed for the 109.

I was closing in on his beam and started firing while I worked my way around to quarter, then fine quarter, all the time reducing my angle of deflection until I was just a hundred yards dead astern before I opened up. I could see my cannon fire hitting home along his fuselage and was glad to give the pilot something to think about other than shooting down my colleague. I held steady, sustaining the cannon fire to make sure he was going down, but suddenly there was a juddering thump. My guns stopped working.

I knew I had probably been hit and jerked around in a left-hand turn with lots of bottom rudder to try getting away from whoever was on to me. The engine began to stammer, and I realized I was in even bigger trouble than I had thought. The engine was still ticking over, but my revs were dropping fast, so my speed was falling. Worse still, a quick glance around showed that several ME 109s were closing on me from two directions.

By this time I was down to about 10,000 feet, with virtually no pull on the prop at all. If I slowed down much more I would be standing still, which is never a good idea when in a large heavy object a long way above the ground. Half-a-dozen enemy planes, a mixed bag of 109s and 190s, were now circling, taking it in turns to try to finish me off. I pummelled my dead gun in rage.

Every attack they made against me I turned in to face head on, and I flew straight at them. This made me harder to hit as a smaller profile, and also an object to avoid flying into. But it also meant that I had to stare straight at the smoke coming from their guns, their lead heading straight at me. Some of their cannon fire hit home into the structure of my beloved Spitfire which had carried me through so many scrapes and up to now had never let me down.

As a Focke-Wulf screamed straight at me, guns blazing, out of force of habit or blind optimism I kept pushing my silent firing button in reply. I even heard my own voice, loud and surreal in the cockpit, shouting 'Bang! Bang!' as I narrowly avoided colliding with one of my tormentors.

It looked as if my career as a pilot, and as a member of the human race, was just about to come to an end. I cut my engine, since it was clearly full of holes and not doing much good. I knew that there are few worse ways to go than being trapped in a cockpit on fire and I only really had two choices – pick a spot to crash-land or bail out. While the journey down on a parachute would no doubt have been much more scenic and leisurely, I knew that it would give the Wehrmacht plenty of time to have a reception committee waiting to catch me on the ground, or perhaps even provide the Focke-Wulf 190s with target practice on the way down. Landing under my own steam seemed to offer a better chance of getting away.

While I was pondering, the German fighters continued to take it in turns to finish me off, but my lack of horse-power and rapidly lowering altitude started to work in my favour. The high-powered enemy planes whizzed by, guns blazing, while I drifted ponderously down. I was going so slowly that they all tended to overshoot. Perhaps, I thought, this was the secret of modern aerial warfare – no engine, no guns. My thoughts were interrupted by the rapidly approaching ground, and rather than finish my new theory of warfare with no pilot, I picked a nice flat field next to what looked like an old Gothic church, on the edge of a picturesque French village.

Coming in to land, I realized that I was a bit too high, and a bit too fast, without flaps, and it dawned on me that I was likely to skid right across the field, straight into the church wall. I knew that demolishing the ancient church was not likely to make a good impression on the locals, and that the church was not likely to make a good impression on me, so I decided to stop at all costs.

As I reached the ground, I dug a wing tip into the field. Almost instantly my plane began a cartwheel, careering over the ground. Flashes of grass and sky alternated as pieces of the plane started to disintegrate. One wing was practically ripped off and a shuddering crunch close behind me told me my fuselage had probably gone too. I finally came to a stop, not too far from the church, which – like myself – was miraculously intact.

6

The Day of Reckoning

The first thing I noticed after crash-landing was that the church seemed to be upside down, but as my head cleared I realized that I was hanging upside down in the remains of the cockpit. The straps had held me in place. I wriggled from the remains, hoping to get out before something blew up, and stood a little distance from the wreckage. Even though my mind was racing, I felt as if things were happening in slow motion. Gradually my hearing and sight came back to normal. I ached from bruises caused by the crash-landing, but remarkably apart from a few scratches there was nothing broken and I was all in one piece.

The same could not be said of my beloved Spit, which had taken me through so much over the previous months. The fuselage had neatly broken in two just behind my seat. The wings seemed to be going in different directions and just about anything else that could be broken was in ruins. Standing for a moment beside the remains of the plane as if at the funeral of an old friend, I thought of all the lessons I'd been given in England, and in training in Canada, on the importance of not allowing your machine to fall intact into enemy hands. Looking at the wreckage, I wondered if they might give me a medal for outstanding destruction.

But the medal would have to wait. One of the German planes dipped low to see if I had survived and presumably to radio my position to ground forces to pick me up. I dived for cover and as soon as the coast was clear hurried into the village, which was little more than one street. If I was expecting a brass band reception, I was disappointed. The village appeared as deserted as a Texas ghost town. Every door was shut, windows shuttered or empty. Not even a dog barked. Then there was a creak as a cottage door opened and a little girl of maybe ten years old peered out.

She took a few steps towards me. I took a few steps back, not wanting to get such a young child in serious trouble for trying to help a foreign airman. But she kept coming, as if odd Americans fell from the sky into her village every day. She held out her hand. I took it and she led me back to her house. I was hauled through the open door and it was shut tight behind me.

I found myself looking at an attractive woman, probably in her late twenties, with a kind, sad face. She smiled and ushered me upstairs.

I deployed the only French I could think of, which was an unconvincing '*Bonjour*', and then started explaining in English that I was an American with the Canadians fighting for the British. She told me in the universal language of those in a hurry dealing with possible idiots to shut up, and tugged at my clothing. Baffled, and probably still a bit shaken from my landing, I was a bit slow on the uptake. She went to a cupboard and took out some men's clothes.

I took off my flying jacket and struggled out of my flying boots. I was about to take off my trousers when I turned to see that both mother and daughter had formed an impromptu audience for my striptease. I hesitated, a bit shy, but the mother pointed out of the window urgently. The soldiers were on their way. I dropped my trousers and pulled on the new ones. The little girl applauded. The new trousers were a bit short but service-able and I pulled on a black jacket that looked as if it might fit provided I didn't try to do up the buttons. I com-pleted my transformation into a French peasant with a pair of clogs. I was offered boots, but like some in-experienced actor I went for overkill with the clogs – a decision I started to regret almost as soon as I teetered and clopped my way back downstairs.

There was no time for a proper thank you, a proper hello or goodbye. This kind, brave woman and her young daughter took me to the back door of their house. I kissed the little girl and hugged her mother, knowing that the soldiers were likely to be coming through the front door as I was hurtling out the back.

In the coming weeks and months I was to become aware of the heroism of ordinary people, risking everything for a stranger. When I left America, I was fighting for some abstract notions, against bullying and for democracy. Now I knew that I was fighting for real people like this woman, and it made me determined to evade capture, get back to England and climb back into the first Spitfire cockpit I could find to continue the war.

Much later, I found out a little about the first person in France to come to my aid. Her name was Pauline Cam, a widow who survived by doing odd jobs around the village. When she heard my crash-landing she sent her daughter out looking for me and got the clothes ready to transform me from pilot to local. The clothes belonged to her husband, who had been killed by the advancing Germans in the opening days of the war. The fact that his clothes were being used to open a new front against the enemy seemed to give her some comfort, though I wonder if as she watched a fleeing stranger disappear into the countryside, dressed in the clothes of the man she had loved, she was getting one last glimpse of her husband, not just an American on the run.

As I clopped my way out of the village I guessed that the enemy had by now reached my crash site and were tearing the surrounding fields and houses apart looking for the missing pilot. I found myself running along the side of a little canal or river and, having watched too many movies about prisoners escaping from chain gangs in the 1930s, remembered that in virtually every one the escapee threw the pursuing bloodhounds off the scent by wading down the middle of a river.

I plunged in. It was not wide, but it got deeper and deeper. Soon I was up to my waist, then my chest. I sniffed. Something smelled truly terrible. The noise of the countryside and the thought of my pursuers being just steps away propelled me on as it gradually dawned on me that the canal was actually some kind of open sewer. A particularly loud noise, perhaps a pursuer's boot snapping on a twig, caused me to submerge myself completely into the foul-smelling murk. I stayed under as long as I could, and when I surfaced, gagging and retching, the coast was clear.

I stayed away from towns and buildings where I could, so as to avoid detection, and following my dip in the sewer the locals were probably very grateful. That night I found a secluded copse of trees and made camp as best I could. I thought of the hobo jungle camps I had used in the 1930s Depression. They at least had the advantage of people and life and a fire to warm oneself, but clearly a fire here was out of the question, since it would attract unwelcome attention. I turned my attention to my little escape kit in a tin, examining its contents in detail for the first time.

The little box contained a map of the Pas de Calais, some French money, a steel file, a tiny compass and some Horlicks tablets. I treated myself to one of the tablets and curled up in a nest of leaves, exhausted.

I woke cold and early as the first rays of sunlight slanted through the trees. For the first time I felt the full impact of the crash-landing and was very stiff until the sun warmed me up. I pored over my little escape map and picked what looked like a sparsely populated area as my objective and kept walking, occasionally allowing myself another of my dwindling supply of Horlicks tablets to stave off the worst of the hunger pangs.

Setting off in the general direction of nowhere, I was soon forced to come into contact with another human being. I found my way blocked by a wider river and, having wandered about looking for a bridge, found that the only way across was via a small ferry boat. I handed over some of the French money from my escape kit to the ferryman. He took it silently, handed me my change and rowed me across. We never said a word, and if he had his suspicions about the silent stranger in badly fitting clothes who smelled as if he had recently been swimming in a sewer, he kept them to himself.

Later that same day, I was walking along a deserted road when I heard the rumble of a heavy vehicle – an army truck. Looking around desperately for some cover, I saw a large haystack in a field that sloped off to one side of the road. I took a running leap from the road and dived into the welcoming hay. Unfortunately it turned out that the hay was just a few wisps used to cover an impressively large manure heap, but I had no choice but to burrow into the dunghill and wait for the vehicle to pass. By the time I slithered out of the bogus haystack I smelled so bad that I figured if the Germans caught me they would probably throw me back again.

The same pattern of fairly aimless wanderings lasted for about three days, and perhaps given an endless supply of Horlicks tablets and a lot of luck, I could have spent the rest of the war shuffling around the byways of the Pas de Calais. As it was, I wanted to get back into the war and above all to avoid spending the next several years locked up in some German prison camp. Given my precarious existence in the Hungry Thirties, I was used to not always having enough to eat, but as night fell for a third time since I had crashed, I knew I had to take my chance and make contact with some locals, hoping that they were on the right side.

At about the same time as I came to that conclusion, I found myself on the outskirts of a village called Quercamps. Instead of skirting around it, I walked down the deserted main street. I could hear music seeping out of a very closed and shuttered tavern. Several voices were raised, singing French songs from the trenches of the Great War. It seemed unlikely that there would be many fascists joining in the chorus, so I rapped hard on the closed shutters. There was immediate silence.

Eventually someone shuffled to the door and opened it a crack. Suspicious faces peered out from behind the owner of the establishment. This was Monsieur Boulanger, an elderly man who smiled a lot but said very little. I attempted to explain to him and his friends in pretty terrible French that I was a downed Allied pilot.

Boulanger listened and conferred with his friends. His left hand had been smashed shapeless in the carnage of the Great War and I could see him staring thoughtfully at this bundle of fresh trouble that had just turned up un-invited on his doorstep. He seemed to reach a decision. He swung the door open wide and welcomed me in anyway. Some of the patrons, delighted to see evidence of resist-ance to the occupying forces, even in the form of one bedraggled and shot-down pilot, moved to embrace me, but a combination of my dip in the sewer, a roll in a dung heap and three nights sleeping rough had obviously lessened my appeal and they satisfied themselves with a few friendly pats on the back.

I was ushered into the kitchen at the back of the restaurant, where Monsieur Boulanger's wife, a quiet but reliable and kind woman, rustled me up one of the few truly great meals of my life. I can see it to this day – an enormous plate of greens and eggs with a mountain of fresh bread. When I had finished devouring the feast, I leaned back and drank hot, sweet coffee as I tried to communicate with these brave, remarkable people who put their lives and the lives of their family at risk by opening the door to a stranger.

The Boulangers had two children, a charming sixteen-year-old daughter called Marthe and her amiable young brother Julien. It seemed that Monsieur Boulanger had been through a lot in the Great War and his wife had her hands full looking after the family and cooking for the restaurant, so it fell to Marthe to look after this strange stray who had fallen from the sky to change their lives.

They made me up a bed in the cellar below the restaurant and fixed me a much-needed bath. That night, I slept the most profound sleep, floating in a sea of exhaustion, surrounded by new friends and feeling safe for the first time in days.

Days passed as I regained my strength, sleeping and hiding during the day in the basement and sometimes emerging into the restaurant when the coast was clear. Marthe took charge with a quiet maturity far beyond her years. Most of the time things were uneventful, but sometimes a German staff car would roll into the village, heading for the only restaurant and tiny bar which doubled as my hideout. When this happened, I clattered my way into the dark cellar, home of old furniture and food supplies. I was usually accompanied by the children, Marthe calm and determined, young Julien frightened but brave enough to want to defend me with whatever stick or toy he had to hand. As we huddled in the basement listening to the sound of jackboots clomping their way above our heads as the Germans made a beeline for the best table, we would smile at each other to keep our morale up and wait.

Above our heads, a simple drama would act itself out each time the enemy visited. Madame Boulanger would pretend to concentrate on the cooking and stay out of sight in the back kitchen. Other French diners would stare pointedly down into their soup, trying not to be noticed. Only Monsieur Boulanger would serve the enemy, a towel over his sleeve, covering the smashed hand given to him in a previous conflict with the same foe. He would serve them with the same enigmatic neutral expression that he reserved for all his face-to-face encounters with the enemy, polite enough not to raise hackles, but reserved enough not to prompt further conversation. When the unwelcome guests had dined on the best Mrs Boulanger could muster, they would leave satisfied, and after a few minutes' silence to make sure they were out of the village, we would be welcomed back to the light and noise from the twilight tension of the basement.

The village grapevine seemed to work well, so we usually had notice when a particularly dangerous visit by the occupiers was coming up. In the meantime, I passed the time talking to Marthe, who was full of hope for life after the war and determined to do her part to make it happen. She would ask me about the bright lights of London and the strange wide-open world of the American West, which she dreamed of seeing for herself some day, and I promised her a welcome there equal to the one she and her family had given me. As days turned to weeks, we became good friends.

Then one night I was awakened by a vigorous shaking. Marthe and Julien were standing beside my bed, wide-eyed with worry and excitement. Marthe urged me to get dressed and get my things together quickly. The Germans were on their way to search the village and my cellar hideout was the first place they would look.

Marthe led me across dark fields, with Julien tailing

along behind. Julien was frightened, but clearly delighted to be out on a night-time adventure, and he so worshipped his big sister that he was determined to come along to see that no harm came to her or his adopted pilot.

I had no idea where we were going as we hurried through the moonlight, but we soon came to a very imposing house outside the village. It was owned by the local mill owner, Emile Rocourt. Emile was an impressive middle-aged man who welcomed me with amiable formality before greeting Marthe like a long-lost daughter. Indeed his own daughter was about the same age as Marthe and it turned out that they were best friends.

Emile was a local politician and dignitary. As far as the Nazis were concerned, he was an obedient local bigwig, but after the war he was decorated for his active role in the Resistance. Assisting me was one of numerous actions he conducted under the noses of the unsuspecting occupiers.

While the enemy troops inspected and searched the village that morning, I was hidden in the mill and looked after by the Rocourt family, who were considered too important to bother with such inconveniences.

When the visit was over and the searchers were gone, I returned to my life in the restaurant cellar, gradually improving my terrible French with the help of Marthe. For some weeks this existence continued, with me being shuttled to the Rocourt mill when my restaurant roost became too perilous. But the strain of playing against longer odds as time went by began to show and I was anxious to get back in the war rather than sit it out while endangering a lot of decent, brave French people. Marthe, as always, took charge. She went away one day and contacted the Resistance – an act that would change her own life as much as mine.

Some weeks later, towards the end of April 1942, she told me it was time for another retreat to the Rocourt mill. As usual we were shadowed by young Julien, brandishing a stick he had picked up on the way, to defend us from any enemies we might come across on the road. But this was no ordinary trip. At the big house Emile Rocourt told me they were expecting a visitor from the Resistance, responding to Marthe's approach for help.

Moments later a man arrived. He had tough, Gallic good looks and a wiry build that hinted at an ability to take care of himself in trouble. He was introduced only as Monsieur Jean. He nodded to Rocourt and then turned his piercing eyes on me, sizing me up. After what seemed like an age, he clearly decided I was worth helping.

He was going to arrange for me to go to a safe house in Lille, then on to Paris, where I would wait for the 'underground railroad' to take me through France to Spain, from where I could make my way back to England and the air war. I asked him when he thought I might be going. He replied, 'Half an hour.'

There was some debate between those assembled about whether I would need papers for the short train ride to Lille. Rocourt suggested that I was about the same age and build as his daughter's fiancé. Perhaps he might be persuaded to part with his identity for the journey. Rocourt's daughter bravely did not say a word, but I could see the tears welling up in her eyes. If her fiancé was asked, of course he would want to help, but if I was caught with his papers he would be arrested and probably shot. I was clearly uncomfortable about this arrangement and luckily Monsieur Jean intervened. Papers would not be necessary for such a short journey. We would take our chances.

Decisions made, we were invited to sit down for a hasty meal before we left. Suddenly my time at Quercamps was over. I had just minutes to say farewells and thanks that could have taken a lifetime. Surrounded by young friends and by men who were risking their lives for a stranger, I had a chance to practise my faltering French. I took Marthe's hand at the dinner table and said thank you to her and to all of them. I promised I would move heaven and earth to get back to England, and that the next time we met their country would be free. Then we were away, being waved off by Rocourt, his daughter, Marthe and Julien, still brandishing his stick.

After the war I discovered that as a result of Marthe's first contact with the Resistance, to help me on my way, at only sixteen she became an active and leading member of the local Resistance. For a year and a half she harried the invaders in every way possible until eventually she was captured. After that she was interrogated, beaten, starved and systematically brutalized as only the Nazis knew how. Eventually she was deported to Ravensbruck concentration camp, where she endured the rest of the war in terrible conditions, but survived with the same quiet determination that had made me admire her so much.

When she was liberated from the camp at the end of the war, her health was shattered. I was able to visit her a few years later, in a free France as we had planned. She sat up in bed to greet me, but she was very weak and was not thought likely to survive for long. We sat together, both in conversation and in silence, remembering. My return visit in peacetime was reported in some of the local newspapers, and I hope it in some way contributed to some belated interest from the French authorities in this brave young woman. Shortly after my visit, General de Gaulle himself came to her bedside in Quercamps and personally pinned France's greatest medal, the Légion d'honneur, on her. Marthe died soon afterwards.

As I stood on a crowded local train to Lille, swaying as I hung from a passenger strap and rubbing elbows with German soldiers and curious, staring locals, I began to wonder if not having a single identity paper was such a small thing after all. But Monsieur Jean was a professional. He rode alongside me, showing just the right amount of boredom and diffidence to fade into the background, and very soon I was breathing a long sigh of relief as we made our way through quiet streets in Lille to the house of a widow who would shelter me.

It struck me that this was the second time since I had

crash-landed that I was being helped by a woman suffering the loss of her husband in the war, and I wondered how many other brave women there were out there, fighting back in whatever way they could and longing for the end of the war, even though they knew that their own loved ones would never come marching home.

I stayed there for a week or so, being kept company by some neighbours of my host – a young man who played the guitar and his sister Juliet. It seemed like a little oasis in the war to be sitting in an apartment with a young man who knew all the latest songs and could strum tunes such as 'J'attendrais'. I would take the guitar and teach him and his sister some songs in return, including a few cowboy tunes I had learned in Texas and New Mexico, like 'Blood on the Saddle'. But in wartime France, the illusion of peace was always fragile. I found out from Juliet that her amiable, guitar-playing brother was on a Nazi death list – a rota of people who would be picked up and shot in retaliation for any action by the Resistance. His crime had been to laugh out loud at a German propaganda newsreel in the cinema. Some fascist sympathizer had squealed on him and days later his name was on the list.

I was horrified. How could he just sit there and wait for his fate? He must come with me to Paris. Maybe we could escape together to Spain and he could resist the fascists in some way from there or from Britain. At first his sister seemed to feel this offered a real glimmer of hope, but when I raised the idea with her brother, he just smiled. He explained to me that if he ran away, they would just put Juliet's name on the list, and if she ran, they would put his mother on the list – or someone else's sister or mother.

I was still struggling with the enormity of this when Monsieur Jean reappeared. I barely had time for a new set of farewells before heading with him on the local train to Paris. This time we had passable identification papers, forged by Monsieur Jean's Resistance contacts. On the journey, I had time to think about the different sorts of bravery that this war was bringing out in people. Perhaps it took a certain amount of guts to climb into a Spitfire cockpit and head for the skies over France, but in reality the quiet heroism of a young man who refused to be silenced in a cinema, then refused to place his family in danger by running away, was just as brave.

Few experiences can be quite as exhilarating as a first visit to Paris, particularly if the year is 1942 and you happen to be an Allied pilot on the run. Monsieur Jean and I walked from the Gare du Nord into the very heart of occupied Paris. Suddenly, as well as being surrounded by civilians, enemy soldiers and policemen ignoring me and going about their business, I was surrounded by buildings and history that had fascinated me since childhood. I walked saucer-eyed as we strolled along the rue Sevastopol, past landmarks like the rue de Rivoli and the bustling River Seine. There, in the distance, was the Eiffel Tower, and right ahead of me rising in all its magnificence was the medieval splendour of Notre-Dame cathedral.

Monsieur Jean was walking at a purposeful pace, not too fast so as not to attract attention, but not dawdling so as to get to safety as speedily and uneventfully as possible. I stopped. He stopped. I explained to him quietly that I had to go into the cathedral. He looked at me as if I had just confirmed some vague suspicion he held about my sanity. I stood my ground. I needed to go into the cathedral. How many Americans ever get the chance to see the inside of that magnificent building, let alone visit it in the middle of a war? He shrugged and let me go in.

For one brief moment, as I stood engulfed by all that medieval magnificence, the soaring stone columns and breathtaking arches, my thoughts rose heavenwards, along with the whispered prayers of a few old ladies in the pews. There, on the run in an occupied city, I felt free, and once again remembered that there were things truly worth fighting for.

When I emerged to reunite with a slightly impatient Monsieur Jean, I was holding something in my hand. He looked amused as he studied my purchase – a postcard of the cathedral. I hastily wrote a note to the teacher in Texas who had tried to drum some French into me some years earlier, with little success. On the card, I pointed out that I had recently gone to considerable lengths to brush up on my dialogue by taking lessons from the natives. Monsieur Jean pocketed my card and promised to get it out of the country. We set off again and arrived safely at a beautiful apartment building, full of Parisian style and charm, near the Porte d'Orée, just a stone's throw from the entrance to the Bois de Vincennes.

As the door to one of the apartments opened, I turned to see Monsieur Jean already leaving. For once it was my turn to watch someone else hurry off. I never found out anything about his life or his family and he never asked anything about me or my life before the war. He was a man who knew the price one paid for such information if captured by the enemy, and he focused all his considerable talents on moving downed pilots from France back to Britain where they could once again go about the task of helping to liberate his country. I never saw him again, nor found out his real name, but I recognized in his rapidly disappearing wiry frame the sort of determination that would win this war at any price, no matter how long it took or how much it cost.

Turning back to the doorway, I was greeted by a beautiful French woman, Giselle, and her husband Josef, who ushered me into their apartment. Josef explained that he too had been a pilot before the fall of France. These days, both he and Giselle worked at small jobs to pay the bills, while helping the war effort in any way they could. They showed me to a small, simply furnished spare bedroom. That room was to become my home for about a month.

What had presumably started as a hideout for a few days, similar to the apartment in Lille, had become a long-term residence. At about this point in the war the 'underground railroad' had been severely damaged by

Nazi success at arresting and torturing some key figures in the escape apparatus. My next stop was due to be Angoulême in the south, but the escape route was at a standstill. Previous routes were unsafe and all along a line from northern France to the Spanish border there were stranded Allied airmen being hidden in French homes, from lofty chateaux to the most lowly cottages, waiting for the routes to reopen.

It may seem strange to someone reading about those times so many years later, but the prevailing atmosphere was not one of the justifiable fear of being caught. These were times when life was lived very much in the present, since no-one knew quite what the next day would bring, or even if there would be a next day. That led to some decisions that one can see now with the clarity of hindsight were not the brightest.

With days passing and May bringing the promise of summer, I was obviously feeling cooped up in the tiny room. Josef and Giselle suggested a few outings to avoid me getting cabin fever. So began a series of excursions which made me one of the only Americans on vacation in Paris in the late spring sunshine of 1942.

One of my favourite outings was to the local swimming pool near Denfert-Rochereau. I have always loved swimming and the physical exertion made me feel free of the cramped feeling that comes with spending too long in one small space. Still damp from the trip to the baths, it was a strange experience to find myself sharing a Metro strap with some SS officer on the way home.

On other days, we went to the zoo, where I would stare at the animals behind bars and commiserate with them, hoping to avoid a similar fate myself. We also went together to the movies, and it was hard not to feel like part of a more interesting movie in real life than whatever was flickering across the screen, usually accompanied by hectoring newsreels of German victories. One of my more practical outings was to a safe dentist, a charming, dignified Jewish woman who treated me in secret for a tooth abscess that was causing me a great deal of pain. She was already on a list to be deported, and even if we did not at that stage know the full extent of the horror ahead, we were wise enough about the Nazis to know that they had no good intentions. Yet despite the threat she faced, she continued to help people, at the risk of making her own terrible situation even worse by helping me.

The general theory of my somewhat freewheeling Parisian existence seemed to be that it was safe to 'hide in plain sight' and this seemed to work quite well provided I did not open my mouth. From there it was a simple step for my hosts to suggest that I could let myself in and out during the day for some welcome exercise. I became a regular walker in the Bois, sometimes sitting on a bench with a sandwich, watching the German troops practising their drills in the open space.

I have had many years to ponder the foolishness of not hiding all day every day in some cupboard, being fed by a straw through the keyhole, but the truth is that no-one can ever know what brings about success or failure in such a strange world of escapes and captures. It may have been that someone saw the comings and goings of a stranger, or it may have been that some unfortunate person at some point in the long and winding escape route was tortured beyond endurance. It may simply have been that the raid was random, based on vague suspicions. Whatever the reason, the reality remained the same, as simple and stark as the reality of the war itself. One night, in early June 1942, about a month after I had arrived in Paris, the front door of the apartment was kicked in, cracking and splintering under the weight of many jackboots. All three of us were dragged from our beds and forced to dress hastily at gunpoint, then held in the living room while a group of German soldiers ransacked the apartment and demanded our papers.

Knowing that the game was up, I tried talking to the one who seemed to be in charge, attempting to explain that I had just arrived and that these people did not know who I really was. They had just taken me in off the streets and should not be blamed for harbouring me.

I had only got halfway through my admittedly thread-bare excuses when I was cut short by a rifle butt in the face. We were dragged into waiting vehicles and brought straight to one of the most feared buildings in the world – the Gestapo headquarters in Paris, near the Opéra. Josef and Giselle were dragged off in one direction, I in another. I never saw either of them again.

After a short spell in a basement cell, I was brought by two guards up to an office. There, behind a large and highly polished desk, sat a grey-haired man in well-tailored civilian clothes, with a face that I hated on sight. He motioned politely for me to take a small seat positioned in front of the large desk while the guards hovered by the wall behind me. I sat down and immediately began gabbling my series of excuses about my hosts. My French must have still been pretty terrible, since the grey-haired man stopped me in full flood with a terse request for me to speak English.

I started again from the beginning in English, but if anything my story sounded even lamer. Once again my interrogator cut me short. He told me to stop worrying about my former hosts and start worrying about myself. I responded that I was a prisoner of war and expected to be treated as one. The man leaned over towards me, confidentially. 'There is only one way I will believe you are a prisoner of war,' he told me. He produced a pen and paper and I had a sinking feeling about where this little civilized chat was leading. 'You can prove you are really a pilot by giving me the names of every person who helped you since you crash-landed. Then we can check your story.'

I gave him the date and location of my crash, but he just sneered. Knowing the location of a downed plane did not prove I was the pilot; and I had been captured in Paris in civilian clothes. It was my turn to sneer – I pointed out that with my terrible French and no German I would not make much of a spy. He countered that I probably spoke such bad French to make my pilot story more plausible.

He was beginning to get impatient. He wanted the names of every person who had helped me from my crash to my capture.

For once I was able to use the truth. Ever since I was a boy I've had a terrible memory for remembering names on demand. I leant over as he had done, as if about to divulge a secret. 'To tell you the truth, I'm terrible with names,' I confided.

This did not seem to have the desired effect. He turned purple and hissed at me, 'You do not seem to be taking your situation seriously enough. Perhaps we can help you.' With that, he tidied his desk and left the room.

He had hardly closed the door when one of the guards hauled me to my feet and grabbed my arms behind my back. The other hit me a vicious punch in the face. I turned my head away and the next blow crashed into my stomach. I tried to clench my muscles but a third crashing blow to my solar plexus left me gasping for breath as he returned to beating me around the face.

He stopped for a second, as if some shred of humanity had been rekindled somewhere inside him, but in reality he had merely stopped to fastidiously take a handkerchief from his pocket, wrap it carefully around his knuckles and then start over again, landing blow after vicious blow on my cheeks, jaw, neck and eyes.

As I came close to passing out, the guards shoved me back in the chair, where I cradled my head in my arms. One of the guards yanked my head up by the hair. As it rose, I saw that the sleeves of my shirt were covered in blood. He jerked my head back until I was once again staring at the grey-haired Gestapo man, who had re-entered the room as silently as he had left.

He waved a piece of paper at me. One of my eyes was so swollen that it was practically shut, and the other one was swimming with blood. I struggled to focus.

'It's in German. I told you, I don't speak German.'

He seemed delighted to translate it for me. It was an order from the Kommandantura. It said that if the prisoner calling himself Bill Ash failed to provide satisfactory proof of identity, he was to be shot as a spy on 4 June 1942. Just as I've never been great with names, I am not much better with dates. I asked him to remind me what today's date was.

He leant over and whispered, 'June the third,' with obvious enjoyment.

He could see I was rattled, but my brain was by now racing, searching for any shred of information that might stop them shooting me without leading them to shoot someone who deserved it less. I couldn't think of a thing.

The Gestapo man pressed his advantage, enquiring innocently if I had happened to come across a Monsieur Jean in my travels. I thought for a bit, but said I didn't think I had had the pleasure. My interrogator began to get irritated once more. He shouted that they knew I had been helped by a Monsieur Jean and that if I wanted to avoid being shot, I should start giving details of when and where I had met him. I brightened and he leant forward eagerly.

'Does he have a very bushy black beard?' I enquired.

Something in my delivery must have seemed less than totally sincere. He shut my file and stood up. 'That's it. You have not cooperated. Events will have to take their course.'

I was dragged out of his office by the two goons, feeling slightly gypped that I was going to be shot without at least a little more haggling. They brought me back to my basement cell and shoved me in, clanging the door locked behind me. I lay on the floor, trying to assess my injuries, feeling loose teeth. Part of me tried to convince the other part that they were bluffing. But why should they, I retorted to my bloody and confused self. If they recognized that a prisoner was unlikely to cooperate, perhaps the Gestapo method was not to waste time beating them or feeding them. That got me wondering if I would at least get a decent lunch to celebrate my last day on the planet. But there was no lunch. No dinner. No anything.

As I lay on the floor, I pondered the strange workings of a world in which an American boy in the Canadian air force, fighting for the British, had ended up about to be shot by Germans in France. I tried to smile, but it hurt too much. I settled down on a rough prison cot for a long, dark night.

My thoughts turned to the cocky young Texan who had told a local paper just after I qualified as a pilot that I was going to bash the Hun for democracy, then come back and write a book about it. I even thought that like Dostoevsky, I now had the useful experience of knowing what it was like to be sentenced to death. Unfortunately this led to the thought that I would not be able to make much use of this information once I was dead.

Most of the rest of the night passed with a jumble of thoughts and emotions. I tried to steel myself so that I would at least not give the Nazis the satisfaction of seeing how frightened I was. One of my strongest thoughts was that I had organized my war rather badly. I had started off with a dislike of bullies and a desire for adventure, but my feelings about fascists were abstract at best. It took actually meeting some of them and seeing their handiwork first hand throughout Europe to know I had done the right thing in joining up. Even if I had known it would end like this, I would still have joined, and I would have been less squeamish in some of my earlier dogfights. It was simultaneously the longest and the shortest night of my life.

As morning approached, I heard the clatter of a food trolley in the corridor outside with the clank of plates and the slosh of breakfast slops, but my door remained stubbornly closed. No food, but no execution yet either. So much for fascists making the trains run on time, I thought. The two parts of my addled brain debated my situation. One side grew hopeful that they would not shoot me after all, but the other just laughed and told the optimistic side not to get my hopes up.

At lunchtime the door clanged open. This was it. The pessimistic part of me was busy telling the optimistic half that it had told me so, when I was handed a hunk of black bread and a cup of sauerkraut soup. I made my first acquaintance with Reich tea, which looked like boiled confetti but tasted much worse. For me, it was a victory feast. The optimist finally bubbled to the surface, reasoning that they would not waste good food, or even bad food, on me if they were about to shoot me. The door clanged open again and I was led out by two guards, who seemed intent on contradicting my theory.

Yet instead of leading me to an execution yard, they brought me back upstairs to the office of my interrogator. I felt it too rude to enquire if he had possibly forgotten something, and since he did not immediately bring up the fact that I was alive contrary to regulations I felt it was not my place to remind him.

He was like a different man. He ushered me back to my chair and started a cosy chat in impeccable English. He told me how well he knew London and what a fine city he thought it was. I agreed politely.

'How is Scott's restaurant these days?' he enquired, adding, 'They always made excellent steaks.'

For a moment I thought he might be speaking in some kind of code, but I realized that this was what passed for polite chit-chat in Nazi interrogations. Since I could not enlighten him about the steaks at Scott's I let him know about a very good Lyons Corner House in Piccadilly Circus where you could get all the salad you could eat for a few shillings.

No doubt grateful for this information, he proffered me a cigarette and even lit it for me. I was just settling in for more homespun Nazi wit and wisdom when he clearly decided the formalities were over.

'You'll never see London again!' he shouted and indicated to one of the goons behind me, who stepped forward on cue and slapped me across the face, sending my cigarette flying with a little trail of sparks. The interrogator pointed to the guard who had just struck me. 'He will see it. He will be in London! Where will you be?'

I felt little need to encourage him by offering suggestions, and he obliged me by telling me anyway. 'You will be dead today unless you give us some names. We are not unreasonable people. Just a few names and you will be treated as a pilot instead of as a spy.'

Like a compulsive eater or gambler, I knew that if I gave them even one name it would be impossible to stop. In any case, following the advice of Monsieur Jean, I had become adept at trying to find out as little as possible about the people who had helped me.

'Just one name,' he coaxed. 'We already have many of them in custody, so you need not worry about giving your friends away.'

I thought, then reluctantly squeezed out one name. 'Monsieur Joseph.'

My interrogator was delighted. He leaned forward. 'Ah, Monsieur Josef. And what does this Monsieur Josef do?'

'He's a teacher.'

The interrogator wrote this nugget down officiously, then turned his cold eyes back to me.

'Where?'

'In Texas. He tried hard with me, but I was never much good at French.'

He turned purple once more. I could tell I was going to pay a high price for stringing him along. But he seemed almost disappointed that our session was ending. He simply got up and left, turning to me at the door. 'You had your chance. You will be shot tomorrow morning. Good day, Herr Ash.'

As he left he nodded to the guards and they commenced giving me the beating of a lifetime. Blows and kicks rained down on me for what seemed like an eternity. A searing pain doubled me over as one of them punched my kidneys. As I started to lose consciousness, they dragged me back to my cell. I could no longer walk properly.

For the rest of that day, I lay aching and bleeding on the rough cell cot. This time I was in no doubt that they meant it and the gradual erosion of one's sense of self and perspective at which the Nazis excelled began to take its toll as my physical condition deteriorated.

But instead of shooting me, they took me out later for another interrogation, and another beating, and another, and another. The days blurred into one long, bloody hell of pain, humiliation and unanswered questions. I can no longer say how long it went on. Perhaps a week, or maybe more. It felt like a year.

By the end of this period the Nazi techniques began to backfire. The mere thought of being shot no longer seemed quite so terrible. I lay, aching and bloody and wretched in my cell, listening to the click of military boots on hard floor outside my door. What this time? Perhaps the final bullet? Or just another beating? Or perhaps it was time for more Reich tea, to keep me alive until the next beating.

Instead, I heard a new sound. My captors loved shouting – shouting at me, shouting orders at each other and shouting at anyone who did not do as they were ordered – but the tone of such shouting always had the same ring to it, of a superior bawling out some unfortunate *Untermensch*. This was different. A blazing row outside my cell was being fought out by two equals. I recognized one of the voices as that of my interrogator, and even though he was no slouch in the screaming department, he was gradually getting the worst of it from whoever was on the other side of this argument. A final bark by his adversary was accompanied by an insistent thump on my cell door, rapidly followed by the reluctant clank and shuffle of the loser unlocking it.

By the time the door opened my interrogator had left already and I was faced by the stern but relatively friendly figure of a Luftwaffe officer and several soldiers. He seemed taken aback by my condition, but he saluted.

'We must leave now. You are now in the custody of the Luftwaffe as a prisoner of war and will be treated as such. But we must hurry. The Gestapo still dispute that you are a pilot and we should leave before they get a chance to have our orders countermanded. Come!'

I needed no further encouragement, but I was in such bad shape after the endless beatings that I needed some help from the Luftwaffe subordinates as I limped my way out of that hellish place, which was something few of its unfortunate inmates ever lived to do.

As the heavy gates of the Gestapo headquarters closed behind me, I could almost hear the sigh of relief from my new captors. The fight between the Luftwaffe and the Gestapo for custody of prisoners was a recurring theme of their war, and a battle that the Gestapo would gradually win. But for now, the Luftwaffe had the upper hand, which was fine by me. In general they wanted to abide by the Geneva Convention, and on a less noble note, they knew that there were hundreds of Luftwaffe prisoners of war being held in camps in England and Canada. If word got out that the Gestapo were beating and shooting their counterparts, who knew what might start happening to German prisoners.

I had plenty of time to ponder all this as I sat on a train, propped up between two Luftwaffe guards. The escort was a bit over the top, since I could barely stand up. As the train rumbled from France to Germany, a group of Luftwaffe pilots stopped by to take a look at me. They were based at St Omer in the Pas de Calais, heading home on leave, and were delighted to discover that the strange single Spitfire pilot they had taken it in turns to shoot at some months earlier was alive, if not very well, and in relatively safe hands.

I could not muster much enthusiasm for a chat. Any

idea that this war was simply something cooked up by our superiors and that the brave little men like us on both sides were simply doing as they were told did not fit my recent experiences. The military might that allowed Hitler and his vile theories of racial supremacy to turn Europe into a giant slaughterhouse of innocent people was based on both collective muscle and individual people doing as they were told, even when they knew in their hearts that it was utterly wrong. Such thoughts might be considered churlish, coming from someone who had just been rescued from death at the hands of the Gestapo by the Luftwaffe, and I do not for a minute compare the actions of the Nazis to those of the average German soldier, but the truth is that their military actions were the only thing that made the Nazi outrages possible. Their well-meant camaraderie, like the dream of the humble foot soldiers on both sides getting together every now and again to play football in no-man's-land or sing a few rousing choruses of 'Hurrah for the next man who dies', belonged to another time, another war and another movie.

I settled down and stared at the countryside as the train rolled towards Frankfurt, and towards my first prisoner-of-war camp, Dulag Luft – as it turned out, the first of many.

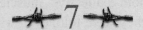

For You the War is Over

My Luftwaffe escort deposited me at a sort of mustering camp for new air force officer prisoners called Dulag Luft, just outside Oberursel, near Frankfurt am Main, some time in June 1942. The camp was the Luftwaffe's main interrogation centre and a sort of transit point from where captured flyers were sent on in batches to the main prison camps. Apparently, at some point in the war a British airman prisoner had carved a giant sign that hung over the camp entrance, reading 'I told you it wasn't a Spitfire' but if I saw it at the time, I must not have been in a laughing mood.

For me this period was one of the lowest points in the war. I was put briefly in solitary confinement, and paced my cell as all the events from my crash-landing to that moment seemed to well up all at once and slap me in the face. I was suffering not only physically from weeks of beatings at the hands of the Gestapo but also mentally as the strain of constant threats of death and the ultimate let-down of months of tension and hiding resulting in only this – a bare cell and an eternity of barbed wire ahead – started to take their toll. A strange feeling rose up inside me, like a combination of food poisoning and utter depression. I felt increasingly disgusted – for allowing myself to be shot down, for letting myself be captured, and most of all for failing the long chain of brave French people who had done so much to help me get away, potentially at such a terrible cost. I smashed my fist into the brick of the cell wall again and again until it was in just as bad shape as the rest of me.

As I watched the blood trickle down my hand, a metal tray with some food was shoved through a hatch. As I stared at the food something struck me mentally with more force than any thump I could give the wall. The food! Every time I had a meal in the cell I immediately started to feel even more low and strangely passive. I started to wonder if they were putting something into the food or drink to make us more manageable. My next experience hinted that this was right.

A man in Red Cross uniform under a white doctor's coat came in with a clipboard. He sympathized with my plight and offered me a cigarette, leaning in closer to ask quietly if the guards were treating me reasonably. He then encouraged me to fill in his detailed questionnaire so that he could get the information to Switzerland as soon as possible and my worried family and former unit could be informed that I was safe and a prisoner of war.

The way I was feeling, I did not think anyone would very much care what had befallen me, but as I stared glumly at the ground I noticed something interesting. Under the bottom of the good doctor's white coat peeked a shiny pair of German jackboots. I took a look at his questionnaire, and sure enough it was crammed full of questions that would be of no use to a worried mother but very handy to German intelligence. I declined politely and told him that since I had fallen from the sky several months ago, another week or two before they found out I was OK would not really matter. He stamped out in a manner that was much less sympathetic than his entrance and the cell door clanged shut behind him.

As was the case with most prisoners arriving at Dulag Luft at that stage of the war, my spell in solitary was followed by a series of interrogations by Luftwaffe intelligence officers who spoke good English, some of them having lived in America or Britain before the war. Their questions, though probing, were not too difficult to deflect and they generally behaved in accordance with the Geneva Convention, which was a welcome change from my treatment by the Gestapo. I could see how this gentler approach might actually pay dividends if used with a frightened young bomber pilot, blown out of the sky on his first or second mission, who had just watched his closest friends burn up and for whom the terror of capture would be replaced with a strange sense of security and the familiar warm tones of an accent he recognized from home. But I had seen the other side of the Third Reich and could still feel the bruises and loose teeth from my last chat with the Gestapo, so I was in little danger of being charmed out of any state secrets. Better still, I didn't know any.

Things started to pick up when, still at Dulag Luft, I hooked up with another downed Spitfire pilot, Paddy Barthropp, whom I mentioned earlier. His luck had lasted from before Dunkirk, right through the Battle of Britain and beyond, in fact right up to a few days before our meeting at the Dulag. Paddy had parachuted when he was shot down over France, and a large German reception committee was waiting for him long before he hit the ground, and carted him off to a local jail. Some of the pilots who had downed him were stationed nearby and came over to inspect their catch. They were decent enough to give him some cigarettes and huddled together for a souvenir photo in which Paddy stands puffing enigmatically before being carted off to Dulag Luft.

Although Paddy was almost out of central casting as the young hard-nosed Spitfire pilot with a devil-may-care attitude to life and death, and a passion for anything fast, including aeroplanes, horses and women, underneath that persona was one of the kindest, most generous-spirited men I have ever known. Years after the war, if any of our old colleagues from either operations or prison camp were in any kind of difficulty, they would always turn to Paddy for help or advice. His arrival was just the boost I needed, and I started to turn from wallowing in self-pity and recrimination to concentrating on getting out and getting back to the war. I was Prisoner Number 757 and Paddy was Number 759. We never did find out who was the mysterious 758.

Filled with newfound zeal for an escape, I approached a senior Allied officer who seemed to be stationed at the transit camp permanently. He had apparently been in the second-hand car business before the war, but I instantly had the feeling that no-one in his right mind ever bought a car from this slippery character. Still, I pressed ahead and told him that I wanted to have a go at escaping from Dulag Luft. He waved his hand airily and told me in a rather patronizing way that that sort of activity was all well catered for in the main prisoner-of-war camp near Breslau, much as if he was talking about day-trip excursions from a holiday camp. After the war, I found out that he had been working for the Germans all the time, so admitting my plan to him was a bit like a criminal announcing to a policeman his intention to rob a bank.

Luckily we were very quickly moved on from Dulag Luft to Stalag Luft III in eastern Germany, now Poland. We were shipped out in a large batch by truck, heavily guarded and unable to see much on the long journey through Germany. Luft III was the main prisoner-of-war camp for Allied flying officers, located at Sagan, some hundred miles south-east of Berlin.

On our arrival, which must have been in late June 1942, we were given a fairly standard 'For you the war is over' speech by the camp commandant, Von Lindeiner. As far as Paddy and I were concerned, our war was just getting going, but it seemed rude to interrupt.

Colonel Freidrich Wilhelm Von Lindeiner was in his sixties, a long-time military man who was already a seasoned soldier at the time of the First World War, during which he was wounded three times and won the Iron Cross twice. He married a Danish aristocrat and did his best to side-swerve Nazi politics, but at the start of the war he was refused retirement and eventually put in charge of a camp that grew to house 10,000 prisoners, including a fair few like myself whose day job was trying to escape. He ran the camp from the time it opened in May 1942, about six weeks before I arrived, right through to the aftermath of what became known as the Great Escape in 1944, when he was relieved of command and replaced by my old friends the Gestapo. It must have been the least welcome of all assignments – apart, perhaps, from the Russian front.

The camp was divided up into several compounds – at that time one for officers, another for sergeant pilots or NCOs and another area, the *Vorlager*, that was exclusively for the Germans, containing their barracks and administrative buildings. The place was surrounded by pine forest and inside it was defined by wooden huts, barbed wire and tall machine-gun posts at regular intervals. We were shown the low warning wire that led to a sort of no-man's-land before the real wire, which was often 20 feet high. Even between the compounds there were double fences of wire, on the far side of which was the compound for the NCOs and later my fellow Americans, though at this stage there were fewer than a dozen of us, all waifs and strays like me.

Our accommodation, particularly in comparison to that given to me by the Gestapo, was pretty good. Men were divided into small groups of six or eight in small rooms. Under the terms of the Geneva Convention, officers were not expected to work, so the main things to fill time were studying, being involved with the camp entertainment through music or theatre, or simply trying to escape. As well as the new surroundings and the micro-geography of huts, exercise yard and watchtowers with machine guns at regular intervals along the endless barbed wire, there was an entirely new language to learn. Guards were goons, for instance; the cry of 'goons in the block' was used to alert anyone doing anything illegal as they approached. Specially trained guards used to sniff out tunnels and contraband were known as ferrets, while our own men, innocently lounging in a doorway while acting as lookout for some escape endeavour, were known as stooges.

Walking through the gates of that massive barbed-wire camp into the prisoners' compound was like finding I had died and arrived in the feasting halls of Valhalla, where a previous generation of warriors were already at home. Over there was Bob Tuck, a truly brilliant fighter pilot who flew both Spitfires and Hurricanes. He had been based at Hornchurch during a remarkable career in which he shot down thirty enemy aircraft before he ended up 'in the bag'. And over there by the wire was the former 242 Squadron Leader, the redoubtable Douglas Bader. At one point, his captors had temporarily confiscated his artificial legs and, regarding this as the ultimate act of war, he became one of the most persistent escape artists of the era. Nearby, standing in the doorway of one of the wooden barracks huts, was Norman Ryder, another Spitfire ace. There was a sea of other faces I did not recognize but was soon to get to know.

Some of the inmates had been prisoners since the early days of the war. One pilot called Edwards had been flying around in an Anson over the North Sea in September 1939 when he was suddenly blown out of the sky by a ship's guns. A German E-boat fished him out of the cold water, which had failed to dampen his anger. He shouted at them that they were fools and that actions like this could even start a war. They gleefully told him it had already started, and that his stay as a prisoner of war was going to be almost exactly the same length as the war itself.

Among the many prisoners I got to know around that time was Bill Stapleton. He had been shot down back in 1940, also flying from Hornchurch. While most of the acres of print about the camps have focused on the obsessive escapologists among us, Bill is a great example of someone who helped many of us get through those tough years in unexpected ways. He had a great streak of humanity in a place where it was in short supply. Bill was also the proud owner of a rare and valuable thing in Stalag Luft III, an old wind-up gramophone with a small but treasured hoard of classical records.

Back at his first German camp, Stalag Luft I at Barth, Bill had begun a tradition after lights out. Lying in the darkness, even among so many other prisoners, men's minds turned to all the things they missed and the loved ones they did not know if they would ever see again. Into this loneliness crept some of the most beautiful music ever composed. It would waft out from Bill's gramophone, across the camp, making us feel just a little bit more free and a little less forgotten.

Bill was able to continue his good work at another camp in Poland, then back in Luft III. It was a good training for a job he is still doing sixty years later, helping to organize the annual prisoner-of-war dinner at the RAF club in London.

Paddy and I quickly gravitated to that small knot of prisoners who headed up the serious or at least serial escape artists. It might seem strange that escaping was something of a minority pursuit, but it is hard to over-emphasize just how much the average pilot had been through even to get there in one piece. Every single one had been through some catastrophic shooting down, parachute experience or crash-landing in enemy territory, usually being a ten-to-one survivor of such an event. I remember a rear gunner of a Whitley that had been hit and force-landed at night in Germany. The crash-landing was incredibly rough, and the gunner had crawled forward in the shattered fuselage to give the pilot an earful for such a duff landing. He discovered that he was utterly alone in the plane. His intercom had been shot away earlier and so he had missed the order to bail out when the rest of the crew had done so, leaving him oblivious at his rear gun post as the plane drifted lazily down and crash-landed itself.

As a result of their experiences of crash and capture, most prisoners were understandably not overly keen on pushing the odds even further by escaping in the heart of Germany. Virtually every prisoner dreamed of escaping, and most were willing to help others get away, but the chances were so slim of making it home, and the dangers of being shot even before you were out of the camp perimeter were so great, that most decided to wait it out.

Nevertheless there were the slightly crazier ones like myself and Paddy, who were determined to escape from the start. Even some of the more adventurous characters tended to think better of escape if they had escaped once and survived but been recaptured and put in the punishment cells or cooler. But for those of us who undertook a second escape attempt, there was usually another and another. Escaping is quite addictive and, like all addictive drugs, extremely dangerous.

Even for the most ardent escapologist, there was a period of adjustment to life as a prisoner and an exploration of the strange world of a prisoner-of-war camp that took some time. True to form, I started by looking for food. Cooking facilities were spartan, with dozens taking it in turns to cook on one little pot-bellied stove in each hut, but the real problem was finding something to put in the pot.

In the early days after my arrival, rations were very bleak – a virtual starvation diet of black bread and a scraping of jam plus the occasional potato. Later, we would rejoice in the contents of regular Red Cross parcels, which transformed our diet for the better. The contents of these depended on where they came from. The Canadian and American ones tended to contain coffee, which was good for bartering. The British ones contained such delights as tinned bully beef, raisins, tinned salmon and always-sought-after chocolate. These parcels were administered individually, but we tended to pool them among our group of room mates and try to make them last all week. But those Red Cross days were still ahead, and at first we had to make do with the barest of rations from our captors.

The atmosphere in the camp was a bizarre mix of prison and British boarding school. Before the war the RAF recruiting policy had favoured bright young men from fairly upper-class backgrounds, many of whom had been boarders at expensive but spartan public schools. Some of my more delicate British upper-crust officer colleagues obviously found the grim fare on offer very tough, while I on the other hand, brought up in the more hungry and precarious environs of Depression-hit America, could munch my way through most things. Still, one particularly well-brought-up pilot once challenged my theory, saying that anyone who could live through several years of the cooking at a top-drawer British boarding school could handle anything the Third Reich threw at us, even if on occasions we felt like throwing it back.

Determined that our stay at this particular eaterie was going to be a short one, and that we would leave without paying the bill, Paddy and I decided that before we could escape, we should be both fitter and fatter to cope with the demands of our journey. We needed food, and lots of it. But there were only two items that could be classed even vaguely as food which were not immediately wolfed down by the hungry masses. One was a green, runny, vile-smelling thing that pretended to be cheese. Most people could not even approach it, never mind put it in their mouths. I manfully munched my way through lakes of the stuff, with a sort of grim fascination and amusement at how each mouthful was worse than the previous one. But man cannot live on green liquid cheese alone, and I was soon on the lookout for something with a little more substance. I found it in the form of Klipfish.

Klipfish is a delicacy virtually unknown even to my generation. It was made of those parts of a fish that would be best kept to itself, pounded into a sort of extrusion. This had then been dried out some decades earlier, at the time of the First World War, into something resembling wood shavings. Some enterprising Berlin bureaucrat had rediscovered it in his quest to find the cheapest possible way to feed the growing number of hungry Allied pilots that seemed to be dropping out of the sky, and so it reached Stalag Luft III in prodigious quantities. Though it started out looking like sawdust, it had to be soaked in water for about a week, and by that time it developed both the consistency and smell of wet dog hair, but tasted much worse. The next step was to cut it into slabs, fry it and then, in most cases, hurl it out of the hut door in disgust. And that was its one great advantage.

I requisitioned a big basket and went from hut to hut collecting the stuff from people grateful to get it out of their sight. I collected basketfuls, barrel loads, and bushels of the stuff. Other prisoners used to huddle around just to watch me, in much the same way that passersby in Detroit had peered in at me as I ate stew for two weeks in my attempt to bulk up enough to end up here in an enemy prison camp. Because I had been through some fairly tough times, I honestly did not find conditions all that bad in the camp, and some of my more sensitive colleagues used to accuse me of being unreasonably cheerful just to annoy them. I agreed that the food was lousy, but pointed out that the prices were very reasonable.

Once we had padded ourselves out a bit with the Luft III diet, Paddy and I knew that the next step was to get fit enough to attempt an escape. The easiest way seemed to be to kindle a bit of interest in team sports, so about a dozen of us set off for an exercise area with a rigged-up ball. The only problem was that we seemed to be playing several different games at once. I was familiar with the wild world of American football. Paddy seemed to be playing Irish Gaelic. Some of the Brits were playing rugby, Australians played 'Aussie Rules', and I think there were a few soccer players too.

As the game progressed the players and ball were passed, thumped, bounced and tackled in every way possible, with heated disputes about whether a goal was a try or a try was a touchdown. Most of the players were in pretty bad shape from the lack of food and the experiences of being shot down. Quite often, while making a charge down the wing, I would pass the ball to someone, only to discover that he had fainted from hunger and exertion and was already lying horizontally on the ground, without the indignity of even being tackled. I thought it was a salutary demonstration of the pitfalls of not eating everything that did not try to jump off your plate, but did not say so, in case they asked for their Klipfish back.

Finally, we judged that we had eaten enough Klipfish and returned to some sort of fitness. Our ponderings about what method of escape to try might have gone on for longer, but for an event that gave us both some inspiration. A month or two after our arrival, I stood with a crowd of others and watched as Douglas Bader, who might have had no legs but who had the heart of a lion, was carted off by guards to Lamsdorf camp, then to the ultra-high-security of Colditz castle.

Ever since his crash-landing, in which he had had to leave one of his artificial legs behind in the disintegrating plane as he parachuted, he had taken the same sort of attitude to the enemy as he had to the loss of his real legs: nothing was going to beat him. I once talked to him about the Battle of Britain, and his analysis was as brisk and straightforward as his attitude to his physical state or the importance of resisting: 'We couldn't have the bastards flying over England, attacking our own land and people, now could we?'

When the RAF was permitted to parachute him a replacement leg he thanked the Luftwaffe by attempting to escape from the hospital even before it arrived. Once he got to Luft III, he had missed no opportunity to attempt escape and encourage others to do the same, all the while tormenting and outraging our captors at every available opportunity.

Shortly after we arrived, there was an attempted escape. The next morning the entire camp was standing outside on parade for hours while the guards took a roll call to figure out how many had got away. Bader decided that guerrilla warfare included waiting until the guards had almost finished, then telling about twenty of us in the dwindling uncounted pile to run over and mingle with those already counted, forcing the guards to start again. Paddy Barthropp and I, being the keen new boys, led the charge. With a whoop we set off, racing from the uncounted herd to the counted one, and others joined in.

The guards at first reached for their guns, thinking it was a mass breakout, but quickly realized that our objective was to make them restart the count. Anyone who has ever been cross at being distracted and 'made to lose count' in the middle of a long sum can imagine the effect multiplied a thousandfold on irate guards in a prisoner-of-war camp trying to find out if anyone has escaped. Paddy and I were grabbed by a group of soldiers and marched off into the guards' part of the camp, and then out of the camp gates at gunpoint.

Normally, leaving the hated wire that caged us and suffocated all hopes of returning to the wider world would have been cause for jubilation, but in this case, as the camp receded behind us and we were shoved and prodded forward at rifle point by seething enemy soldiers, there seemed to be little cause for celebration. Our spirits sank further as we saw that they were taking us off the path and deep into the murky pine forest that surrounded and isolated the camp.

We marched deeper and deeper into the forest, into the gloomy permanent twilight caused by the thick pine branches blocking out even the smallest rays of optimism from the sun. Each tread of a jackboot on a twig sounded like a gunshot as we marched forward with a row of guns trained on our backs. Then, in a clearing carpeted by pine needles, we were ordered to halt.

We were roughly pushed to our knees, side by side, as our unseen captors stood behind us, their guns pointed at the backs of our heads. The ground felt soft and cold beneath my knees and we could hear our own breathing. I had learned in the Gestapo cells in Paris just what it felt like to be waiting for my own execution, but this was different. I felt the endless, powerless gnawing of time passing with almost glacial slowness as we waited for the end, and yet the same time seemed to hurtle forward as it ticked away our last few precious seconds. Waiting for a Gestapo cell door to swing open seemed easy in comparison to waiting for a bullet in the back of the head. Paddy was praying; I was relying on his rather better relations with the Almighty, with whom I did not correspond much, to work for both of us. After a few minutes that stretched like an eternity, the soldiers told us to stand up and herded us back to the camp.

As they marched us back in we were almost glad to see the welcoming barbed wire, at least for a few seconds, after which our attitudes returned quickly to business as usual when we were hauled before the camp commandant, Von Lindeiner. He tore us off a strip and in order to discourage such adventures in the future, particularly as we were relative newcomers whose bad habits he thought might not be as solidified as those of our mentor Douglas Bader, he gave us each two weeks in solitary confinement in the punishment cells or cooler on iron rations.

The punishment cells were simple concrete affairs with nothing but a bare bed, sometimes not even that. The ones at Luft III had a small, high window with bars, through which interesting noises of the world outside sometimes wafted in. After what I had been through, my first stint in a cooler seemed strangely tranquil for a day or two, but the twin evils of boredom and gnawing hunger soon made me long to return to the camp. Gradually, over the coming years, I would get a lot of practice at how to survive such spells in solitary, to make the bliss of silence last a little longer and to pass the time by living more in my own head than in the grim reality of isolation and semi-starvation.

When we got out of the cooler we bumped into Bader, and Paddy expected at least a pat on the back. Instead he asked us where we had been as he hadn't seen us around. Luckily he smiled before both of us exploded.

Bader appreciated anyone who was willing to bring the war to the guards. He was an inspirational leader and really practised what he preached. Not everyone in the camp was as fond of him as we were. There were many who felt that his constant goon-baiting risked losing us valuable privileges that helped us plan bigger, better escapes. Equally there were those who just wanted a quiet life, people for whom any of us escapers were at best a necessary evil.

Finally, the authorities had enough of Bader's incessant warfare and effectively admitted defeat – which is why we saw him being hustled off to another camp. At first it looked as if he would not go quietly. The commandant marched in about forty armed guards and we and other Bader supporters lined up in our droves, ready to do anything he told us, even if it resulted in a bloodbath. Some of the cooler heads in the camp prevailed on him not to start anything when there were so many trigger-happy guards aiming at us and he satisfied himself by knowing that he was demonstrating a valuable lesson to us as he left. Here was one man, without even the use of his legs, whose actions had tied up at least forty enemy soldiers away from the war effort. We might not be able to fly any more, but as he put it 'we can still bloody well fight'.

As he was marched out, he stopped in front of the lines of menacing guards with their guns at the ready. The enemy troops were baffled as he walked along the line looking at them until they realized that his ultimate act of defiance was to take an inspection of them. We stood around the barbed wire at the gates, cheering him and saluting as he was taken away. That was it. Paddy and I decided it was time for us to escape.

This Drain Leads to Poland

One of the problems with thinking up an escape scheme and acting on it was that such activities were not organized on the sporadic, freelance basis that has been the hallmark of so much of my life. Even in those early days, the camp had a well-organized escape committee. Four stony-faced escape experts would listen to and evaluate hare-brained escape plans and either give the OK or forbid them. We waited nervously outside a hut for our audience with the committee, covered by a range of prisoners casually lolling at strategic points against nearby hut walls, operating an invisible lookout system to warn of any enemy presence in the vicinity.

Compared to selling this hard-nosed bunch your escape plans, getting past the guards was thought to be relatively easy. Almost any scheme, even one that sounds brilliant at its time of invention, starts to sound faintly demented when you pitch it to an audience who look as if they are trying you for your life. And in a way, that's exactly what they were doing. Escape from a German camp was, even at the best of times, a risky business. If you were not shot on the way out, there was a considerable chance that an enterprising German civilian or policeman would regard you as easier to capture if dead.

Then there were the dangers of travelling across occupied territory. The senior member of the committee who listened to our escape plan, Lieutenant Commander Jimmy Buckley of the Fleet Air Arm, later made a brilliant escape himself, which ended in a tragedy we will come to later. He was a small, tough career navy man with an unblinkingly honest eye and a strong sense of humour. He was older than most of us and his job was to ensure that some of us had the chance to live to be a little older than we were. Only one in about a hundred escapees made it back to England, and even those prisoners who were recaptured undamaged often fell into the hands of the Gestapo. I did not fancy my chances with them a second time.

Paddy and I outlined our scheme. It is said that most great ideas come to people when they are in the bath, a long tradition presumably started by Archimedes when he shouted 'Eureka' having discovered that an object immersed in water displaces an amount of water equal to the object's weight. In Stalag Luft III, we did not have the luxury of baths. We stayed relatively clean dousing ourselves under a cold water tap, and once a week the guards herded us into a shower block in the *Vorlager* or German section of the camp for a welcome warm wash. And that is where the idea for the Great Shower Escape was born. Unlike Archimedes, we did not want to displace a volume of water – we just wanted to displace ourselves. The escape committee listened in silence, then asked a few questions and kicked us out while they discussed it. They called us back and, much to our astonishment, agreed. The escape was on.

The first step in our escape strategy was to become 'ghosts'. That was the camp code for someone who had managed to disappear within the camp and evade detection until eventually the authorities decided they had really escaped and gave up looking. Admittedly, this type of escape had the rather obvious drawback that you were still inside the camp, but the theory was that once you were a ghost, you could escape at a more leisurely pace, unencumbered by roll calls, head counts, bed-counts and curfews.

Our plan was to vanish during our weekly shower. We had noticed that inside the shower there was a small drain and trapdoor leading to a compartment where the water could be turned off at the mains. It would be a bit snug, but the two of us would squeeze into the compartment and hope that the guards did not notice two fewer coming out than went in. If we could go undetected until that night, we just had to avoid several hundred guards in their own part of the camp and cut our way through the *Vorlager* fence to become real escapees rather than ghosts. Whether we graduated from prisoner-of-war ghosts to real ones would depend on what the Germans did if they caught us.

Support from the escape committee meant a great deal more than mere permission to put our plan into action. We were kitted out with a compass, a hand-drawn map of the area which used the experiences of previous escapees and – most importantly to us in those hungry days – a generous supply of 'the Mixture'. This was a sort of cereal concoction of oats, chocolate and sometimes dried fruit, all of which were considerably more valuable than gold dust to us prisoners. Much of it came from other prisoners pooling their gifts from home or making donations by bartering one food for another. It was used as an easily portable high-energy food for those on sanctioned escapes. Some of my more cynical brethren who knew of my ever-hungry appetite even suggested that getting my hands on a prodigious amount of the Mixture was my primary motive for risking life and limb on an escape.

We marched into the showers as normal, but quickly dived into our soggy hiding place under the grating and waited. All would now depend on our colleagues' ability to distract the goons long enough for them to miscount or not count at all as the sweet-smelling squad were returned to the compound. After that there would be further roll calls, but the bigger gatherings were easier to fix.

As we hid in our soggy roost, the rest of our colleagues took their time with their weekly shower, which we experienced second-hand until one of them had an argument with a grumpy guard. Our colleagues knew that one of the best ways to distract a guard was to irritate the hell out of him. Unfortunately they decided to start the process rather early, when they were in mid-shower. Normally we got two blasts of hot water – one to soap up and one to rinse off. One of the prisoners began an interesting conversation with a guard about Adolf Hitler's parentage. Starting off by being merely rude, he progressed to calling Hitler so many choice names that the guard did exactly what his tormentor wanted and lost his temper. To punish the prisoner for badmouthing the Führer, the goon withheld the second blast of hot water and our colleagues were herded out, still covered in soap, back to the compound.

When it came to the bigger parade-ground counts or *Appells* there were all sorts of stunts that could be pulled. Men would wait until they had been counted once, then duck down and crawl to the end of the row so that they would be counted again, covering for someone hiding, or someone who had already got out and needed time before the alarm was raised. Since time immemorial *Appells* had consisted of men standing in rows five deep, making counting easier for the more mathematically challenged of the guards. One amazingly effective tactic was to occasionally line one of the sections of men up in four rows instead of five; the goons simply counted the neat front rows and multiplied by five rows as always. This only worked if there was a neatly divisible number of escapees and gave the prisoners as many head-count headaches as the Germans.

Another brilliant ruse used at another camp, Marlag O, was a dummy called Albert RN made by John Worsley. He was very realistic, dressed in an old navy jacket, with his elbows out and his hands shoved in his pockets, so he could be held up between two real prisoners. Other convincing dummies were made by Dutch prisoners in Colditz and by Germans in an escape from Canada, but our own dummies tended to be more basic, designed to fool mass headcounts, or papier-mâché 'sleepers' snoozing in beds vacated by escaping prisoners.

But these were all scams for other times, not for a huddle of damp prisoners in a conspicuous line. Our comrades were marched back from the *Vorlager* to the compound, with their grumpy guard. But the guard on the compound wire was neither grumpy, sleepy or dopey – nor any of the other seven dwarfs. Like many of the camp's eagle-eyed ferrets he was a worthy adversary, on the lookout for any manner of wickedness which we might try. The best we could hope for was another distraction that would make the guard lose count, or a bored guard who would not bother to count in the first place. Instead our fellow prisoners were counted meticulously. Their efforts at distracting or enraging were met by prods from a rifle to keep quiet. The wire guard was puzzled and counted again. Then again.

Paddy and I waited in our cramped, soggy roost, every second seeming like an eternity. Then the game was up.

The steamy shower air was filled with the noise of running jackboots, whistles blew, sirens blared and guard dogs barked themselves into a frenzy.

A squad of guards with guns at the ready burst into the shower room but missed us at first. Then we heard the dogs arriving, sniffing and snarling, and we knew it was only a matter of time. Paddy and I looked at each other. We could shred the map to stop the searchers finding out what we knew, but our pockets were crammed with the Mixture. With minutes to go before we were caught, we adjusted our plans. Escape would have to wait. The best we could manage was not to let the Mixture fall into enemy hands.

As more and more goons, ferrets and growling Alsatians descended on the shower block, Paddy and I crammed mouthful after mouthful of the Mixture into our gullets. Then it was all over. The trapdoor was flung open and we found ourselves looking up at a ring of rifles pointing at us and snapping Alsatians straining at their leashes. We emerged soggy, with our hands up and our faces covered in chocolate, which I think they took to be some kind of ingenious camouflage. I dropped the last of the Mixture for one of the Alsatians, hoping that he might remember the good deed when we met again on some future escape attempt.

From there it was a short, sharp march to the solitary punishment cells of the cooler. In the coming years I was to become a regular resident in cooler cells, in this camp as well as others in Poland and Lithuania. Some kind souls have even suggested that I was one of the half-dozen real-life role models for the Steve McQueen made-up character of Hilts the Cooler King in the film of *The Great Escape*, but if I was, no-one told me. It is true that at this stage in the war there were not too many American pilots in the camp, and fewer still who ended up in the cooler on a regular basis, but the reality was that no Americans got away on the Great Escape. By then I was in a different compound, not to mention locked up in the cooler. Anyway, my movie-star skills at riding motorcycles over barbed-wire barricades might have left something to be desired.

As further punishment for our shower escape attempt, Paddy and I were added to a list of about ninety other incorrigible escape artists chosen to be purged from Luft III to a punishment camp in Schubin, Poland – Oflag XXIB, where conditions would be harsher and we would not be able to corrupt the minds of our more docile colleagues. Without much ado, Paddy and I joined Jimmy Buckley and what seemed like half the most accomplished escapologists from the camp, and were loaded into train carriages and trundled in the general direction of the eastern front.

The list of prisoners with us read like a *Who's Who* of recidivist escapees, many of whom later became the nucleus of the Great Escape team. Alongside Lieutenant Commander Buckley and fellow navy flyer Peter 'Hornblower' Fanshawe were the senior British officer (SBO) Wings Day, who had asked to be moved with us, Major Johnny Dodge, known as the Dodger, and Jimmy

James. Then there was Eddy Asselin, a superb French-Canadian tunneller, and escape intelligence officer Aidan Crawley, who went on to become a Member of Parliament. Aidan had shared our salubrious surroundings at Luft III, so Paddy and I felt that we were in very good company, or very bad company, if you happened to be a ferret.

It must have been around October 1942 when we rolled through the bleak landscape of Poland in a series of shipments on our way to a new home. For nearly every one of us crammed in those third-class carriages on the way to Schubin in the autumn of 1942, escape was an almost all-consuming addiction, a full-time job. We were not daft enough to think that getting out from behind the barbed wire would mean that we would get home, but at least if we were captured we would be living up to our duty to tie up as many Axis troops and resources as possible to divert them from the war effort, and there was always the thought that, just like winning the lottery, a few people occasionally did get home.

There cannot have been a single POW – or 'kriegie' as we called ourselves, short for the rather more unwieldy *Kriegsgefangener*, meaning prisoner of war – who did not think about escaping. Yet out of the total pool of all prisoners, maybe only a third in an average camp would have been actively involved in escaping-related activities. Most of the other two-thirds would assist if possible behind the scenes and undergo some hardships to help, while a small rump simply wanted to wait the war out and seemed to have taken the Germans at their word when they announced to each of us on arrival that 'For you the war is over.'

The majority of non-escapees concentrated on filling their time with education, sport and reading. The biggest enemies were hunger, cold and the crashing boredom that comes from being a prisoner with no release date other than the end of the war. For some, survival after a terrible flame-filled air crash, often in the case of bombers with the loss of other crew members, had so scarred them that keeping their heads down and surviving the war was about all they could manage.

But the third of the population which constituted the pro-escapers and their helpers was more than enough to keep our jailers fully occupied. Maybe only 5 per cent were committed to getting outside the wire at all costs themselves, but none of us would have done so without the help of the remaining 25 per cent involved in keeping an eye on the guards over long, dull shifts as stooges or helping prepare anything from documents to clothes and maps or digging implements. Within that 5 per cent of die-hard escapers, for most sensible people one escape attempt was usually enough, and on its failure, or re-capture after a successful escape, some decided to concentrate on supporting activities in the future rather than tempting fate. But for the last 1 or 2 per cent, escaping became a way of life.

While others worked on concerts or education, we ate, slept and breathed schemes for escape, from the ingenious to the insane. Of the whole prisoner population, fewer than 1 per cent ever got to the other side of the wire and less than 1 per cent of that number escaped all the way to England. During the course of the war only about thirty Allied prisoner-of-war pilots made it home. Still, we all dreamed that we might be the one to accomplish that rarest of achievements, the home run.

Even before we all arrived in Poland, the effect of having so many career escapologists together in a few train carriages was starting to be felt. Johnny Dodge the Dodger was fearless almost to the point of comedy. Nothing was going to stop this remarkably brave man escaping, short of a bullet.

The American-born Dodge was old enough to be the father of most of the other prisoners. Just five days after the start of the 1914–18 war, and three years before the United States got involved, Dodge sailed for Britain to join the fight. He emerged from the carnage of the western front as a colonel with the Medal of Honour, still only twenty-five. Like most experienced soldiers, he was called back into service at the outbreak of the Second World War. In the chaos that followed Britain's defeat in France and the Dunkirk evacuation, Dodge was captured but he managed to escape. The second time he was caught happened to be by the Luftwaffe, a twist of fate that saw him spend the rest of his war as a rare soldier among flyers. He was tall, big-boned, remarkably good-natured and very well liked, yet despite his calmness and the fact that in his mid-forties he was a lot more mature than some of us, it was often Dodge who led the charge on escape attempts.

That day, as the elderly train wheezed its way towards the camp at Schubin, Johnny Dodge got permission to use the lavatory as the train paused at some signals. Modestly leaning over the door, he set to work levering off a few planks with a hidden implement to enlarge the lavatory window, and when the noise of the flushing toilet had subsided he was off and running. Unfortunately he was in the middle of a vast open field through which the railway line sliced, with not so much as a lettuce leaf to hide behind. He was spotted in a matter of seconds. Prisoners who saw him making his mad dash cheered him on, but guards started to open fire. Still nowhere near any cover, he knew the game was up and turned, hands up and smiling, as if he had been struck out in a baseball game rather than being two seconds from death. Afterwards he played the incident down in his amiable way, telling friends that the guards were not aiming too accurately. As he was marched back on the train, to be dealt with at our destination, he shrugged at one of his captors and said, 'No harm in trying!'

The trains rolled on for thirty-six hours, and we squirmed in our third-class wooden seats, not allowed to move, stand or even lie down on the floor. Occasionally the train would wheeze into some quiet station and we would study the civilians, getting tips on how to dress to blend in on future escapes. At this stage the locals were still bustling about with no sign that they expected to lose the war. The Russian front had reached what would later prove its high-water mark for Germany and it would soon be downhill all the way. But for now soldiers on leave from the *Ostfront* still proudly wore their red insignia from the Russian campaigns, and the civilians stared at us with a mix of curiosity and contempt.

After two days of travel in the cramped carriages, with rather more attentive guards, we arrived at a sleepy station called Altburgund and were marched down the deserted main street of a village, eventually reaching the gates of Oflag XXIB, the Schubin camp. It was situated about 150 miles west of the Polish capital Warsaw. The invaders had declared it part of a new German province called Warthegau, which the Poles did their best to ignore.

A ragged line of prisoners and their Luftwaffe escort were kept waiting outside the gates like unwelcome door-to-door salesmen. One of our senior guards eventually argued his way in and we waited. Eventually I was fascinated to see Feldwebel Hermann Glemnitz, one of the senior ferrets who had accompanied us from Stalag Luft III, leaving the compound looking irritated, while the rest of our Luftwaffe guards had still not even been allowed inside the camp. It looked as if relations between the army – this camp was run by the Wehrmacht – and the air force in the Reich were not all that rosy. But Glemnitz was not a man to shirk his duty. As the senior German NCO at Luft III he was the leader of the attempts to keep us in. He was generally well respected, even if his name, when spoken by any of us prisoners, was always preceded by the epithet 'that bastard'. This respect was partly because he was depressingly smart at sniffing out tunnels, partly because he treated us with some respect, and partly because he had been an experienced pilot himself in the Great War, which seemed to give him some understanding of how we felt.

As Glemnitz stomped out of the compound it was obvious he had been given short shrift by our new captors. After months of trying to stop us leaking out of Luft III, Glemnitz was obviously having a little difficulty letting go. When the army had said a frosty farewell after the handover at the gates, he had insisted on going inside to attempt to tell the new army management about the wicked ways and wiles of the new arrivals. The duty officer in the camp, a pompous and thoroughly nasty fascist Czech called Simms, had taken great umbrage at a mere flyboy such as Glemnitz daring to tell the army how to run their prison and had virtually booted him off the premises, sending him on his way back to Luft III with a Wehrmacht flea in his ear.

So angry was Glemnitz at this treatment that as he was saying farewell to some of us prisoners he confided the whole sorry exchange, complimenting us by saying that if he was a gambling man, he would be laying bets on a mass breakout within a month, and it would serve the army blockheads right for not listening to him. He did everything but wish us luck, and we assured him that we would do our best to make his dreams come true.

Our Luftwaffe guards soon became small smudges of blue-grey uniforms hurrying back to the railway station to return to Luft III before the rest of the prisoners still there decided to start their own escaping spree. We were handed over to some nervous-looking German soldiers who herded us into the camp and left us to our own devices.

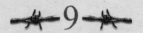

New Country, New Tunnel

The punishment camp at Schubin, Poland – Officers' Camp or Oflag XXIB – was built around the grounds of a former girls' school, centred on a big building called the White House with a host of smaller ones dotted around. To these had been added the ubiquitous barracks to house the captives, though unlike those of many of the other camps, these were made of brick. There were twelve barracks, six on each side of the school's former playing fields. These huts were little more than huge shells, without even ceilings; just bare rafters through which the Polish wind whistled day and night.

Because of its previous function, the camp looked strangely attractive, with trees and gardens dotted about a few old, scenic buildings including a big white house and a chapel; but the reality was very different. Despite the landscaping, the surrounding rings of barbed wire and guard posts were very real.

Inside the barracks there were two-storey bunk beds and a table and benches for every twelve prisoners. These were housed in one giant room, partitioned by lockers, with a central walkway. A wall of conversation and cross talk between prisoners along the length of our communal barn made it one of the loudest prison camps in the history of the war. Despite the cacophony, grim conditions and lack of privacy, morale at the time of our arrival was remarkably high.

Although conditions were spectacularly grim, we felt as if we had arrived in escapers' paradise. The place was run by Wehrmacht units, rather than the devil-we-knew Luftwaffe. These guards, some elderly, some invalided out of units on the eastern front and others simply trying to avoid any front whatsoever, had none of the Luftwaffe's hard-earned expertise in stopping our escapes.

We were delighted to see that there were about two hundred RAF prisoners already installed, the remnants of an equally grim camp at Warburg, and for a while the area buzzed with reunions between men who had last seen each other over a pint of beer in some sleepy English pub some years and a few lifetimes earlier.

Then it was down to business. Once we had studied the camp as a place to live, we took a long close look at it as a place to leave. Paddy Barthropp commented that the designer must have had a drop of British blood, since some of the buildings were conveniently close to the prison wire, with some of the huts only about 70 feet from the outer perimeter, which meant that tunnels could be shorter. The basic fact was that the place had not been built as a prison, and it is always harder to guard a place that was not specifically designed to keep people in. The layout of the buildings created several blind spots where the goons in the watchtowers could not peer, while clumps of trees and some steep slopes gave us more chances to hide.

Best of all, we were in Poland, and that meant that if we got out and managed to knock on a door we were just as likely to be helped as not. This was in stark comparison to Luft III in the heart of Germany, where every Nazi boy scout was on the lookout for escaped flyers and every blonde-haired apple-cheeked lass would sooner stick a *jugend dirk* dagger in your ribs than help you. To discourage such collaboration the occupiers had the simple remedy of shooting any Poles who helped escaped prisoners, no matter how briefly or ineffectually, and their family as well. Despite this threat, thousands of ordinary Polish people risked their lives to help escapees.

On arrival at Schubin, I found myself in an utterly alien position – invited to become one of the hard-faced veterans on the escape committee, whose job was to stress test the mad escape ideas of people like me, and decide which should be allowed and supported. Paddy was also on the committee and our friend Aidan Crawley was in charge of security.

The idea that I should tell other people what to do or what not to do never came very naturally to me. I think people tend to do their best work when they are working together, following their own instincts. But in a war, sometimes we do not have the luxury of walking our own path. Effectively, by joining up I had recognized this, however instinctively or from an apparently emotional basis. I agreed to serve on the escape committee, though secretly I planned to escape as soon as possible, and soon be too far away to have to make such tough decisions about who should stay and who should go. Even if the odds on getting home were not ones any bookmaker would care for, at least our escapes added to the general sense of unease among the German population, with the thought that even in the heart of the Third Reich, there might be a scruffy, hungry American lurking behind every hedge.

Crouching down in the compound, I examined a handful of the rich Polish earth. It was well drained, allowing freedom to tunnel, though requiring decent shoring to avoid collapses in tunnel walls. I took a trip into one of the vast huts, already filling up with prisoners grabbing bunks and a few trying to give themselves some feeble privacy by hanging up their spare clothes like curtains beside their bed.

One bunk was as good as the next, so a group of us, including myself, Paddy, Aidan Crawley and Eddy Asselin, picked a corner of the barn-like Hut 6, barricaded off by a few lockers, and set up shop. The first thing I looked at was the construction of the beds. The bed boards were perfect – not perhaps for sleeping on but ideal ready-made sturdy tunnel supports. At the end of each hut was a bare concrete wash area, and some distance away were the latrines, a grim row of thirty-six holes in a wooden bench, located above a reeking pit in a nasty black shed. Before we could do any further inspection of our no-star accommodation, the German army decided it was time for them to take a look at their new inmates and they called an *Appell*.

The event was a near riot. We met the man who had ruffled Glemnitz, Captain Simms, a caricature of Prussian pomposity with a vicious streak which he took out on both his own subordinates and any prisoner who caught his eye. At that first *Appell*, Simms was appalled that we were not turned out like new recruits on a parade ground. He screamed and shouted at us and at the guards, who screamed and shouted at us again. Much to their surprise we screamed and shouted back.

Over the following months Wings Day, as senior British officer, attempted to work with the pompous Simms and his laconic camp commandant. It was not love at first sight. Despite the fact that the commandant was the same rank as Wings and therefore on an equal footing, in accordance with both military custom and the Geneva Convention, once Wings had introduced himself as the senior officer and stood at ease, the commandant barked at him to stand to attention. He didn't care what rank Wings was; he was just another British prisoner and he should not speak unless ordered to do so. If he had known Wings a bit better he would have realized that he had just made a very big mistake. Wings simply told him not to shout at an officer of equal rank, saluted, turned on his heels and left. From then on the two waged their own private war, which Wings was determined to win. Addressing a group of us a short time later, he declared his intention to get men out of the camp not just in ones or twos but in large numbers. He would have done it anyway, but he told us that the camp commandant had been 'damnably rude' and refused even basic requests concerning food parcels, sanitation and mail. So in return, Wings was going to ensure that as well as giving the Third Reich a headache catching us, his secondary aim would be to chop the commandant down like a tree.

Wings Day, a tall, angular man, had a special place in escaping history. While he was in effective charge at Stalag Luft III, given free rein by his superior Group Captain Massey, Wings had taken a bunch of quirky runaways and tunnellers and their disparate freelance efforts and turned them into a coordinated escape force. As one wag put it during one of our frequent debates about politics and the future of Britain after the war, Wings Day had already nationalized tunnelling.

Though very likeable and extremely popular with the men, Wings was also a bit of an old-school officer – hence his indignation at his treatment by the commandant. He expected his own people to behave with a certain amount of military discipline, which was often lacking among those of us who were civilian-volunteer types as opposed to the career military men with whom we rubbed shoulders. One day, some time before Christmas 1942 at Schubin, Wings gave a somewhat routine telling-off to a group of NCO orderlies who had been transferred to the camp with us, including one called Wareing. Wings did not think that being locked up was a good enough reason for them not to apply themselves to the job of orderly with the same spit-and-polish zeal expected of them in a barracks at home. Even Wings had to see the funny side when Wareing, on a trip with other orderlies to get coal supplies from the local village, managed to slip away, steal a bicycle and pedal all the way to the port of Danzig, where he hopped on a ship bound for Halmstad, Sweden. Ironically his ticket to free- dom was a coal boat, and he was back in London in time to celebrate Christmas 1942. This was the first successful home run from Schubin, for which he was awarded the Distinguished Conduct Medal.

For the rest of us, it was business as usual until we could follow in his footsteps. One excellent reason for cranking up our escape activity was to get away from the appalling conditions, which made Luft III look relatively like a five-star hotel. We were assailed by a novel version of the biblical plagues, the main ones being famine, pestilence and ice.

In terms of famine, hunger was a constant factor in our lives. A normal day's ration would consist of a thin slice of black Reich bread for breakfast with margarine, sometimes jam and a cup of boiled confetti pretending to be tea. Reich bread was to bread what Reich tea was to tea – one step down from baked sawdust. Lunch would be a few sad leaves of cabbage boiled to oblivion and called soup, and the evening meal either another slice of the grim bread or maybe a few small potatoes. Gradually we dwindled to a fraction of our former weight.

Those of us who made frequent visits to the cooler for two or four weeks of solitary punishment were treated to a bread and water diet for the duration, which made the incorrigible escape artists even thinner. If this kept up, I once confided in Paddy, we might be able to slip between the strands of barbed wire, or perhaps disappear altogether by turning sideways. In another of our endless food conversations, shortly after emerging from another stretch in the cooler, I suggested a great plan that had hatched as I lay on the floor in solitary. Paddy leant in eagerly to hear the details. My plan was to lure some of the more vicious guard dogs into Hut 6 where we could do away with them, eat them in a feast and then dress up in their skins as very large guard dogs and wander out of the front gate, stopping for a pee on the commandant's trouser leg. Paddy was up for it, but the dogs must have got suspicious and stayed away from our hut for a few days.

The pestilence surfaced mainly in the form of jaundice, which spread rapidly in our poor living conditions, reinforced by the inadequate diet, until at one point almost half the camp was down with it. An even more common pestilence came in the form of lice and bedbugs, which infested every corner of the barracks, from the concrete floors to the rafters where the ceiling should have been. The lice were huge brutes with a red V on their heads and we spent a good deal of time every day finding them and crushing them with a satisfying pop against a thumbnail. A combination of tunnel dirt, sewage and the ubiquitous lice made us not the most fragrant of guests, but the guards still insisted on hanging on to us.

As for ice, bitter arctic winds whistled in from the Baltic; as winter of 1942 arrived, snow fell in vast drifts and temperatures plummeted to minus fifteen and below. The football pitch now doubled as an ice skating rink. This had an added advantage. The Germans had underground microphones to listen for tunnelling activity, but the noise of fifty ice skaters on rickety home-made skates drowned out even the noisiest burrowing.

As our thin uniforms failed to keep out the cold and we huddled around the brick stoves, half numb and unable to think straight with the mixture of chill and hunger, Wings Day continued to demand better conditions. The commandant was as unhelpful as ever, though he finally cracked and rustled up some moth-eaten greatcoats taken off the Polish cavalry when they surrendered.

His one other gift was a huge supply of badly made French wooden clogs, which were no use for keeping our feet warm and clearly designed to stop us escaping, or even walking more than a few yards at a time. As I studied one in the chill of the barracks one evening,

I thought back to the foolish young man on the run in France who had chosen a pair of clogs for his quick getaway. How long ago was that? Nine months? Or maybe a lifetime? Studying the clogs, I and my colleagues had a brainwave. They might not be much good to walk in, but they could still keep our feet warm. I opened the brick oven door and threw them in.

The only other way to keep out the cold was to find more food, and once again we were back to the famine part of our famine-pestilence-ice cycle. On good days we were able to share the contents of a Red Cross parcel, though we tried to save as much of these as possible for 'escape food'.

At Schubin, our basic escape concoction of the Mixture evolved into two entirely new subspecies. These were called Fudge and Goo. Fudge was built around cocoa, while Goo's main ingredient was dried cereal with vitamins. Other key ingredients from our Red Cross parcels that ended up in our escape concoctions included milk powder, sugar and dried fruit. Both versions had the consistency of fudge or caramel, depending on the individual batch, since producing the stuff was not an exact science.

Many of the veterans from Stalag Luft III called all such mixes dog food, which baffled some of our newer arrivals, since it tasted so much better than anything else we got to eat. The origins of the name came from a time at the Sagan camp when some over-zealous cooks had made such a prodigious batch of the stuff that supply of the Mixture temporarily outstripped demand for escaping. To avoid the surplus falling into enemy hands, those responsible dug a hole under Hut 62 and hid it for future use. That night the hungry inhabitants of the hut could do nothing but listen as a guard dog on patrol sniffed out their hidden treasure, dug it out and started wolfing it down with loud slurping noises and grunts of delight. From then on it was dog food.

The basic recipes at Schubin were devised by David Lubbock, a Fleet Air Arm officer who had been a dietician in a previous life. His basic aim was to make the best use of the food from the Red Cross parcels without leaving escapees with the headaches or nausea that came from eating relatively huge quantities of sugar and fat after months of a virtual starvation diet. By the end of the war, like old wine connoisseurs, some of us used to debate the relative merits of the escape mixtures from half-a-dozen camps. In comparison to our usual fare, they were all like nectar.

The fact that there was a dietician in the camp is a clue to one of our greatest strengths. Many if not most of us had joined up after some other experiences in life, and if you looked hard enough, you could find people of every possible trade, skill and profession represented in the camp, from engineers to medics and artists to accountants. In the world of an escapee, every single one of them had a skill that could make the difference between discovery and a home run. They were all forgers, scroungers, tunnellers, surveyors and tailors in waiting.

This camp would be the first to function as a pure escape factory, building on what inmates had learned from Luft III, Luft I and Dulag Luft. In turn, the hard lessons we learned in Poland were later put to good use by those involved in the Great Escape, who included many of my Schubin accomplices.

Wings made sure that we teamed up with the prisoners who had come from Warburg – including some very experienced escape artists – and did the same with the increasing number of my fellow Americans, who were being shot from the skies in bomber crews on a regular basis. The Prussians might let their inter-service rivalries surface, but for us the only enemy was whatever kept us on the inside of the wire. The senior officer 'Hetty' Hyde, who was rarely seen without a pipe clenched between his determined jaws, knew Wings from their mutual time at Dulag Luft, and soon an unholy alliance was born, with those from both Warburg and Luft III contributing all their escaping experience.

The Warburg officers, as you might expect, were keen on team-effort assaults on the outside world and our first joint effort was based on a brilliant escape they had managed at Warburg. Not long after our arrival, two teams were put in training for Operation Forlorn Hope. This began with two groups hiding at the ready after lights out, one inside the barracks, the other huddled in a blind spot between the machine-gun posts. The boundary lights blinked brightly around the perimeter fence as always. Then there was a loud bang and the lights went out. Our enterprising army colleagues had fused the electricity generator. Seconds later both teams were charging for the wire, neck and neck as if in some competition at a military show. They were carrying scaling ladders like some medieval horde involved in the siege of a castle. Both teams got their ladders up against the wire. But then, with another muffled bang, the lights came back on.

My friend Aidan Crawley groaned. As the man in charge of security for escapes, a job at which he generally excelled, he knew what this meant. The Germans had an emergency secondary lighting system which we had failed to spot. Suddenly the whacky race to the wire was run in reverse. Amazingly, the would-be escapees made it back to safety, mostly unscathed. The guards did not know this, and on discovering the ladders were convinced that some of us had got away. There followed a long, cold night in which we were turned out of our barracks and counted and recounted. To gain a small crumb of comfort for our failure, we all tried to make the counting as difficult as possible. Even Wings Day, who did not normally share our passion for goon-baiting, joined in and was discovered only after some hours perched in a pew in the camp chapel, apparently having a quiet word with the Almighty.

As well as the failed mass escape, there were a thousand smaller schemes afoot in those first weeks and months. At first, our approach to escaping from Schubin was less than subtle. As our eyes roved the camp we saw dozens of potential ways out – under the wire in tunnels, over the wire by vaulting or climbing, through it with cutters or through the main gate by hiding or in disguise as anything from a guard to a Red Cross inspector. We were up and off like a wayward bunch of school kids who find themselves let loose in a chocolate factory.

What our army guards lacked in experience, a few of them made up for in thuggishness, in stark contrast to the majority of Luftwaffe guards at Luft III, as I discovered on one of my first escape attempts that winter.

I had decided to diversify from my usual tunnelling and wire-cutting habits to try strolling out instead. A work detail of non-officers and Russian prisoners was being herded out to some unknown destination for the day. Sliding alongside them, my uniform hidden under a long coat, I waited until the guards were distracted and then slipped into the column. I marched along with my head down until I got to our destination, a local railway station. There we were detailed to unload a goods train, while several bored guards trained their guns on us, just in case we got any ideas. When the guards were looking the other way, I managed to roll myself under the train. Looking up at the sooty, oil-smeared wheels, I prayed that the train would not move and rolled as quickly as I could to the other side of the line. I ended up crouching on the far side of the train while the bustle of the loading continued a few feet away on the platform.

I looked into the distance. There was about half a mile of desolate open ground, and then a line of trees marking the edge of a wood. I looked back towards the guards. That was a great deal of open terrain in which even a bad shot could pick off a fleeing prisoner. But the woods were calling me. It was too tempting and I set off like a greyhound at a racetrack.

Seconds later a shout went up and what I hoped were warning shots whistled over my head. The German officer surveyed the distance I would have to run to escape, evidently with some amusement, and ordered several soldiers with pushbikes to cycle around either side of me. There are few experiences more depressing than racing as fast as you can for an unattainable target while your enemies overtake you in a leisurely manner and are waiting for you, guns at the ready, just in front of your objective.

They expected me to give up meekly, and indeed if I was smarter I would have, but having got that far, I decided I might as well really go for it. I attempted to charge through them as if I was an American footballer, determined to score the winning touchdown. I was brought down by a rifle butt in the face and got a very severe beating for refusing to halt.

I was thrown, battered and bruised, into the Schubin cooler. Like many things at the camp it was not in the most logical place, being outside the inner wire in which we usually lived. The guards had been so busy battering me that they had not searched me very well, and so I unpeeled a piece of sticking tape I had patched on my leg and took out a very tiny file that I had hidden in it. I started to work on one of the three thick iron bars that covered the small window.

Part of my punishment was a bread and water diet, and the bread was Reich bread. Every time I was left alone, I would saw for hours on end with my tiny file. When I took a break for my Reich bread, I at last discovered a good use for the stuff. If chewed enough and mixed with powder from my cell walls, it blended in brilliantly with the cement that held my cell bars in place. Each day I was able to cover up my handiwork with Reich bread putty and, when the coast was clear, continue with my sawing.

After a week, I was through the bottom cut on one of the bars and about to start on the next. But by this time the goons were starting to learn how to keep us on the hop, and for no apparent reason they changed my cell. I started on the bars in the new one. A few days later when cleaning out my old cell, a guard noticed my handiwork. I was searched and my file, by then pretty blunt anyway, was confiscated. I was sentenced to another two weeks in solitary, without the aid of escaping equipment.

But the one thing they could not confiscate was my mind. There was hardly a night when my dreams did not take me soaring back to London – to the kind people and the theatres, the music and the last train to Hornchurch. To kick-start my nocturnal adventures, my brain imagined every possible type of escape. I catapulted myself over the wire on a giant rubber band. I burrowed out through the walls like one of the mites in the German cheese. I soared on home-made glider wings, and sometimes the guards kindly left the gates open. But no matter how brilliant or bizarre the escape, I still woke up in solitary.

During the day I passed the time by remembering poetry I had learned at school in Texas. I got so good at it that I could start a day knowing only a fragment of a poem and end it by being able to visualize the entire page in the poetry book where I first read it. Whether this was evidence that we are all gifted deep down with a well of memories of even the smallest things that happen to us, I do not know. I was certainly glad that the Gestapo did not subscribe to the theory, as they might have tried even harder to extract my forgotten memories. Alternatively, it is perfectly possible that the bits of poems I conjured up had very little to do with what the poets had written down, but with no books allowed and no-one to challenge me, the versions in my head were word perfect.

I got out one lunchtime after my double stretch and was enjoying wolfing down as much Red Cross food as possible in my hut when two of my friends, Mike Wood and Bill Palmer, started telling me about a break they had planned for that same night. I really could have done with a rest, but the one thing time in the cooler does for you is to make your priorities very clear, and mine was escape.

As soon as darkness fell, we slipped out of our hut and made our way down to an area where a natural hollow and a small vegetable patch gave a little cover from the searchlights that swept back and forth from the guard towers all night. We wriggled through the vegetable patch, smelling the earthy night smells and listening to the night-time noises, fearing that every little sound was a guard on patrol.

I found myself trying to huddle under a potato plant that was about six inches tall, and I began to wonder why I kept on doing such stupid things, reasoning that I would probably have another month in the cooler to figure it out. Then the other Bill cut the wire. It was stretched so tight that it went off like a gunshot as it whipped around and nearly caught us. An incredibly loud twang, like the first note of a crazed bluegrass banjo solo, filled the air, echoing away along the fence.

A dozen lights snapped on, sirens wailed and the three of us dived in different directions. There was no way to get out without cutting more wires and no time to do so. We tried to make it to cover and I lay still, camouflaged again as a very unlikely potato plant. A light shone directly on Bill and Mike and they were carted off at gunpoint for a long stay in the cooler. But amazingly, as I lay still, a guard examined the minimal damage to the fence and walked away, almost treading on me as he passed by in the darkness. When the commotion had died down I crawled very slowly back to our hut and fell into a long sleep in which I was too exhausted to escape, even in my dreams.

Soon after this disaster, several of the hastily started 'blitz tunnels' which were underway almost from the day we arrived were found. A blitz tunnel was a short tunnel, designed to be dug quickly and used for a lightning escape under the wire. A mixture of over-zealousness, not enough planning in the construction or security aspects, and a large dollop of bad luck meant that one by one nearly all the tunnels were discovered. The ferrets were a bit shocked that one of them started underneath the altar in the chapel, but the fact that the enemy had '*Gott mit uns*' or 'God is with us' written on their belt buckles didn't mean that we could not look to the same source for inspiration.

Another of the tunnels, as yet undetected, says a lot about what sort of leader Wings Day was. The tunnel started underneath his own senior officers' mess table. Perched at the table, Wings had determined that our future tunnels needed to be bigger, better and with cast-iron security. Instead of a couple of hopefuls scooting out the second the tunnel broke, we would aim to get people out in the dozens, maybe even the hundreds. That way we could keep many Germans occupied looking for us. This was the thinking that sowed the seeds for a later breakout from Luft III, the Great Escape.

But having dozens of people on the outside meant dozens of sets of civilian clothes, escape rations for more people than ever before, mass production of everything from compasses to maps and, most important of all for those hoping to travel in style, forged documents and passes or *Ausweis*. Our pool of talent from all walks of life was suddenly called on to go into overdrive.

In order to maintain security, each part of the operation was known by the name of a shop in Britain. The people who turned blankets and spare uniforms into anything from bogus German uniforms to business suits or peasants' garb were known as Gieves, after a famous gents' outfitters in London; likewise Gamages was our security network. The map makers were known as Cook's Tours and those in charge of concocting escape food were named after Lyons' celebrated Corner House restaurants. Those who specialized in dying cloth were named after Pullar's of Perth, a big dry-cleaning company in Scotland. If they heard the names, the Germans were baffled, as of course were those of us from America.

The Pullar's of Perth group, under the leadership of John Paget, needed immense coordination and the support of almost everybody in the camp. The only way to dye the volume of cloth that would be needed for so many sets of clothes for escapees was to do it under the cover of our regular laundry day. On one day each week the huge cauldrons used to prepare our communal soup were requisitioned and used to boil our flea-ridden clothes. The washing went on in each of the barracks and gave cover for the dyeing that was being done in the cauldrons. Every time a couple of guards appeared, any of the heavy overcoats that were being dyed were hastily bundled up and shoved in kit bags, which were then smuggled to the tunnels or hidden in the barracks. In some cases it took weeks to get them dry.

The world of the dyers and tailors was fraught with problems. There were only two main sources for cloth with which to make civilian clothes – old uniforms and blankets. The tailors were delighted at first when a consignment of blankets arrived from Britain with encoded instructions on how they could be turned into rather natty suits, but a quick look at the results presented an obvious problem: they were too good. This was after all wartime, and strolling about the Polish countryside dressed like a Piccadilly toff was not much better than wearing an RAF uniform. Instead, old threadbare Polish blankets, smoothed down with a sharp knife, provided a much more credible wardrobe for next season's well-dressed escapist.

We were fortunate to have with us at Schubin one of the greatest forgers of the war. Eric Shaw produced apparently typewritten letters with a tiny paintbrush and magnifying glass, knowing that a single slip on a single tiny letter could cost a man his freedom or maybe his life. His passes and letters of authority to travel on business from companies such as Krupps Engineering were truly works of art, and his work was a far cry from my job of burrowing in the mud, but just as important.

And so, for those above and below ground, days turned into weeks and weeks to months, and my first Christmas in captivity approached. The run-up to Christmas is always one of the toughest times for any prisoner. It is a time to spend with family and loved ones, not isolated in freezing conditions with a few hundred men even more glum than oneself. It was a time when bad news from home – whether of death or of marriages disintegrating under the strain of enforced separation – could hit very hard.

Every POW camp in the war had its own stories about suicides or virtual suicides as men pushed beyond endurance finally cracked. Sometimes the trigger was a letter from home. While we Americans knew these as 'Dear John' letters, the British called them Mespots. I was interested in this word – it sounded like mess pot, which in turn sounded like something that might involve food, my only main interest apart from escaping. In reality the name came from the British inter-war campaign in Mesopotamia, a place so miserable and far away from home that it prompted a flurry of long-distance break-ups.

Many of the most remarkable Mespot letters became almost legendary, the stories moving from camp to camp with the prisoners. One told of a wife who wrote to tell a prisoner that she now had two babies by an Italian prisoner of war at a local camp at home, but added that she would make it up to him by buying him a motorbike after the war. Another told how a complete stranger rushed up to her under cover of the blackout and presented her with a bouncing baby which she had decided to keep. In some camps such letters were even pinned up on the noticeboard as a way of sharing the misery and avoiding individuals suffering alone or being whispered about.

Not every letter from home brought such news. Most helped keep prisoners going, reminding them what they were fighting for and giving them something to work for. Some of the most welcome Christmas packages included board games and playing cards. It was not just that a few rounds of the Monopoly board helped remind us of strolling down more interesting streets at home: the boards themselves contained escape materials, ranging from maps to blank passes. These helped to supplement the painstaking work of our forgers and cartographers.

Perhaps our most remarkable piece of post that December 1942 was a message from Buckingham Palace. The letter was brought in with a certain amount of reverence by one of the senior guards, Rittmeister Reimer. Reimer was a rather rotund and jolly-looking ex-cavalry officer who would have made a good Santa Claus compared to most of us half-starved inmates. He was amiable and did his best to look wounded if we were not quite as jolly in return, but anyone who took him for a fool was badly mistaken.

He handed the letter to Wings. It was a Christmas card from the King and Queen, with a photograph of them and the two princesses in London. It had probably wound its way through the Red Cross or other neutral diplomatic channels, then through the more chivalrous sections of the Luftwaffe, to somehow arrive safely in the heart of enemy territory.

As we passed it gently from hand to hand, I thought back to the time when I met the King on that rain-sodden air strip in Lincolnshire, exchanging a few words as the rain dripped off our noses to form an egalitarian puddle at our feet. He was a naturally shy man, who had no desire to be king but ended up with the job after his brother abdicated, just in time to hand him the crown and a one-way ticket to a world war. He and his wife stuck it out in London during the Blitz and earned respect and affection from thousands who were also suffering from the equally egalitarian bombs. I also thought of the parties in London and my boisterous city nightlife being interrupted by an unexpected introduction to his wife Queen Elizabeth. It seemed as if all these events had happened to someone else, in another century or on another planet. I've never been much of a monarchist, and always figured that the Boston Tea Party was a good idea, but getting that card did wonders for our morale. In some strange way it was a little civilized gesture that said that even in the wilds of Poland in the bleak midwinter we were not completely forgotten.

For every letter from royalty, there were a hundred Mespots. Whether because of bad news from home or just from the strain of captivity, physical or mental, there were some poor men in Schubin who escaped the wire only when carried out in a pine box.

Poor old Flight Lieutenant 'Pissy' Edwards had been very badly shaken by a particularly traumatic crash before his capture, and during his time in captivity he had become less and less stable, gradually becoming what we called wire-happy. His unhinged arguments and nervous ticks could be irritating to men already cooped up and spoiling for a squabble, but he was harmless, and most of us did our best to look after him. When he announced one day that he was 'fed up with this place', no-one paid much attention. Minutes later, when he strolled over the death wire, the low warning wire some yards in front of the main fence, and started to climb the perimeter barbed wire in broad daylight, it would have been easy to take him down and bring him somewhere to lie down for a while. Instead an army guard called on him to halt just once. He climbed on feebly, not getting very far up the wire. The nervous guard aimed low but shot him in the groin and he dangled briefly on the wire like a broken doll before being taken down. He was tended to by the camp doctor, but died of his wound.

When I and some others who had rushed to the edge of the death wire protested, one particularly vicious guard known as the Blond Beast was all in favour of mowing us down too. Machine guns and rifles were clicked at the ready as a menacing crowd of prisoners gathered to support us, but some of the more moderate guards cooled the situation and we were spared. Instead, I was marched back into the cooler as punishment for raising my voice and fist against a guard.

Years later, when watching the film *The Great Escape*, I noticed that it portrayed a similar, tragic moment in which an officer is shot down on the wire and a protesting American is led away to the cooler. As far as I know, such an event never took place at Luft III, but the real-life tragedy at Schubin was burned into the minds of anyone who saw it.

Back in the cooler, I tried to conserve my strength. Iron rations and isolation were the main forms of punishment.

There were now so many guards around during the day that escape from the cooler was impossible, and just to make sure that I didn't try something during the less well guarded night shift each evening the Blond Beast came into my cell and removed my shoes. He took them away, returning them, sadly unpolished, along with my Reich bread in the morning. Sometimes it was difficult to tell the two apart.

Every evening as he stole my shoes, he would play a little game. 'Who is winning the war?' he would ask me, amiably. The first time, I replied, 'We are,' and got a mighty back-hander in the face, which sent me sprawling to the cell floor. The next night he was back for more. He asked the same question. This time, showing that I might be stubborn but was not entirely stupid, I changed tack. 'You are,' I replied. I got an equally hard punch in the mouth, apparently for lacking sincerity in my delivery. This continued night after night. Each night he asked the same question, and each night I tried a new potential victor for the war, including the Chinese, the Patagonians and the whirling dervishes, but none of them seemed to make him happy, and my bruises multiplied.

Things were pretty grim, but with some really creative thinking, I managed to make them even worse. If I jumped up and clung to the window bars I could peer out at the road that ran along the outside of the camp. One day I heard a commotion. Whips were cracking and men were shouting. I had not heard any noises like that since my childhood vacations in Texas and New Mexico. It was the sound of a herd being driven. Yet the one sound that was missing was that of the cattle.

Hauling myself up by the bars, I saw that instead of cattle there was a moving mass of about two hundred young women. Members of the local fascist militia and some German soldiers were driving them along the road with whips and sticks, herding them like animals towards the nearby railway station. I am not sure if they were Jews destined for the extermination camps or young Polish women destined for the forced brothels on the eastern front.

Not since the 1930s when I had sat with my blood boiling while I watched American newsreels showing the Nazis' treatment of Jews and communists had I felt such a red rage welling up inside me. And this time it was no purely abstract experience. I now knew just what I was fighting against, and that I would fight against it while there was breath in my body, whether by escape or sabotage, or back behind the guns of a Spitfire if I could manage it. Something inside me snapped. The year of abuse, captivity, beatings and a thousand tiny humiliations boiled up into one overwhelming desire to fight back and to defend these poor women who were going through everything I was and probably things a hundred times worse. Through that tiny barred window, I screamed at the fascists herding the women. I shouted and swore and cursed, throwing every vile word I could at them. Some of the women looked up, and I like to think that this small voice of defiance gave them a little comfort in the human hell which the Nazis had created for them.

The Blond Beast and the other guards came running into my cell to see what all the commotion was about and tried to pull me away from the window, but my grip was like iron on the bars. I continued to pour out abuse at them, at the fascists and at the whole corrupt edifice that was reducing Europe to rubble. I was so enraged that I hardly felt the blows raining down on me and the gun butts smashing my hands until I finally let go of the bars and fell to the floor, where the kicking continued.

As I lay curled up and semi-conscious on the bare concrete floor, the guards returned with wood and nails and boarded up the tiny window, then left me, clanging the cell door locked behind them. My face ached and my back and stomach throbbed from where I had been kicked while on the ground. I was badly bruised, but I knew I would have time to heal before they let me out. I felt the cold concrete against my battered cheek as I lay utterly alone in the darkness. But I was glad I had raised my voice. Human beings are surrounded by a universe many sizes too big for them and the ability either to shout out in anger or to laugh in the face of chaos are the only truly noble options available to us. That shout, or that laughter, even in the black infinity of the universe, is an absolutely new and pure thing, filling the void and going on, echoing off among the nebula, with an entirely human significance.

━✳━10━✳━

Digging for Victory

When I emerged from my latest stint in solitary I was even thinner but more determined than ever to get out. Christmas 1942 was nearly upon us. In fact it was the night before Christmas and all through the house there were scruffy, uniformed creatures stirring. Down by the vile latrines, a group of us were engaged in activities other than the obvious ones. Reasoning that even the most diligent guard would be reluctant to rummage about in an open sewer, we decided that this would be the ideal place to start a tunnel. It was the closest building to the wire, though still a long way from the perimeter – about 150 feet; but that could not be helped, so we just got started.

At first we worried about the German defences against tunnels, the most prominent being their network of microphones planted in the ground at varying depths, and designed to pick up any digging sounds bigger than the local moles. Through Aidan Crawley's excellent intelligence network we soon found out that this was not a big problem. The microphones were in fact too sensitive and anyone tromping around above ground would more than drown out any tunnelling noises far below. We decided to be on the safe side by taking the tunnel depth down to 17 feet below ground, while scores of our helpful fellow prisoners took long walks and stamped their feet to keep out the cold, deafening some unfortunate guard given the tedious job of listening to the soil for eight hours at a stretch.

If the authorities could think up some tedious jobs, we were not to be outdone. The first thing we needed was someone to occupy the unenviable post of 'throne stooge'. This involved sitting on a particular toilet seat for hours on end, guarding our tunnel entrance and also ensuring that our own colleagues did not unwittingly add to our miseries when we were working below.

Eddy, Paddy and I, along with perhaps a dozen willing helpers, chose the end toilet hole of the communal latrine. This last seat was beside a wall that divided the latrine building in two. Under the concrete floor, the dividing wall continued, separating an underground sump on one side from a huge sewage pit on the other. We chipped away around the toilet seat until the 'throne' was effectively a removable tunnel entrance. Below it, we made a hole in the dividing wall and made up a removable dummy wall in case the ferrets ever held their noses and peeked in. The hole was just large enough for a man to squeeze through. In the sump we hollowed out a huge working chamber. The best thing about the latrine was that all our normal convoluted antics to get rid of soil from tunnels, whether by storing bags in the huts or acting like penguins by shuffling small amounts onto the ground from bags hidden in our trousers, were no longer needed. We shovelled the dirt from the sump into the latrine pit on the other side of the wall.

Once we had a big-enough chamber to work in, we started the tunnel. This was to become one of the most successful in the war. Since Eddy Asselin was in charge of the operation, the tunnel was called Asselin, and if any ferrets overheard the name rather frequently in the following months, they must have assumed that Asselin was a particularly popular man, which indeed he was.

Edmund Asselin was only about twenty-one, but had as much nerve as he had style. He was a French Canadian from Quebec with my own squadron, and had been shot down shortly after I arrived in Britain. He was an outstanding planner and organizer. The organizing genes seemed to run in his family, since on news of Eddy's capture his mother Beatrice set up and led the Canadian support organization for prisoners of war, which helped to keep us alive with very welcome food and clothes. I had encountered Eddy briefly as a fellow RCAF Spitfire pilot, but he had been shot down before we had much of a chance to get to know each other. By the time we renewed our acquaintance in Stalag Luft III, Eddy was a charismatic veteran of all aspects of life in kriegiedom, from tunnelling to playing poker for the back pay that was building up in our absence. Before the war he had been a star football player for Loyola College in Canada. He was immensely likeable and tried to be helpful to his fellow prisoners, but he also had a very well-developed streak of ambition and we all had an unshakeable sense that no matter what happened, Eddy Asselin would come up smelling of roses.

Unfortunately, roses were not what we smelled of as we started the Asselin tunnel. Entering the tunnel was a daily experience of horror as I wriggled through the hole where the toilet seat was and my face came to within a few inches of the great stinking lake of sewage. I thought back to the day I was shot down over France and found myself wading through the river that turned out to be a sewerage ditch. I seemed destined to spend a great deal of the war swimming in unsavoury seas, which is how I generally regarded the Third Reich and all its works.

After we had got past the grim, stinking lake, a wriggle through the wall brought us to the working chamber and the tunnel entrance. We dug with scoops made out of old tins with wooden handles cut off brooms. Virtually every prisoner in the camp was persuaded to relinquish at least one bed board, though a small minority whined about this further assault on their comfort. By now there were thirty of us working on the project, and we were expected to lead the way in all such sacrifices. As the tunnel progressed, every single bed board from my own bed was cannibalized as a tunnel prop, and I ended up sleeping on a criss-cross web of string.

We worked on the tunnel in three shifts of eight each. I mostly dug, along with Eddy Asselin and some of our other close associates. The next shift dispersed the earth, mostly into the latrine pit, and the third concentrated on shoring up and securing the tunnel after each digging session. Day after day we progressed, sometimes only a few inches a day, depending on the saturation of the ground and the number of interruptions as the goons patrolled or inspected. We celebrated after 10 feet, then after 25, inching our way towards freedom like the mites in the German cheese.

Emerging blinking into the early evening sunshine one day from a long shift underground and trying not to look as grubby as I felt, I saw an animated debate going on between an old Polish worker and one of our comrades, who was Czech. It turned out that the old Pole was the driver of the tanker vehicle that had the unenviable job of pumping out the latrine and departing with the contents every few weeks. His tanker had the optimistic nickname of the honeywagon, and he was complaining bitterly that his honeywagon was half full of gravel every time he emptied it. Luckily he turned out to be a Polish patriot, and instead of giving us up to the guards, he agreed to help in another escape.

The Czech pilot, whose real name was Brycks but who had changed his name to Joe Ricks to avoid retaliation against his family, persuaded the driver to allow him to get inside the honeywagon and drive to freedom. Wings Day and the rest of us on the escape committee considered it a good plan, since the Germans were no more keen on poking around in a tanker full of sewage than they were sticking their heads down latrines, but we worried about the old man, who would certainly be shot if the plan went wrong. We decided to approve the escape, but to allow it to take place only at the same time as our mass breakout from the tunnel, which would be how the commandant would assume Ricks got out.

Joe Ricks, a short and immensely tough Czech with the broad face of a prize fighter, was quite a character. As well as being invaluable because he spoke both Polish and German as well as heavily accented English, he was something of a Romeo and was carrying on a long-distance romance with a farmer's daughter who passed by each day on the road outside the camp. Somehow he persuaded a Polish worker who came into the camp to carry his messages of affection and she sent hers by return. Ricks had more reason than most of us to want out of the camp, but perhaps less reason to get as far away as possible.

As the entire camp turned into a hive of activity above and below ground, the ferrets started to get suspicious and threatened to lock us up earlier in the evenings to stop us lurking around in the early evening darkness of a Polish winter. Loud protests about the effects on our already failing health were heeded, partly because the camp authorities knew that if we came down with something like typhus, the germs would demo-cratically decide to infest their men too. But our freedom was curtailed in another way. Simms, the unpleasant security officer, ordered in an extra company of guards and from then on our two *Appells* a day rose to three, four and even five. For these, whatever we were doing, we had to stop, cover our tracks and show ourselves in a matter of minutes.

Underground, when not disrupted by a cry from above of 'Goons in the block', we were making steady progress, now at the rate of two or three feet a day. We had turned an old army kitbag into a bellows, pumped by a man in the entrance cave pushing a wooden handle in and out for all he was worth. The pump was joined to an air pipeline made of dried Klim milk tins from our Canadian Red Cross packages. Luckily, the tins were slightly smaller at the lid end, so if you cut out the bottom they fitted into each other like ready-made tubing. Despite these efforts the tunnel, as it grew longer and longer, passing 60 feet, became a suffocating place. Each trip down it required a little more courage, and the need to blot out the thought of all those tons of earth pressing down on you, knowing that a cave-in would leave us trapped, breathing mouth-fuls of mud and unable to go forwards or backwards.

The presence of light became important, not just to work by, but to steady our nerves and to remind us that there was a world above with sky and fresh air, waiting for us to return. We experimented with different forms of light and settled on a sort of lamp fuelled by margarine with a wick made from a boot lace. The margarine had been slowly simmered for hours to get rid of the water content, but as we clawed away at the dirt, the air would become worse and worse until eventually even the margarine lamp would go out. After that, we worked on in stifling darkness, trying not to think about the amount of unstable earth directly above our heads.

It is hard to convey the real sense of claustrophobia that comes from an hour of stabbing away at a wall of Polish mud in a tunnel so narrow that you can get only one arm forward to work at the face and which stretches back behind you so far that it takes half an hour to wriggle back to safety and sanity at the tunnel start. The experience assaults every sense. We felt the cold clay around us, pressing in on us and seeping into our bones until we almost became part of the tunnel. The loss of sight in the darkness when the lights went out was total. No glimmer of light had penetrated that wall of mud in a million years. Even when the margarine lamp flickered, it only served to emphasize the blackness around it – what Milton once called 'darkness visible'.

Our sense of smell was overpowered not only by the stench from the yellow and brown clay through which we wriggled but also by the nauseous waves of filth which sometimes flooded in from the latrines. We even had to taste the tunnel when a shower of earth fell from an unshored roof: it filled the mouth of any unfortunate digger, gaping wide for oxygen in the stale void of the tunnel. The only sound was the slapping and snapping of home-made knives and scoops, digging into the mud, or the wheezing noise made as some heroic character far behind pushed for all he was worth to keep the bellows operating and the air circulating feebly in our Klim milk tin pipeline. Sometimes when you stopped for a rest the silence was so deafening that it made you want to shout just to hear a sound, but the knowledge that a few feet above us the guards' hidden microphones were reaching into the ground like inquisitive, greedy fingers made us stifle any sound and return to our digging.

We moved the dirt back in a big bag tied to a long piece of string. After hacking away at the tunnel face, I would scoop the dirt into the bag and give a sharp double tug on the string. From somewhere far back in the opening cavern I would get the answer of a double tug on the other end of the string and the heavy bag would start to be hauled back along the tunnel. At the other end another team would dump the cans of dirt into the main latrine and prod the unpleasant contents around with a pole to avoid any tell-tale blockages.

As our work progressed the strain on our string grew greater. One day there was an ominous snap and a loud curse from far back in the tunnel. Unable to turn around, I had to wriggle back yard after yard to find the bag and then to grope around for both ends of the broken string to make a running repair before crawling back to the tunnel face. When the string snapping became a regular event, we realized that we needed men positioned in the middle of the tunnel, hauling back to that point, and another at the end.

As the tunnel grew there was a gradual, almost imperceptible change in our attitudes. The grumbling and cursing about the grim conditions continued, but now they were tinged with excitement and an unspoken feeling that maybe this time we would not be discovered. Once we passed the 100 feet mark, instead of measuring how long the tunnel was so far, we started to talk about how far we had to go.

Apart from lack of air, the terror of collapse and the fear of discovery, a surplus of sewage was sometimes a more immediate problem. While the proximity to the latrine helped us to get rid of the tunnel dirt, when the latrines flooded with winter rains or a blockage, a vile liquid would pour in on us as we dug. One of the toughest jobs was making sure that all the diggers were remotely clean after hours of working naked in the dirt. Those same smells made our tunnellers less than popular with their room-mates in the big, open barracks, and there were rumours of celebrations planned for after we had escaped.

The tunnel was only 2 feet square, and cave-ins were a constant fear, despite the sacrifice of so many bed boards from so many prisoners. Working in the suffocating, stinking world of a claustrophobic 2 feet of tunnel, hacking my way through yet another 6 inches of what seemed like an eternity of muck with a bent tin, I had plenty of time to ponder. I wondered sometimes why I did not just settle down to life as a kriegie. Then I could have been clean, lying back on a lumpy straw mattress staring at the place where the ceiling should have been in our hut, with nothing to worry about but the fleas. Better still, the mattress, rather than the tunnel, would still be supported by bed boards. But then I would remember all the bravery of the Londoners, and of the French men and women who risked their lives to save mine. I would remember the beatings I got at the hands of the Gestapo and from thuggish guards. Most of all I would remember that without resistance, this life was all the world could look forward to and that the fate that was already befalling the Jews, socialists, Gypsies and trade unionists would sooner or later be waiting for all of us. And so I dug.

At about that time we had another casualty, but whether depression or accident was the cause we would never know. A young officer called Lovegrove was involved in the attempts to map our surroundings for the tunnelling teams. He had just had some bad news from home when he climbed up to the very top of the biggest building in the camp, the White House, which housed our command staff. There was a sickening thump as he plummeted to his death some 40 feet below. I like to think he simply slipped, but there were few of us who did not at least think about suicide at some point in our captivity. The life of a prisoner of war is full of strange ironies, and when Wings Day was permitted to attend Lovegrove's funeral with military honours in the nearby village, he was able to see and memorize the very details that Lovegrove had been trying to map when he died.

Week after week we burrowed in the muck and the

mire, expecting every day that the ferrets would find the Asselin tunnel and for all our work to come to nothing, but still we dug. One of the hardest parts of digging the tunnel was that we were on virtually starvation rations, so any physical exertion was twice as tough as it should have been. Eventually by the start of March 1943 it was almost ready, more than 150 feet long. All but the last few feet had been clawed out by tired, impatient hands over three months. Eddie and I would dig the last section out on the night of the escape. If the calculations of our engineering and surveying comrades were right, we should emerge in a small ditch containing a potato patch on the far side of the perimeter fence.

Our plans to wait for the perfect moment were given a sudden jolt. Wings had got news that plans were afoot to send us back to Luft III. As well as intelligence received from our own methods of bribing guards to find out what was happening sometimes even before the commandant knew, there was word from the secret services back in London, often through our intelligence officer Aidan Crawley. He had several prisoners who had agreed to encode messages into their letters home, which were then forwarded by the recipients to the War Office, who would reply using a complex code based on specific page numbers of a German-English dictionary. One of the code writers was the young Dane Thalbitzer, a fellow tunneller who was to team up with Jimmy Buckley on our escape.

The implication of the news that we would be moved

soon was stark. If we did not act right away, all our weeks and months of eating dirt would be wasted as we were carted back to Luft III. It was time to make a decision about who was going and when. The tunnel was completed on 3 March and we decided to make our move on the fifth, using a relatively moonless night for cover.

The decision about who should go was fairly simple. In order to have any hope of avoiding alerting the guards, the escapers would have to be sealed in the tunnel for several hours after curfew but before the breakout. That meant that the maximum number who could go equalled the maximum number that could be shoehorned into a damp, airless hole in the ground and left there for several hours without suffocating. The final number of thirty-three was arrived at, half to be nose to toes along the tunnel, the other half crammed into the cavern at the start of the tunnel. Some of the tunnellers worried that the air would give out and that the end result would be thirty-three prisoners who were killed and conveniently buried themselves, but our semi-scientific calculations suggested that we would be OK.

Most of those chosen were the team who had helped to make the tunnel. To this group were added some senior escape personnel, including Johnny Dodge, the Dodger, who had tried to jump from the train on the way to Schubin, as well as the senior British officer Wings Day himself. Wings figured that since he was going to be thrown in the cooler for presiding over our escape anyway, he might as well at least give them a run for their money.

Our security chief Aidan Crawley was also on the list. In fact, had we but known it, we were in very august company as we squeezed into the tunnel to await our fate. Aidan Crawley would later become a Member of Parliament in Britain. Among the other escapers were Anthony Barber, a future British Chancellor of the Exchequer, and former bomber pilot Robert Kee, who went on to become a world-famous historian. They were squashed alongside the first and greatest leader of escapes during the war, Jimmy Buckley from the Fleet Air Arm. Those of us who had done the tunnelling were given priority. We decided to go in pairs, with Eddy Asselin and me being the first pair, numbers one and two, with the job of completing the last few feet in the hours before breakout. Paddy and his escape buddy Wilfred Wise were just a few people back in the horizontal conga line at numbers seven and eight. With characteristic self-control, Wings Day awarded himself the last place out, alongside his escape partner Squadron Leader Dudley Craig, who was also no slouch in the escaping department, having earlier attempted to stroll out of the camp at Barth dressed as a guard, clutching a rifle made entirely from wood.

In addition to the real escapees, ten other prisoners volunteered to hide in the attic of the main building, the White House, so that if we got away the Germans would think they were looking for even more runaways. If they could remain undetected until the camp was evacuated in a few months, they could then slip away when it was deserted. In the meantime they would be kept supplied by the small number of their colleagues who would know they were hidden inside the camp.

Earlier on the last day before our night-time escape, the bouncing Czech Joe Ricks and his escape companion Squadron Leader Morris, clad head to toe in hooded overalls, waited in a quiet corner behind a building, out of the lines of sight of the guard posts. The brave old Pole had parked his honeywagon there as promised and the two men squeezed through a specially adjusted top hatch. Mercifully, the driver had done a good job of washing out the interior, and a large bucket of sewage hung under the inside of the hatch, just in case some zealous ferret decided to peek inside. As always, they were not so inclined, and the honeywagon drove out of the camp, bringing the lucky Joe straight to an assignation with the local farmer's daughter, I hope by way of a bath tub. Normally, our escape kit was kept as small and light as possible, but Joe had special dispensation for an extra piece of vital equipment – a huge bottle of eau de Cologne that was an expensive trophy from our bartering system from some unfortunate guard.

After the last *Appell* at about five o'clock we sauntered a few at a time to the latrines, since we thought that even the doziest guard might raise an eyebrow if confronted by a delegation of thirty-three men all heading for the latrines at once. For added cover one of our frequent POW rugby matches was taking place on the exercise ground above, England versus Australia. As we ambled in, no-one noticed that more people seemed to go into the latrines than came out. Wings Day allowed himself one of his wry smiles as a junior escape officer chose his words badly when he came to him to say, 'It's time for you to be put down, sir.'

As Eddy and I went in through the latrine first, we prayed it would be for the last time. We were followed one by one by the other thirty or so. Being wedged at the front of 150 feet of dark, cramped tunnel was bad enough, but with the men lying head to toe all the way back behind us, even a slight tunnel collapse would mean the end: it would take hours for each man to wriggle backwards, allowing the one ahead to do the same. At least Eddy and I had the last bit of tunnelling to occupy us, spreading the dirt back on the tunnel floor. Soon, with thirty-odd men in dyed greatcoats clutching bags and laid end to end in a tunnel, the air became stifling. Naturally, until we broke the tunnel, it would be worst at the tunnel face end. The air pump was working overtime with exhausted men taking it in turns to push the kit-bag bellows in and out like galley slaves at the oars, but the air it pulled in was from the latrine pit next door, so it almost made matters worse. Then came the next torture – there was a leak from the cesspool next door and we were soaked by the vile concoction. If ever I wanted to escape, that was the moment.

While Eddy and I dug like demons, the rest could do nothing but lie there suffocating, wondering what was happening. Hissed messages were passed forward from one man to the next in a giant, smelly version of Chinese Whispers. A message that started off as 'Hurry up, we need more air' after passing through fifteen whispered versions would come out as something like 'What's happened to the bear?' and an equally confused question would make its way back until someone, worried about the level of whispered hubbub, hissed, 'Shut up!' His message was duly muttered noisily all the way up the line.

But if our entry into the outside world was going to be less than glorious, at least we were prepared for the possibilities. Never before had an escape attempt for so many provided the escapees with such good equipment. The entire camp had worked non-stop. We had civilian clothes, forged documents, accurate maps, compasses, escape food and more. The escape would also be something of an experiment, with every possible mode of travel and strategy being applied. If we managed to get all thirty-three out, we would be able to see which techniques worked best outside the wire. Not all of us wanted to travel in comfort on trains, exchanging pleasantries with some Gestapo officer checking tickets, and those of us who intended instead to tramp across country while avoiding contact with the enemy were collectively known as the 'hard arses'.

At last, with a triumphant shove of his home-made trowel, Eddy was through to the surface. He passed me a lump of earth to dispose of on the tunnel floor and I felt a clump of grass on it. The scent of living plants joined the wonderful rush of fresh cold air which will forever be linked in my mind to the smell of freedom. Men further back along the tunnel gasped and gulped in great lungfuls of it. We had reached the outside world.

Eddy carefully cut the roots of plants out of the way, handing down the debris to me, which I trampled into the tunnel floor. Then came the moment of truth. Eddy cautiously poked his head up and we both blessed the mathematical geniuses who had helped survey the tunnel route. It came out exactly where it was supposed to in the potato ditch, just outside the wire. Eddy froze as a guard on his rounds inside the perimeter strolled past. He didn't see a thing. The reality was that all the lights pointed inwards to illuminate the camp and, as we had hoped, his entire attention was focused on the inside of the wire, looking out for prisoners scurrying from the huts or making for the perimeter fence. The only things likely to be outside were stray cats. Eddy made his move, squeezing out and spraying tunnel dirt down the vertical exit shaft as his feet scrabbled on the walls.

Then it was my turn. The guard was on his way back, so I waited, feeling that my head sticking out of the tunnel must look as big and luminous as a pumpkin. When he had passed by on the far side of the wire I squeezed out of the tunnel mouth and commando-crawled from one potato ditch to another, inching my way along under the cover of the ditches until I was nearer the woods. The silence held and I waited for the right moment to make a last terrifying dash into the trees.

I scurried forward, half-crouching, half-running. My every footstep sounded like someone dropping an entire set of crockery, and every twig snap sounded like a rifle being cocked to finish me off, but seconds later I made it to a stand of trees where Eddy was waiting, panting from the exertion.

Seconds later we were up and off, the first two out of a successful tunnel at Schubin, with the camp eerily illuminated behind us. It was March 1943, coming up to a year since I was shot down. I figured that if I hurried I would be back in London in time to celebrate the anniversary.

As the remaining thirty-one started to emerge, Eddy and I took off, heading in the general direction of the Baltic Sea. Not far behind us Lieutenant-Commander Jimmy Buckley, astutely teamed with a young Danish pilot who spoke fluent German, was aiming to make for Denmark, then Sweden. I knew the young Dane with a broad, likeable face as John Thompson, but his real name was Jørgen Thalbitzer. He had risked his life at the start of the war to escape to Britain and become a pilot with the RAF, changing his name to avoid retaliation against his parents in occupied Denmark. Danny Kroll and Otto Cernay, a Pole and Czech, were going to 'hide in plain sight' as labourers heading back to Warsaw. Danny was a short, incredibly hardy Pole, a former fencing champion who caused some consternation among guards and prisoners alike by regularly washing naked in the snow outside the huts. After the fall of Poland he had made his way to France to fight on under Polish General Sikorsky, and after the fall of France he had made it to Britain to continue the fight from there. Even after his own fall, like mine from a Spitfire over France, he continued his war on both sides of the wire. He was one tough customer and one of many who were involved both in this venture and the later Great Escape from Luft III.

As befitted an intelligence officer, Aidan Crawley was planning to stroll onto a train, waving a letter introducing him as a travelling engineer working in a Krupps factory. The letter was on beautifully headed paper, forged by our fellow kriegie Eric Shaw. Nearby, but pretending not to know him, would be German-born Flying Officer Stevens. He was a brave man. His advantage was that he spoke native German. His disadvantage was he was Jewish as well as a German fighting for the British. If he was captured and either of these interesting facts came out, he knew he would be both tortured and executed. Others who let the train take the strain included future historian Robert Kee and a colleague.

Then there was my pal Paddy Barthropp and Wilf Wise, 'hard arses' on foot like myself, as were Wings and Craig, though it took over an hour before it was their turn to make the dash for the cover of the woods. As person after person scurried out of the tunnel, one unforeseen problem was that each man kicked some dirt back down the tunnel as he scrambled out. By the time Wings had done his final job of extinguishing the margarine lamps and wriggled his way forward, the end of the tunnel had narrowed alarmingly and he was barely able to squeeze out, covered in mud. It was midnight, and all thirty-three were out.

As Eddy and I scurried away through the woods, we listened for the tell-tale firing of shots and the mournful wail of the alarm siren, but the night was as quiet as it was dark and cold. By the next morning we were far away, but with one small part of us wishing we could be a fly on the wall for the next *Appell*, just to see the expression on the face of pompous little Captain Simms.

The feeling you get from being free, after so many months when the barbed wire at the edge of the camp represents the limits of your horizons, is like no other freedom. It is sharpened by the fact that you are in enemy territory, hundreds of miles from home with nothing but a few handfuls of the Mixture in your pocket and half the guard dogs in Germany hot on your heels. Never, before or since, have I felt more alive.

Eddy and I managed to evade capture for about a week, hiding in hedges and sometimes sleeping in barns. We wolfed down our escape supplies, drank from streams and occasionally liberated some vegetables. On the first night we hid in some woods and sat perfectly still as what seemed like half Germany passed within a few feet of us, shouting and beating bushes, waving flashlights. They came within inches of finding us. When they had passed by we quietly moved on. The nights were cold and that night we sought shelter in a particularly large barn, hoping that the inhabitants would not find us, or that if they did, they would be patriotic Poles.

One of the most frightening moments came when we were forced to cross a bridge at night. We knew that the Germans had thrown a cordon around the camp and that every road and bridge had sentries posted on the lookout for us. Normally we would have skirted around to find some quieter spot to cross, but the river was deep and there was little cover, so we decided to risk the bridge. There was one sentry at each end, luckily huddled in a sentry box to keep out the cold and only occasionally marching up and down the bridge to keep a lookout. We crawled along the side of the bridge in the shadows. To our frightened ears every tiny noise we made as we scrabbled across sounded like an explosion. At one point a guard stood peering over the opposite side of the bridge, no more than 10 feet away from us as we kept perfectly still. When he went back to his sentry box we continued our crawl and breathed a long, quiet sigh of relief when we reached the shelter of the woods on the far side.

We woke one morning, about six days after our escape, to find ourselves held at bay near a railway crossing by a group of ethnic German farm workers brandishing pitch-forks. A farmer's wife returned with some soldiers and shouted at them to shoot us there and then. When they refused she tried to wrestle the gun from one of them so that she could do it herself. They restrained her and searched me. One, who spoke some English, found a letter from my mother in Texas. He translated it for the amusement of the others. It told how she was baking apple pies to send to the local prisoner-of-war camp for the German boys, because she felt sure that the German moms would be doing the same for me.

While our escape was a great success in terms of getting the German army out looking for us, the down side for anyone hoping to get home was that we had become such a sensation because of our large numbers that every Hitler Youth, German farmer and spare soldier for a hundred miles was spending every waking hour looking for us. Reports of how many troops were tied up in the search for that first week vary greatly, from the modest to the near impossible, but the most common one is that we were being hunted by 300,000 regular troops, police, militia, civilians and Hitler Youth. It is a very satisfying thought to have tied up so many enemy troops, even for a week, though for that one week I would have been much happier if they were looking for someone else.

What with the chaos of thirty-three prisoners running around and being recaptured, returning us to the camp was not a top priority. We were thrown in the civilian jail in a little town called Hohensalza. I was added to what was already one of the most bizarre groups of prisoners gathered in any jail in history. Polish pimps, mobsters and petty thieves rubbed shoulders with those who had resisted the invaders and Jewish people trying to stay out of the death camps. Alongside them were German deserters and Axis soldiers whose papers had been lost, and now two stray escapologists.

Eddy had been pretty shaken up by what we had been through and our rough treatment. I at least had the advantage of being a serial escaper who regarded such problems as an occupational hazard, but Eddy, the man who guided and masterminded every aspect of the tunnel, was deeply disappointed that all those months of pain and planning and dirt had led to a dusty jail full of deserters only a day's truck ride from where we had started. Eddy was a practical man, and he confided in me as he lay on his jail bunk that he wanted to get home, if not now, then eventually, and he felt that if he continued to join the small band of obsessive escapers he would be unlikely to see the end of the war. Modestly, he described his mother in Canada running the prisoner-of-war association as 'the only hero in the family'. He suggested that he might try his hand at some of the non-escaping activities to fill in his time in a less life-threatening way, if ever we were lucky enough to be returned to the camp rather than shot or interrogated by the Gestapo. He was interested in many things, politics and poker being his favourites.

I did not press him. Each man had to decide for himself what was right in terms of the balance between suffering and defiance, between risk and foolhardiness. For me the issue was simple. I had joined the war to resist and I would keep resisting with every breath until I escaped or until the enemy helped me to get away from it all on a more permanent basis, 6 feet underground, and not in a tunnel. My escaping gene was just as much a part of me as my instinct to keep breathing.

Eddy was a survivor, a philosopher, a helper of others but also someone with a finely developed sense of when to push and when to step back in the cause of self-preservation. Maybe that's why he made such a great poker player. Having decided on his strategy for the rest of the war, he yawned, stretched and joined in a game of cards with the motley group of pimps, deserters and refugees with whom we shared our cell. Very soon, as always, Eddy Asselin was winning.

Once he got back to Schubin camp, Eddy did as he had said, both there and later in Stalag Luft III, where he ran a vast and never-ending poker game, racking up huge amounts of money in back pay from those less sharp of mind. He also participated in the frequent political debates about the future of the world after the war and when he went back to Canada he became hugely successful as a leading light in local politics in Quebec, then for a time as a Member of Parliament in Canada and finally as a lawyer and a judge.

I particularly remember one character in the cell, Stefan, whom I fleetingly got to know and like. He was a German soldier and something approaching a deserter king. I think Stefan had had too much of the sun in North Africa and decided not to bother with the rest of the war. He was amiable and ruled over a kingdom of demoralized and cynical prison lags as if the jail was the only sanctuary of sanity in a world gone mad. He enjoyed music and I taught him a few of my cowboy songs, such as 'Blood on the Saddle'.

Towards nightfall, the warders would go off duty, leaving the prisoners to their own devices. One of the most surprising sights of the entire war for me was when I saw Stefan casually get up, stretch, take out a hidden key and let himself out, locking the cell door behind him. I tried to coax him into letting me out too, but he pointed out that the guards would not have to look too far for the guilty party. He said that as long as he was back in his cell by morning, and kept the guards well stocked with contraband and cigarettes, he could come and go as he pleased.

Having spent more than a year risking my life to get out of prisons, the thought of escaping nightly only to lock myself in again each dawn was a tough one to get my battered head around. I asked him why he did not leave for good. Stefan just smiled through the bars at me and shrugged as he headed off for a night on the town, calling back 'Where to?' Before I could think of a reasonable answer, he was gone.

Next morning, while Stefan was back in his bunk, sleeping off a busy night, the soldiers came to take me and Eddy back to the Schubin camp, and a long spell in the cooler, which was doing a roaring trade.

By the time we were returned to our rightful box, virtually all the thirty-three escapees had been recaptured. Actually there were thirty-four, since an enterprising South African squadron leader called Don Gericke had seen the morning after our escape that the tunnel was miraculously still undiscovered, grabbed his escape kit and popped out the other end of the tunnel in broad daylight, strolling along trying his best to look like a Polish workman. He did not get very far, but gained high points from us for initiative, and even Eddy Asselin admired the fact that he was smart enough to get someone else to do all the digging.

The rest of my fellow escapists had some equally hairraising travels to report, but they did so always in the great low-key way that was one of the hallmarks of much of the courage I witnessed in the war years, when coming inches from death was usually described as 'a spot of bother'.

Paddy and Wilfred had made for the railway line, where they planned to jump the train, but the only thing on the track was one of those strange hand-pumped contraptions that resembles a see-saw on wheels which featured regularly in comedy chase scenes in old Buster Keaton movies. It was manned by four railwaymen heading west and the escapees decided not to risk hitching a lift, so they slept in a cold, damp quarry.

After wandering about the next day but not getting too far, they crept into a farmer's barn for the night and slumped exhausted in the hay. They woke with a start as the entire floor of the barn was apparently moving. It was a shoal of huge rats, attracted by the rare allure of the Mixture, and they did not seem to care much which brand of escape food was on offer. The men thrashed out and chased off the apparently fearless creatures and were preparing to flee when an elderly couple came out of the farmhouse and presented them with hot tea and bread. The old folk were clearly terrified of German troops finding the escapees, since they knew that while Allied pilots would probably just be put back in prison, they or any locals who helped would be shot on the spot. Paddy and his companion moved on, heading in the general direction of Warsaw.

They had made Warsaw their objective because they had a contact with the Polish Resistance, who were hoping to get three crews out of the country. The other two crews were Poles and Czechs, who had already made the rendezvous; Paddy and Wilfred would be the last. As it turned out, they were lucky they did not make the rendezvous, since all four of the other pilots disappeared without trace, probably found and shot by the Gestapo as part of their no-quarter war on the Polish Resistance.

Increasingly tired and bedraggled, the two moved through a forest plantation and spent a third cold night in an old and long-deserted graveyard with wolves howling in the forest around them. By this time Paddy was suffering from a bad case of trench foot and was having difficulty walking as it ate away at his left heel. The next morning they were delighted to discover the railway line again and this time they had more luck, jumping a slow freight train, where they shared a box with two nervous and untethered horses.

Ironically, the train rolled into Hohensalza, where I was to be jailed myself just a few days later. The men hid while the train carriages were shunted around and found to their dismay that they were left in a single carriage in the middle of the station. They knew that they would be discovered if they stayed, but the station was alive with people, including German guards, soldiers and pro-German civilians. They made a dash for it, but were soon cornered by armed guards. They were paraded as the town's prize catch by Polish collaborators and Hitler Youth, then interrogated by the local Gestapo. After that, much to their relief, they were returned to Schubin.

As they were driven towards the camp, the car was slowed to a crawl by an old man walking down the middle of the road at a snail's pace. The car horn honked and the soldier driving the car cursed at him, but he was apparently deaf or senile – for whatever reason he just ignored the driver and kept on walking. The soldier jumped out and started to beat the old man, who crumpled to the ground. The guard dragged him to the side of the road and continued to kick him viciously until he stopped moving. Paddy has never stopped wondering if the old man survived the attack. To both of us, the event always summed up the Nazi brutality and arrogance we were fighting against.

Two others of the foot-slogging 'hard-arse' variety, Wings Day and his partner Dudley Craig, after they became the last of our group to struggle out of the ever-narrowing tunnel, made south in the direction of the town of Gneisen. They were perhaps less well equipped than our urbane friends on the trains: all they had were a couple of cigarette cartons with phrases scribbled in

Polish declaring them escaped British officers and asking for help.

Wings was already suffering from a bad case of jaundice and he said afterwards that the whole escape seemed like a sort of semi-surreal dream in which he faded in and out of focus. He felt little of the usual mix of excitement and fear that were part and parcel of an escape, only the need to keep stumbling on in the hope of freedom. On their first day out they thought they would be captured when a group of Polish farm workers found them hiding in a haystack, but the Poles, instead of handing them over to the authorities, risked their lives by sharing their lunch sandwiches with the escapers. Wings thought that the chunky bread and sausage he shared with those Poles was one of the best meals of his life. That night they were again discovered by Poles on another farm and awarded four fried eggs each. They might not have been getting very far, but at least they were being better fed than in many months.

They walked most of the night, through swamps and over barbed-wire fences, and reached Zinn railway station, where they intended to hop a freight train south, but even at night the freight yard was floodlit and a hive of activity. They stumbled on in the dark.

Just as they were going to go to ground for the day, they ran headlong into a young blond boy and had no choice but to show him their cigarette-carton phrasebook, which by now was getting well thumbed but seemed to have done the trick with a variety of brave

Poles so far. The boy beamed when he found out who they were and gestured urgently for them to follow him. He installed them in a safe, warm barn and departed as they collapsed exhausted in the hay. Wings' jaundice was getting worse and he shivered and sweated uncontrollably as they waited for the boy to return, hoping he would bring food and help. Gradually they fell into fitful sleep. They were awoken by the jab of fixed bayonets, surrounded by German troops and captured. The angelic child who had helped them turned out to be a fervent Hitler Youth, living in an all-German enclave. At first they received rough treatment, but when it transpired they were British and not as the German troops thought escaped Russians, they were treated a little better.

The highlight of Wings' escape was something he learned as he was being driven back to the camp. The police chief in the town of Posen had ordered road blocks thrown up all over his jurisdiction to catch the escapees, but being in a hurry he had driven through one of these, assuming his own men would recognize him. They didn't and he was shot dead at his own road block.

When they had arrived back and been thrown in the cooler it was already so crowded that Wings had to share a single cot in 'solitary' with Aidan Crawley, a big man who snored like a buffalo.

Of the other escapers, those who spoke German and travelled by train got farthest. My friend and our escape security supremo Aidan Crawley got all the way to

Innsbruck in Austria, a distance of some five hundred miles. He had the supreme satisfaction of resting back in a comfortable train seat as he stared out the window at rows of hundreds of troops fanned out across fields looking for us. Robert Kee and a colleague did well to get to Bromberg railway station, where they bought tickets for Berlin and beyond, though Robert had fallen in a water-filled ditch along the way and did not look altogether presentable. They had forged documents declaring them to be foreign workers and managed to pass several checks until they had a narrow escape. They made the mistake of having a whispered conversation in a railway station toilet, not realizing that one of the cubicles was occupied. The eavesdropper came out, washed his hands casually, then reported them to a Gestapo man on the platform, but their cover story and forged paperwork held up and they were allowed to go on. Finally, they were caught at Cologne, where they were spotted by the smallest of details: they were wearing leather air force issue boot laces rather than the normal German cloth ones.

Others travelling by train reached the Ruhr and one got as far as Hanover. The quality of the forged documents from Schubin was such that two of the train escapees got through five identity checks along the way, including some by the beady-eyed Gestapo, while Aidan managed to get through seven checks on the long ride to Innsbruck, using sleepy local trains where possible.

The man who stayed out longest from our escape was probably the honeywagon Romeo Joe Ricks. Once he had climbed out of the sewage truck and liberally doused himself with his escape kit eau de Cologne, he decided to stay in the vicinity of the camp for a few days, enjoying a romantic interlude with the farmer's daughter whom he had fallen for through the camp barbed-wire fence. After that, he hooked up at the farmhouse with Otto Cernay as planned and he set off with a spring in his step that allowed him to walk all the way to Warsaw in a few weeks. The pair managed to stay free there for more than three months and joined the Polish Resistance, but they were eventually recaptured when enemy forces surrounded their safe house after a tip-off and they fell into the hands of the Warsaw Gestapo, with whom they had a predictably rough time. They were saved only by the intervention of the commandant at Luft III, who sent a letter saying they were escapees and they were shipped back to our alma mater at Sagan, Stalag Luft III.

In another way there were two men who did stay out longer; in fact they stayed out for ever. Lieutenant Commander Jimmy Buckley of the Fleet Air Arm was the first and perhaps the greatest of all escape leaders in the RAF camps. He had first been shot down during the defence of Norway, but managed to get back to British lines before the evacuation, and then flew in Coastal Defence operations until shot down over France and captured in summer 1940. He had the unenviable job of setting up an escape committee at a point in the war when defeat looked more likely than victory.

The first time I had faced Jimmy as a new arrival at

Luft III, eagerly pouring out my slightly half-baked escape plans, he had seemed like a man chipped out of granite. He was small and dark, about forty, a tough navy flyer to his bootstraps. But when he was not weighing up the life-and-death matter of which escapes to support or forbid, his eyes always had a spark of humour and in any waking moments not occupied by escape plans, he would write brilliant comedy sketches for the prisoners' theatre groups to perform.

Jimmy had been the first 'Big X' or chairman of the escape committee at Dulag Luft, then at Luft I, Luft III and finally Schubin. Along with Wings Day, Jimmy Buckley had dug the very first RAF tunnel while still at Dulag Luft transit camp, a year before I had dropped in to the same mustering point. Seventeen of them had escaped but were all recaptured.

Jimmy's sense of humour sometimes even crept into the serious business of escaping. When the committee was discussing the plans of my friend Roger Bushell, later the leader of the Great Escape, to slip away by hiding in a sort of kennel which was home to a goat mascot just outside Dulag Luft, someone enquired 'But what about the smell?' to which Jimmy replied, 'Oh, I'm sure the goat won't mind.'

Jimmy and his Danish partner Jørgen Thalbitzer, aka John Thompson, made their way north from Schubin on foot, hoping to reach the port of Stettin. The pair were great friends, though utterly different. Jimmy was an older, tougher senior officer with a wry sense of humour, while Thalbitzer was a brawny, amiable youth of around twenty-one, with a great appetite for both adventure and laughter. While Jimmy had been blown out of the sky along with five of the planes under his command, risking their lives to defend the evacuation at Dunkirk, Thalbitzer had an even more spectacular tale to tell.

In April 1940, when he was only nineteen, he had watched silently as the Third Reich marched into his native Denmark and decided that flying for the RAF would be the best thing he could do to get the invaders out. He had recently gained a sports pilot licence from a Danish flying club. Since the journey from Denmark to London presented a few problems, he decided to take the scenic route. He landed himself a job as a refrigerator salesman and accepted a posting to far-off Turkey. He made the perilous trip through Axis Europe, arriving in Istanbul in January 1941. There he made contact with British officials, who helped him plan an even more extraordinary route to London, by which he travelled south around the entire coast of Africa by tramp steamers and sailing vessels, somehow eventually reaching England.

At about the time I was shot down in spring 1942, young Thalbitzer was visiting Winston Churchill at Downing Street, where he presented the Prime Minister with a cheque for some £40,000 raised by Danes in Britain, enough to buy three Spitfires, one of which would be flown by the newly appointed Pilot Officer Thalbitzer. When he first told us the story in the camp, I remember thinking that while as an American I certainly was unusual in volunteering for this war, Jørgen had gone one better by volunteering and buying his own aeroplane.

Just three months later, Thalbitzer was forced to cash in his new Spitfire for a lifetime's supply of free barbed wire when he was shot down over France. He crashed into overhead electric cables and barely managed to escape from being fried as his Spitfire lost a wing and fell upside down to the ground below. He evaded capture for about two weeks before being given away by a French farmer, who handed him over to the police when he asked for food. Some weeks later he rolled into Stalag Luft III, where he immediately fitted in with our small group of enthusiastic escape artists and quickly earned himself a ticket to the punishment camp at Schubin.

After the escape he and Buckley marched north, avoiding all contact and making their escape supplies last as long as possible, guided by a compass made out of a bottle cap and a piece of pen. About a week later they were spotted by a group of farmers waving shotguns and they took off, with bullets whistling over their heads. Luckily the farmers missed, but they cornered them in a field. Jørgen explained in fluent German that they were Danish sailors whose steamship had been sunk by a mine in the Baltic and who were heading for Stettin to get another ship back to Copenhagen. Jimmy Buckley added an indignant '*Ja*' or '*Nein*' where it seemed appropriate, which probably accounted for his entire repertoire of German phrases.

The farmers were die-hard German settlers who had

heard on the radio that escaped pilots were travelling in pairs in the area and gave their story little credence. They sent one of their number off on a bicycle, pedalling furiously in the direction of the local police station. He soon returned with a policeman who examined their papers, which included *Ausweis* and Danish passports, all forged by hand in the Schubin camp, and listened to their story. He read a letter, also brilliantly forged in Schubin, from a seaman's mission in Danzig, urging the reader to offer every assistance to the stricken sailors. He took a second look at the official German eagle stamp in their passes, counterstamped with an ornate and very impressive but entirely fictional seal of the Danish Consulate in Warsaw, then saluted and handed them back before rounding on the unfortunate farmers and yelling at them for frightening innocent Danish sailors in their mad pursuit of stray prisoners. The farmers slunk off and the helpful policeman escorted Buckley and Thalbitzer to the local train station, where he made sure they got tickets to Stettin for free and waved them off.

Their luck started to wobble when they reached the port, since there were no Danish vessels and none expected in the near future. They set off walking again and then jumped a freight train to Rostock, where once again there were no Danish vessels. So they moved on again with a combination of their remarkable forged documents, Thalbitzer's fluent German, a plausible story and Jimmy Buckley's quiet nerves of steel, which saw them through numerous checkpoints and past inquisitive locals. Finally, two weeks after their escape, they reached the small port of Flensberg and found two schooners heading for Denmark. They picked one, which proved to be the second to leave, and were cursing their luck when the ship's captain got word that the other earlier ship had hit a mine and exploded *en route*. They stopped cursing their luck.

They made it safely to port in Copenhagen and Thalbitzer, knowing that Jimmy Buckley would be safest out of sight, left him on board and headed for his family home. He found his father Billy buying a ticket on the local railway station platform and tapped him on the shoulder. His father remembered him appearing 'like a sunburned sailor'. Billy hugged his son like a ghost returned from the dead and Jørgen was able to spend a few remarkable days with his family as plans were made to get him and Buckley away to neutral Sweden. Thalbitzer sent friends to fetch Buckley from the boat and he almost made a run for it, mistaking them for Gestapo men, but they persuaded him they were friends and took him to a safe house, where they gave him fresh, clean clothes which he said 'make me feel like a gentleman again'.

With help from the Free Danish forces the pair were taken up the coastline and given a two-man canoe made from wood and canvas for the short crossing to Sweden. They pushed off from the shore at 10.00 p.m. on 28 March 1943. It had been raining all day, but that night was still and perfectly calm as they disappeared into the darkness with the armed Resistance fighters waving them off. They were never seen alive again.

Some months later, Billy Thalbitzer got a call from his Free Danish contacts to say that a body had been washed ashore. He was able to identify a signet ring on the left hand as one he had given his son some years earlier. Jimmy Buckley's body was never found. It is possible their canoe was hit by a larger vessel in the dark. Thalbitzer still had on his heavy overcoat and gloves, suggesting that he never had time to swim for it.

Somehow, even in occupied Denmark, the RAF managed to get a wreath of flowers to Thalbitzer's funeral, marking the passing of a brave young man with a sense of fun and an even greater sense of freedom, but Jimmy Buckley had to make do with a different memorial, in the minds of those who survived. Thanks to his blend of caution, courage and humour, I and every other person who ever escaped from the camps in which he was our first leader or Big X owe him a great deal, probably our lives.

Some of these stories trickled back to me in the cooler as other escapers were recaptured, while other stories only reached us long after the event. I stared at the concrete walls and bars and wondered if it was all worth it. Eventually all good things must come to an end, and one day the cell door of the cooler was flung open and I emerged squinting and covering my eyes from the bright sunlight. The Blond Beast looked surlier than ever when I was released and I soon found out why. We were all soon to be transferred back to Stalag Luft III.

For me, this meant reunion with many former friends,

even if it was in a camp where escape was much harder. For the Blond Beast, in disgrace since our mass breakout, it meant an inevitable transfer to the Russian front, where things were not going all that well for the Germans.

The one advantage to being back in the compound was that when I emerged from the cooler I was able to relish the exact details of what had happened inside the camp after the escape. A group of friends – including Ollie Philpot, who later made one of the greatest escapes of the entire war as one of the Wooden Horse team at Stalag Luft III – welcomed me back to the 'real' world. They told me how after our escape they had lain awake waiting for the tell-tale siren or the noises of shouting guards and growling guard dogs and they had heard the most amazing sound – total silence. They could hardly believe it when the 8.00 a.m. *Appell* parade was called and the alarm had still not been raised.

The newer, more excitable prisoners hastily threw on their clothes to hurry out for a good place at the show, but the camp veterans knew better. They methodically put on layers of clothing and shoved what food they could into their pockets. The *Appell* after any escape, never mind one where more than forty prisoners were missing either as escapees or 'ghosts', was liable to last all day, with endless hours being spent as the guards tried to work out how many prisoners they had and how many had been mysteriously subtracted.

As luck would have it, the camp security officer, the

obnoxious Simms, was taking the parade, along with one of the most hated and bullying young guards, an Aryan giant known as the Butcher Boy. Simms strutted towards the line of senior officers, in which the senior British Officer Wings Day and his deputy Major Dodge were conspicuous by their absence. At first Simms thought it was another of those strange British jokes, but gradually it dawned on him that they had escaped. He barked orders to the Butcher Boy, who scurried off, much to the mirth of the assembled prisoners. About eight hours too late, the sirens sounded, telephones rang and sleepy guards were turned out of their beds.

Meanwhile Simms counted the men. He furrowed his brow and counted again. Now trembling with rage and confusion, he stamped back to the stand-in British senior officer, Wing Commander Ryder.

'There are too many! How is this?' Simms' voice rose, along with his blood pressure, and Ryder shrugged as if he was just as baffled as Simms. The irritable little Czech fascist who had made our lives a misery with his pomposity and lack of humanity started counting again. This time he saw something different. Instead of the usual five rows deep, on this morning the prisoners were in neat rows of four. On discovering our ruse Simms, now ready to have a heart attack, barged back to the senior British officer.

'You know we count in fives! We *always* count in fives! Why have you put your men in fours?'

Ryder took his time, looked at the men and then,

almost apologetically turned back to Simms. 'Well, there seemed more of them that way.'

The rows of prisoners erupted into the loudest cheering and laughing that had ever been heard in that god-forsaken camp. Their delight helped keep out the cold as they were forced to stand in the open for the rest of the day while every available guard tore the camp and the surrounding grounds apart looking for the missing prisoners or evidence of an escape.

A guard searching the perimeter found the tunnel exit, but the ferrets were so afraid of booby traps or cave-ins that they sent a reluctant Russian prisoner down the tunnel at bayonet point with a rope tied around his waist. Much to the guards' surprise, he emerged quite some time later from inside the latrines. Meanwhile the content of the latrines was hitting the fan for the unfortunate German officers: both the pompous Simms and the camp commandant were taken away to a court martial and a one-way ticket to the Russian front. The commandant might have had time to ponder the irony that when Wings Day had come to him six months earlier to complain about the state of the latrines, he had sent him packing with the reply, 'They are latrines. What do you expect them to smell like? Anthony Eden's hair?' To every prisoner in the camp, they now smelled like victory. Wings might have escaped for only a few days, but he had won his war with the commandant.

Later on that first day after the escape a huge fleet of buses pulled up outside the camp and hundreds of SS troops and Gestapo SD Intelligence men marched into the camp in single file. Here was proof positive that our theory about tying up German troops and resources by our escapes was true.

The Nazis shoved the confused and leaderless guards to one side and kept the prisoners out of the huts while they rummaged and ransacked, but since they were not trained ferrets, they had little idea of what exactly they were looking for. Ollie Philpot told me that the SS troops discovered an illicit barrel of home-brewed beer in one hut. Instead of smashing it, they asked how much it was for a glass. They were charged fifty pfennigs each and a roaring bar trade was soon under way until the barrel was drunk dry. One of the most difficult things to get inside a prison camp was German currency and to be caught with even a single German banknote meant a long spell in the cooler, but now the SS were only too eager to form an orderly line to meekly hand it over. It was lucky that they were only interested in the beer, since a more enquiring search might have revealed that the barrel had a false bottom in which were concealed all the remaining forged documents in the camp. Pressing their advantage, other prisoners opened up a thriving retail outlet for chocolate and cigarettes and more useful cash rolled in.

Some hours later, after finding very little, but laden with chocolate and cigarettes, the SS men marched smartly back to their buses to continue the search in the surrounding countryside.

The Gestapo ran things for a few weeks after the

commandant and Simms disappeared to their court martial. As well as a new commandant, the camp needed a new *Abwehr* or security head to replace Simms, and the jovial Rittmeister Reimer found himself promoted. Despite his amiable and jolly nature, he was all too effective from our point of view, and in the final months of our stay he found several of our remaining tunnel projects.

The replacement commandant, a rather Gothic-looking Austrian, was in place for only a few weeks or a month, but he seemed a more reasonable character, despite having rather theatrical tendencies. No doubt knowing that he was next for the Gestapo high jump if any more tunnels succeeded, he took to strolling around in the evenings after we had been locked up, like an extra from a Dracula movie. He wore a black officer's cape that was buttoned at the neck and then flowed open down to the ground. In his hands he usually carried a mysterious black device, looking for all the world like one of those cartoon drawings of an anarchist clutching a black bowling ball with a fizzing fuse, helpfully marked 'bomb' – and strangely enough that was exactly what it was. He would stalk around the open areas and then choose a nesting place for his device, which must have been some kind of small mine. He would then scratch a hole with his highly polished jackboot, deposit his mysterious object and stroll to a safe distance away, while his minions got as far away as possible. Then he would stand, head forward as if he was praying and cape flapping, peering at the ground like an old crow waiting for a worm. There would be a muffled boom and a small shower of earth would fly in the air.

The commandant would then step forward and inspect the small crater he had made. Perhaps disappointed that he had not created a new and unexpected entrance to a tunnel, he would nevertheless stroll off, apparently satisfied, to repeat the whole process a few days later. While the unexpected bangs were not good for the nerves, most of us agreed that if he was busy engaging in such theatrical but harmless gestures while we got on with the humdrum business of escaping, his interest in fireworks was only to be encouraged.

Our mass escape had made the Wehrmacht look foolish. The army were meant to be showing the Luftwaffe how to deal with us, but their camp was leaking like a sieve. The date for our departure was brought forward and the German High Command was glad to give the Luftwaffe another go at keeping us in our place. Who should arrive to escort us back to Stalag Luft III, grinning like a Cheshire cat at the downfall of his Wehrmacht foes, but our old Luftwaffe jailer, Feldwebel Glemnitz, there to make sure that we went 'home' without any detours.

When he had us marched out of the camp and into the town, he discovered that the army had laid on trucks for our journey. Knowing our propensity for escaping from such vehicles, and assuming quite rightly that many of us were armed with files to saw our way out of the trucks, he had us marched back to the camp, where he argued with the army once more until we were all put into nice escape-proof third-class trains.

'You are officers,' he smiled. 'You will be so much more comfortable this way!'

─✳─ 11 ─✳─

Over the Wire

By spring of 1943, the tide of the war seemed to be turning both in the east and in north Africa. The invincible tone of all Nazi propaganda boomed out over the camp loudspeakers began to have just the faintest trace of doubt lurking somewhere in the background. It was starting to strike the smarter soldiers of the Fatherland that their thousand-year Reich might not be around quite as long as planned. This was to have repercussions for us prisoners of war. Since the early days of the war there had been a power struggle between the Luftwaffe and the Gestapo for the control and the running of the camps. In a way my rescue from the Gestapo in Paris had been a microcosm of this bigger battle. At first the Luftwaffe won most of the skirmishes, but as the tide of war turned, the Gestapo started to make its move.

It might seem strange that two such forces would fight

over the privilege of trying to keep tens of thousands of young men against their will in camps all over Germany and the east, but the High Command recognized our potential value in any negotiated settlement. If things went badly for Germany, we prisoners would turn from a liability into an asset in the form of a large body of hostages who could be shot or freed depending on how negotiations went.

Nearly every Nazi at this period, or at least those who were not so deluded as to be still convinced of victory, thought that the most likely scenario was a truce in the west with their old Anglo brothers, swiftly followed by a joint Holy War against the Red Menace in the east. They, like the so-called appeasers of the 1930s in Britain and America, who were perfectly happy for Hitler to rampage as long as he did it in the east, underestimated the determination of the people of both west and east to finish what the Nazis had started. Those same ordinary people who had joined up in their droves to fight Hitler did not think of the Russians as anything other than an ally. It would take years of the Cold War rhetoric to replace that friendship with mutual fear.

So, some time in May 1943, it was back in the creaking trains for us, and back to the Fatherland. At Stalag Luft III, business was booming, the number of prisoners there having risen from about 2,000 to a peak near the end of the war of 10,000. In my absence the camp authorities had opened a new RAF compound as well as a third compound for downed pilots of the USAAF. It was good to glimpse so many Americans, if only through two layers of barbed wire and the deadly no-man's-land in between that was covered by the machine gunners in the watchtowers.

I was reunited with many of my old friends and started to help with a tunnel which, like most in Luft III, was a triumph of meticulous planning and engineering skill. Above ground, camp life went on but was now more structured. There were amateur drama groups and debating societies as well as all the usual sports groups and an army of gardeners supplementing their diet with home-grown vegetables. Yet even in these gentle pursuits the world of escapology was never far away. The gardens were liberally sprinkled with tunnel dirt to get rid of the mountains of the stuff we had to shift, and later, during the Great Escape, much of the tunnel spoil was tipped into a huge cavity under seat number thirteen of the prisoners' theatre.

By this time, Red Cross parcels were arriving more regularly and a flourishing commodity market had opened up with a few spiv-like prisoners trading in futures of Canadian butter or British corned beef and bribing guards for information about what would be in the next Red Cross shipment so that they could buy up whatever would become scarce while offloading what-ever would be plentiful. It seemed sad to me that some people spent their time cutting deals with guards while fleecing other prisoners rather than trying to escape or just getting on with life as a prisoner, but they were always in the minority. Others thought they were an admirable example of entrepreneurial spirit. Similarly there were a handful of sharks who specialized in long-running poker schools where the more foolish players ended up owing literally years of back pay. Luckily, the majority of prisoners, if not anxious to get themselves shot while escaping, were more interested in helping other escapees than in being reduced to the miserable state of preying on each other. My old escape buddy Eddy Asselin and I never did manage to see eye to eye on that one, yet we stayed friends.

While my first love remained escaping, I was really missing the music that had been such a part of my life since that wonderful first time in Texas when I heard classical music seeping out of a church hall into the night air. Music played an important part as the backdrop to so many of my adventures – listening to the cello solo by the woman I was in love with but never talked to at the National Gallery, while the sirens wailed and the bombs fell; or staring at the ceiling in my room at the airfield as the sound of Bach or Schubert mixed with the noise of Spitfire engines.

Apart from the welcome serenades by Bill Stapleton at lights out that I mentioned earlier, there was not much chance of hearing classical music in Luft III. There were few records and even fewer gramophones, and while we had a few hidden radio receivers, using them was much too dangerous for entertainment, or indeed for anything but brief bursts to grab the news from the BBC in London. In every camp, there was only one place where classical music was sure to be played, and that was on the gramophone or radio in the German officers' quarters. I remember risking a long spell in the cooler, or even being shot, by slipping out of my hut after curfew and crawling and running between the huts until I reached an internal fence that separated us from a hut full of off-duty German officers. One of them listened to classical music radio broadcasts from Berlin, and I crouched by the wire, spellbound as the music drifted across, an unwitting gift from my captors. I was always puzzled by a culture that could produce and appreciate Bach or Beethoven also being responsible for the chaos and atrocities of wartime Europe, but if music was the one thing on which we could call a truce, that was fine by me.

During my years of captivity, I started to realize how much the creation of Hitler's regime was down to the terrible conditions imposed on Germany after the First World War that resulted in economic collapse and mass unemployment. Not for a minute do I condone the people who sought salvation in Hitler or his crude, vicious political theories, but it is too convenient not to see the role that the victorious west played in helping to create the monster in the first place. The western leaders, with exceptions such as Churchill, were not too bothered about Hitler so long as his hostilities seemed to be pointing east towards the 'Bolshevik peril' in Russia or aimed at weaker countries such as Poland or Czechoslovakia, a place that the pre-war British Prime Minister cynically called 'a far away country about which we know little'.

By the time I got back to Stalag Luft III, it also felt like another country. If the camp and the Allied prisoners had changed in my absence, so too had the guards. The ferrets were even more sophisticated at discovering tunnels. There is now some evidence that they did not always act immediately by shutting a tunnel when they detected it. If it was still a long way from the perimeter, they would let us slave away oblivious, knowing that we would otherwise only start a new one that they might not detect. Then, when it looked as if we might be getting somewhere, they would pounce and cart the diggers off to the cooler.

The ferrets used listening tubes to detect the sound of digging underground. They measured soil levels under the huts to see if we were dumping spoil from the tunnels there. They even took to driving heavy vehicles over the area between our huts and the perimeter fence to make our underground earthworks collapse. Despite all this, the tunnelling continued. When one was discovered, we would break another one.

Paddy and I both got involved with the tunnelling plans, and covering for other people's escape activities, but having spent so much time in the cooler and being a rather obvious serial escapologist, I started to find that it was difficult for me even to go for a stroll around the perimeter fence without attracting attention from the guards. This made working towards escapes even more difficult, and I did not want my own unwelcome celebrity with the ferrets to make matters worse for my comrades.

I had to find other ways of occupying myself, one

of which was trying to satisfy my hunger for news.

In a prisoner-of-war camp there are only a few possible sources of news. There was the rumour mill. Someone had heard that the Allied invasion was about to happen. Someone had heard that a senior American officer had been captured and the Allies were going to stage a daring commando raid to rescue us all along with him. Someone else had heard that the SS were going to shoot us all, or that there was a new batch of Red Cross parcels at the local train depot. Virtually all the rumours turned out to be untrue, particularly the good ones, so kriegies developed a sort of split personality, eagerly adding to the output of the rumour mill while regarding all such 'sure things' with healthy scepticism.

Then there was news from home. Every letter from loved ones was eagerly pored over, and those bits that had not been obliterated by the censor's pen were read and re-read. They opened a door to a world we had almost forgotten. It was a place where people went to parties and where children made things to bring home from school. Other people got married, sometimes to the sweetheart of the prisoner reading the letter. Part of us delighted in being able to peer into a world that felt very far away, but the effect could also be to make us feel more forgotten, if not by the letter writer, then by the rest of the world, which seemed to be getting along just fine without us.

My own letter writing, not prolific at the best of times, gradually dwindled in the course of the war, with the exception of occasional over-cheerful replies to my mother's worried letters. Because I read books more than I wrote letters, a girl who worked at one of the book charities that sent us books from Switzerland started to write to me. Apparently in an attempt to keep my morale up, as well as sending crateloads of improving classical literature, she would always include a letter, giving the details of her weekend spent in the pawing embraces of her boyfriend. No detail was regarded as too steamy for inclusion, and I could probably have started a thriving black market in second-hand pornography. Instead, since I've always thought that making love was not much of a spectator sport, I buried my head in some volume on medieval romance and pretended not to be thinking about escaping.

Another source of news was from the Nazis themselves. In their regular propaganda broadcasts over the wheezy loudspeaker system, the details were usually nonsense – all Nazi triumphs and heroic repelling of the Russian hordes – but if you listened carefully for place names you could usually follow the rough reality behind the lies on a map, watching which way the place names mentioned in each bulletin seemed to be moving – east or west.

Slightly more reliable broadcasts could be obtained from the BBC in London, but this involved building and hiding a secret radio receiver. Luckily, expert radio operators were being blown out of the sky as part of bomber crews on a regular basis, and several of these clever people dedicated their entire time in the camp to the simultaneous pursuit of the news and evasion of the ferrets.

The secret radios – there was usually at least one hidden in every compound – were ingenious contraptions. One of the earliest was put together at Luft I and brought in pieces to Luft III. It was mostly made from scrap materials, but the valves had been bought from bribed guards, as was usually the case.

Hiding places had to become ever more ingenious. In Luft III, one radio was smuggled in inside a football and another hidden under a toilet, while at Schubin one had been hidden inside the working gramophone player belonging to Wings Day. Later, in the central compound at Luft III, some enterprising Americans stole a radio from the infirmary and reassembled it to fit inside a table leg, which was nailed under the table top with four long nails. Two of the nails were used as terminals for the power supply and the others were used to connect the earphones.

There were different methods of disseminating the news, but since it was clearly impossible to bring listeners to the radio without also bringing a lot of interested ferrets, the most common network was one of reporters and readers. Each night a radio operator would listen with headphones, often quietly repeating the news for another prisoner who was an expert in shorthand. These men would then ensure that the news was read out to groups of prisoners the following day, usually under the guise of some education class. Sometimes, when those whose job it was to stand on a chair and tell a huddle of prisoners the news were unable to make notes or write it down, the news was a bit sketchy, but at least most of them refrained from adding in bits to make it more exciting.

On one occasion the guards unwittingly obliged in the transfer of news from one compound with a radio to another where theirs had been found and confiscated. One of the shorthand experts was allowed to give shorthand classes to the prisoners in the other compound, and each day his sample shorthand exercise bore a remarkable resemblance to the previous day's news from the BBC.

The prisoners who devoted their days to supplying news to thousands of isolated and information-hungry kriegies played a vital role in stopping the camps turning into little inward-looking worlds. Many of them went on to very successful careers in print journalism or broadcasting.

Listening to the progress of the war in the outside world rekindled my desire to get out and see what I was missing, and when I heard a rumour that sergeant pilots from the compound beside us were to be sent to a different camp at Hydekrug in Lithuania for non-commissioned officers, I could not resist attempting to escape. The fact that I was not an NCO did not deter me. If I could get to a different camp, I could use the period of chaos at the founding of any camp as a happy hunting ground for future escapes with untrained guards and fresh routes for new tunnels.

I found a plucky New Zealander called Don Fair who was more than willing to swap identities if it meant he did not have to get sent to the wilds of Lithuania. He would get a free promotion to flight lieutenant into the bargain. The only trouble was that Don Fair was in the central compound next door, on the other side of two tall barbed-wire fences covered by guard posts and machine guns. So I said my farewells to Paddy and my other friends and, with their help, prepared for an escape from one compound to the next. The guard towers and walking patrols had the area covered, but most of their attention was directed to the outer perimeter. My friends caused several distractions – a mock fight and a noisy football game – while I loitered on one side of the fence and Don Fair strolled innocently on the other. When the guards were looking the other way we both raced for the fence from opposite sides, crossing the warning wire that meant you would be shot on sight beyond that point, then climbing over the barbed-wire fence that was 10 feet tall but felt more like a 100 feet while I was clambering it, waiting at every second for a bullet in the back.

We both made it to the no-man's-land, which was perhaps three or four yards between the fences. We crouched down, hastily shook hands and swapped identity papers. Then, with a quick look around to make sure that the guards were still distracted, we were off again, climbing the wire into the other man's compound, across the terrible open space and over the warning wire to safety and the continuation of our innocent strolls. I never got to see or speak to Don Fair again, but for the best part of a year my parents got letters from someone called Don whose handwriting looked very much like their son's, and who seemed to know rather a lot about their son's former life in Texas. Meanwhile, somewhere in New Zealand, the Fair family was probably getting letters from someone they had never heard of called Bill Ash, telling them he missed them and was looking forward to coming home.

✦ 12 ✦

A Tour of Lithuania

The departure from Stalag Luft III was made more interesting when the camp commandant Von Lindeiner turned out in person to see us off. Since he had had several occasions to have a close look and a shout at Flight Lieutenant Ash, usually when I was *en route* to the cooler, I shuffled to the back of the parade in case he got curious about the uncanny resemblance between one Don Fair and the roving prisoner Ash. I remember the normally reserved commandant called us 'his boys' and urged us not to escape, hinting that the days of chivalry were coming to an end. I think he was a decent man and was genuinely worried about what would happen to us when we left the relative safety of Luftwaffe jurisdiction for a world full of Wehrmacht and Gestapo types. I smiled to myself, thinking back to Paris. As far as I was concerned, the world of chivalry had apparently ended some time back in 1933, when Hitler came to town.

As we marched out, I could see some of my old friends in the other compound, standing by the wire to see us off. There was Paddy, and over there was Bill Stapleton. Even the senior British officers, Wings Day and Group Captain Massey, were there. Wings Day took off his cap and waved it at us. I found my hand reaching up to wave back but shoved it resolutely back in my pocket. This was not a good time to draw attention to my unauthorized departure.

As we passed the senior German officers, we were marching in pretty impressive formation for a ragtag bunch of prisoners. The senior British NCO barked the order 'Eyes right!' and we marched out like soldiers. The Luftwaffe officers held their salute until the last man had left the camp. I marched along, trying to look inconspicuous, hunched within a huddle of my tallest new NCO friends, as the wire gates were shut behind us and we marched under the watchful eyes and machine guns of our guards to the local railway station. As Stalag Luft III receded behind me, I hoped that I would never see it again, but if I had been able to see into the future, I might have been surprised at just how glad I would be to be back there.

Many of my new NCO colleagues had originally come from another camp, Stalag Luft I at Barth. They were a very interesting combination of career soldiers and a majority of wartime volunteers, a mix which had previously led to some lively differences of opinion about discipline and democracy. The attempts to run their previous camp along the rather rigid lines of the King's Regulations by some career senior NCOs had met stiff resistance among some of the more dogged individuals who had only recently left civilian life and were determined to fight on their own terms. Some of them came from families who had lost a previous generation of soldiers who, by obeying orders, had charged to meaningless deaths from the trenches of the First World War. These men were not about to do the same. While knowing that an army without rank and regulations will never get anywhere, I naturally felt a closer affinity to these characters. They could be tough and disciplined when they needed to be, but they did not need to be shouted at by those for whom barked orders on parade grounds and spit-and-polish regimentation were the order of the day. So the NCOs had achieved a remarkable thing: despite several hundred years of army tradition, they had effectively voted in their own leader to run their affairs. This man was recognized not only by the prisoners but also by the German authorities as what they called the 'Man of Confidence'. He was the remarkable Jimmy 'Dixie' Deans, a sergeant who the men decided was a general.

Jimmy was a brave but very low-key man from Scotland, and a brilliant example of someone who could use his head as well as his heart. He spoke excellent German and was always turned out very neatly in regulation uniform with a collar and tie. He tended not to waste words, but said what he meant and meant what he said. Jimmy was proof positive that you don't have to shout to be a commanding presence, and the camp authorities knew that as well as we did. He worked hard to make his compound run as well as possible so that the escape committee could work in peace, and despite incredible hardships and dangers, he never lost sight of both of those at times contradictory necessities. In a world where most people liked to pretend that the war would be over in a few months, or at least could not bear to face the thought of further years behind the wire, Jimmy was prepared to look the possibility in the eye. When he was captured in September 1940, he had made a calendar for himself. It ran from the day he made it to the end of May 1945.

As we sat on the train with our guards and a shouting German officer ran about issuing orders, some of my new NCO colleagues stared goggle-eyed at a smartly dressed German civilian guzzling down a tankard of beer in the station cafeteria on the platform. The man got up from the café and approached the hyperactive German officer in charge of the train. He had a stern conversation with him and the officer seemed to cringe and nod. One man on the train muttered, 'Gestapo,' but another man replied, 'No, it's not. It's bloody Grimson.'

George Grimson was eventually destined for Hydekrug, and he was perhaps the most remarkable figure in the camp, which was crammed with amazing people. A stocky man with close-cropped fair hair, he had a pugnacious manner that put some people off, but he was actually quite reserved underneath. He had been shot down in 1940 and had started to gain a reputation as a man of great nerve when he was at the camp in Barth. There his escape attempts had included impersonating a guard as he strolled out of the gate, with the advantage that he spoke good German and could use his natural manner to bark at guards and distract them from searching him or checking his identity. He had escaped a few times but been recaptured.

How he came to be drinking beer and convincing the train officer that he was a Gestapo man while the rest of us were being herded off to the Hydekrug camp is a typical Grimson story. Back in Luft III, in the NCO compound we had just left, he had dressed as an engineering ferret, one of those who wandered around the camp testing telephone lines and repairing the lights. With his German forage cap set at a jaunty tilt and a ladder slung over his shoulder he had shouted a warning to a machine-gunner guard in a tower, then stepped over the death wire and marched up to the perimeter fence.

Grimson had borrowed the ladder from the camp theatre and, equally theatrically, was wearing a large box with electrical cables dangling from it and a gauge that looked like an ammeter. Once he reached the fence, he put up his ladder and started testing light bulbs. When he was at the top of the wire he dropped some tools down the other side, accidentally-on-purpose. He swore loudly in German, then asked the guard in the tower if he could climb over to pick them up and then walk around the perimeter to the entrance to come back and continue his work. The bored guard nodded and that is what Grimson did, although he forgot about the part where he was supposed to come back. This got him into the German sector of the camp, where he hid for several hours before marching through two gates and presenting his forged papers. Suddenly, he was outside the camp and when he was in a quiet spot he peeled off his ferret costume to reveal a smart suit underneath, giving him a new identity as a roving Gestapo man. In an act of spectacular chutzpah, he had booked himself as a security representative on our train. He hopped on at the back and the train pulled out.

It was early summer in 1943. The trains they loaded us on were cramped but otherwise not too grim. Each coach was divided into three wired-off sections, with the middle section containing half-a-dozen nervous German guards armed with machine guns and grenades, though to throw one of them without themselves becoming what the bomber crews liked to call strawberry jam was at best unlikely.

Our captors took us on a wandering route of minor lines to the north and east, possibly because the more straightforward routes were disrupted by Allied night-time bombing, which was starting to pick up. At one such stop Grimson alighted and saw the train off, looking stern and Gestapo-like before continuing his journey. He made it to Stettin on the coast, where he made some useful contacts among the slave labour workers from many countries, but while he was still searching for a neutral ship that would take him, he was caught up in the hunt for an escaped Russian prisoner who had killed a German NCO during his escape. The Russian and Grimson were both captured and spent what Grimson later described as a very enjoyable night, locked in a filthy cell and passing the time by having races and jumping contests with the bed bugs. They became so engrossed in the bed-bug Olympics that the Russian protested loudly at his game being cut short as he was led out to a courtyard where he was executed. Grimson was put on a train to Hydekrug, this time travelling third-class without his swastika lapel badge. He joined us a few days later and immediately became active in our fledgling escape committee.

By nightfall on our own train journey we were shunted into a marshalling yard on the outskirts of Berlin. Soon we heard the heavy throb of aircraft engines overhead as Allied bombers rolled over the city. The sky was illuminated by swivelling searchlights and a wall of anti-aircraft fire lit up the sky. The dull crump and shrill whistle of bombs falling and the louder crash of closer hits filled the night air. Many of the NCO prisoners were bomber crew and they clapped and cheered from this unexpected ringside seat as the German capital took a pasting.

As the prisoners got more boisterous and jubilant, the guards got more nervous, their fingers twitching close to their gun triggers. The guards were not just nervous about us. They had rather more experience of being on the receiving end of such bombing and they knew that a rail-way carriage in the middle of a Berlin siding was not the safest place to be when Bomber Harris's men were dropping explosives all around us.

Some of the prisoners started to goad the guards, enquiring if they were from Berlin, and not surprisingly the guards began to cock their machine guns as fear turned to menace. The quiet, commanding voice of Jimmy Deans told the guard-baiters to pipe down. Jimmy did not hate fascists any less than the rest of us, but he knew that a carriage full of dead prisoners killed by guards who had been pushed too far would hardly help the war effort. We would wait until we got to the new camp, and then carry on our escape attempts with all the skills we had built up over the years.

In June 1943, we arrived at Hydekrug camp in Lithuania, Stalag Luft VI, not far from the town of Memel on the Memel peninsula. The place was a strange, swampy, mist-shrouded backwater, not far from the Baltic coast. It was like a promised land for escap-ologists, for there were indeed better opportunities for departing suddenly than at Luft III. When we entered the camp, many of the prisoners flopped down in the long grass and lay soaking up the sunshine, grateful to be any-where but Stalag Luft III, but within weeks the grass had been trampled by a thousand captive feet into the prison yard dust with which we were all too familiar.

Hydekrug was a converted barracks, and as such was a bit more solidly constructed than most of the

German camps, which, from POW enclosures to concentration camps, were mostly built along very similar lines of communal one-storey huts and barbed-wire fences. In Hydekrug the four long accommodation huts were built of brick and whitewashed on the inside. There were big old brick ovens at each end of the rooms which helped to stave off the bitterly cold Baltic winters. Personally, I planned to be far away long before the stoves would be needed for heating. The commandant had other ideas and was already building two new compounds alongside us to accommodate prisoners from the vast numbers of American and British bomber crews who were now raiding Berlin both day and night and being denounced as 'Luftgangsters' in the Nazi media.

At first I was regarded with a mixture of amusement and bafflement by some of the down-to-earth and hard-nosed NCOs in the new camp. The idea that an officer would willingly muck in with the ranks to the extent of deliberately swapping identities to join them in the wilds of Lithuania struck some as funny and others as slightly demented. Luckily, word quickly went around that I was an experienced if not altogether successful escape artist and I found myself in the reluctant role of veteran escapologist for a new generation keen to learn.

Alongside a small group of experienced escape artists, forgers, tailors and allied trades were an increasing number of new arrivals, mostly survivors of horrific crashes or bale-outs from burning bombers shot down during the city raids of preceding weeks. Some of them looked to the veteran escapers for advice on anything from tunnel construction to surviving the loss of colleagues or the separation from loved ones. Our escape committee, which included me, Jock Alexander, George Grimson, Paddy Flynn and several others, christened our escape activities the Tally-Ho Club. This sounded terribly upper crust and English to me, so naturally it was a club I was proud to join, even if it was one I hoped to get thrown out of by escaping.

Inside, I still felt like the same young Texan, hardly up to such tasks, with no idea where I was going or how to get there. The only thing I was certain about was that wherever 'there' was, it lay on the other side of the wire.

The guards at Hydekrug were tough. Major Peschel, their security officer, and his team of ferrets worked ceaselessly to uncover our tunnel and other escape preparations, and at first they had considerable success, mainly because of over-enthusiasm and lax security on our part. Despite their little victories over us, however, the guards' morale was low and getting lower as things worsened for the Germans, with the eastern front gradually becoming a quagmire. Our meagre rations got even smaller, and gradually as weeks turned to months it became hard not to suffer from some kind of malnutrition.

The news of Russian advances redoubled my resolve to get out and stay out. I even considered some plans of heading east rather than west, conveniently ignoring the fact that to reach the Russian front lines I would have to somehow get through the German rear.

While I was pondering my options, I and the rest of the escape committee were also making preparations for the bold Grimson to make his next bid for freedom. This one would be different from almost every other escape of the war. Grimson was going to try not to get away but to set up an underground railroad for future escapees. It took some courage to attempt to escape, but to deliberately stay in occupied Europe to help others took a very special man.

The first part of the plan was to get Grimson out of the camp. Several schemes failed without the guards even knowing they were happening. Then Grimson hit on the idea of using his skills of deception to get him out disguised as a guard. In good weather the roll calls took place on the football field and a dozen guards would take up positions around the field. When the counting and shouting were over, they would walk back across our compound, through the gates to the *Vorlager* or German area where the guard room was. On the day of Grimson's bid for freedom we managed to keep the count going until dusk and at the end of the parade there was one more guard than at the start. He was resplendent in a German greatcoat and his rifle looked menacing if you did not look too closely to see that it was made entirely of wood carved from bed boards by a talented sergeant called Webster.

Grimson strolled out with no problems, and changed in a lavatory beside the guard room, then made his way to a store room where we had all his supplies and paperwork waiting for him. He ambled out of the camp as a well-dressed civilian and was soon on board a train to Innsbruck. He made it all the way to a village south of Danzig, where he was looked after by Polish patriots, and from there he set out to build an escape route through the Danzig docks to Sweden.

He stayed out for several months, snatching sleep in railway stations for a few hours at a time and moving from one rented room to another, constantly in fear of capture, but along the way he made contact with the Polish Resistance and with those who were willing to help escapees either for moral reasons or for money. Bravest of all, he made several trips back to Hydekrug, where he met intermediaries who carried messages back inside the camps. He helped another prisoner called Flockhart escape and got him on a boat bound for Sweden. Ten days later, Flockhart was back in Britain, while Grimson continued his one-man war in the Baltic.

But such bravery alone is not always enough, and good luck never lasts for ever. One of our brave Polish helpers on the outside was uncovered following a shoot-out between German troops and members of the Resistance. Afterwards, Poles were tortured and shot and the Gestapo trail started leading back, through Poles and guards who had assisted him in the camp and on the outside, to Grimson. The escape committee sent him a short message: 'Get out of the country. Position hopeless,' but by then it was too late. Rumours of Grimson's arrest circulated, and then – nothing.

It is almost certain that Grimson was captured, interrogated then taken out and shot by the Gestapo, but no trace of him was ever found, during or after the war. In a strange way this gave him an immortality that fitted very well with his bravery. As if he was a Robin Hood or a ghost, for the rest of the war both the Germans and more than a few escapers would look over their shoulders, half expecting to see Grimson, on the loose again.

In the months leading up to these events, a group of us had started a long tunnel, aiming for the edge of a grove of birch trees beyond the perimeter fence. Our experience had taught us that half the battle with a tunnel was keeping the entrance concealed for long enough to allow the tunnel to reach cover outside the camp. Having learned from our successes and failures at Schubin and Luft III, we chose another latrine as a starting point, both to discourage the ferrets from snooping and to give us somewhere to lose several hundred tons of tunnel dirt.

We started with the same sort of arrangement, a tunnel entrance underneath one of the toilet seats, then a precarious tightrope walk along an underground brick wall just a few feet above a cesspit sea of sewage that led to another underground foundation wall and another hole. Climbing through this brought us to a vast, hollowed-out chamber and the start of the tunnel. But we had hardly got started when we realized that there was a fundamental problem. The high water table meant that as we added tunnel dirt to the latrine, the sewage level rose until it very quickly reached the level of the entrance to our tunnel and flooded it with unmentionable liquid. We thought we were at a standstill until someone – I think it was a kriegie called Jack Catley – came up with one of those indecently brilliant ideas that can turn any situation around.

At the end of the long line of toilet holes was a wall, and on the far side of the wall was a small laundry room with three huge hot-water boilers. They weighed a ton, but could be deconstructed into three parts, a base, a boiler and an outer metal sleeve for insulation. We moved the lot out of the way, dug a manhole through the stubborn concrete beneath and excavated a new cavern as the starting place for our tunnel. Up above, we re-assembled the boiler so that it could actually be lit and working while I and the other diggers were toiling below. Even the most suspicious guard, peering at a huge bubbling vat of clothes, would not dream that it covered the entrance to another world. Having worked in half-a-dozen stifling holes in the ground by now, I knew that ventilation was one of the most important factors in how long and how efficiently we could dig. With this new arrangement, the tunnel acted as a flue to the boiler fire. We poked unobtrusive air holes to the surface from the tunnel and the draw of the fire sucked the air from the surface and through the tunnel to the boiler, giving us the first air-conditioned escape tunnel in the Third Reich.

There was no shortage of willing diggers, but despite

the secure entrance and better air, the work was hard, and it seemed endless, marred by cave-ins and flooding in the soft swampy loam of Lithuania. Because of the high water table we could not dig down too far, yet we could not make the tunnel too shallow either, since if we did the German microphones would pick up the noise of our burrowing.

Our shoring to prevent further collapses was once again achieved by purloining bed boards, and once again the majority of the camp showed willing and donated at least one each, while the escapers were again expected to lead by example, by sleeping on a bunk bed apparently held up by air and string. To make sure that the tunnel roof was not also defying gravity by staying up, former mining engineers and several university lecturers in mathematics who happened to be among our diverse talent pool calculated the amount of shoring needed.

While this work went on, Dixie Deans had his hands full as the leader or Man of Confidence in the camp. We desperately needed both information on the new locality and materials for escaping, from clothes to document-ation. The passes or *Ausweis* changed with incredible frequency and there was no point in spending six months of incredible hardship working to get out if we were to be let down by a forged pass that turned out to have expired a week earlier. There was only one way to get such in-formation, and that was from the guards. Some of them were incorruptible, either out of loyalty to the Fatherland or just a healthy fear of being shot by the Gestapo if discovered helping the enemy in even the mildest of ways. But others were susceptible, mostly to greed, a few to excitement, others to getting their own back on some superior officer who had just bawled them out, and towards the end of the war an increasing number recognized that it might be a good idea to be in the Allies' good books if it came to swapping places, with them ending up as the prisoners.

Dixie Deans knew that the way to a guard's heart, or at least to his *Ausweis*, was through his stomach. Our Red Cross supply of chocolate and our relatively generous supply of cigarettes were the envy of all the guards. Some would provide nonsense information in an attempt to get their hands on a few squares of chocolate, but it quickly became obvious who was supplying useful items and who was just a chocoholic. Some of the guards took insane risks for the sake of a handful of cigarettes or a mouthful of chocolate, but the war did strange things to people on both sides.

Our biggest problem in this respect was not the ferrets, but those of our own who had set up as prison commodity brokers. They bought and sold everything from chocolate and cigarettes to musical instruments and paper, trading with the enemy for personal profit. Wars are a good time for people to focus on what they must do to win, and just as industries such as coal and steel had effectively to be nationalized in Britain as part of the war effort, so we kriegies decided that trading in the new camp should be run to benefit everyone rather than making a few spivs rich. We needed to bribe the guards and that meant we could not afford great lurches in the value of cigarettes or chocolate. We also needed the profit created by the trade to be available for the 'purchase' of what we needed for escape – ranging from bits of German uniform to parts for radios and the all-important travel papers.

As usual with such cultural changes, it did not happen without a bit of a struggle, and it probably would not have happened at all had it not been that we were in a new camp where we could start from scratch. Most of all, it would not have happened were it not for the remarkable persuasive powers of Jimmy Deans.

A few of the would-be tycoons objected to the curtailment of their pursuit of riches and one young guy, recently arrived, complained bitterly about his rights being trampled on. Jimmy was a generally low-key and quiet man, but he had a real authority and on this occasion he turned himself up to full volume. He roared at the grumbler, 'Rights? The only bloody right you have is to eighteen inches in the ranks!' referring to the statutory width allowed to each man when in line on parade. 'Good men are out there getting killed in the air every night and other good men are in here risking their lives trying to escape, and you talk about rights? Get out of my sight!'

After that, there were no more problems. A flamboyant character called Nat Leaman ran the trading side of things from then on, with all proceeds being funnelled into escape activities and general welfare for the camp. From this arrangement grew a sort of prisoners' store known as Foodaco which used cigarettes as currency and once again, profits from this went to where they would do most good for escapes, rather than into a few bulging pockets. Those who wanted to make a fast buck transferred their energies to gambling for vast amounts of back pay on cards or roulette. Luckily for them, Eddy Asselin was still fleecing all comers back in Luft III; otherwise they would have been lucky to walk away still wearing their uniforms.

Apart from that one justifiable outburst, Jimmy Deans' presence was a constant calming factor in the camp. He enjoyed a rare break from the endless decision-making and problem-solving with a walk around the camp each day, usually with his pal Ron Mogg, who was another enthusiastic member of the escaping fraternity.

As with the other camps, the 'Dear John' letters or Mespots continued to roll in, increasing in number as the war dragged on and the periods of forced separation between prisoners and their loved ones grew longer, often many times longer than the time they had spent together in the first place. One day a young man who had just pinned his sad rejection letter from home to the noticeboard for all to see ran out just as Edwards had done at Schubin and crossed the death wire, the strain too much for him. As the man started to climb the fence, Jimmy Deans shouted at the guards not to shoot and then marched across the death wire himself, gambling that the guards in the machine-gun towers would recognize him and hesitate from pulling the triggers. Arms raised, he walked slowly across to the man, who was now sobbing, clinging to the barbed wire and waiting for the bullet that would put him out of his misery. Instead he heard the quiet, calm Scottish voice of Dixie Deans, who gently disentangled him from the wire and led him back to safety, their every step covered by half-a-dozen nervous guards with fingers on their triggers. The man was handed over to Paddy Pollock, a great Irish doctor and another unsung hero of the camp. After that, Jimmy simply continued his walk with Mogg, and went back to talking about camp laundry arrangements.

There were times when being a man of few words was definitely in Jimmy's interest. As our tunnel grew, and became what some people claim was one of the finest to be dug in the course of the war, reaching over 150 feet, Jimmy was summoned to the commandant's office. The commandant had heard there was a tunnel and forged documents in the camp and asked Deans if he knew any-thing about them. A few hours earlier, Jimmy had been on a secret inspection of our earthworks and had con-gratulated us on our progress. He looked the commandant in the eye and chose his words carefully, saying he did not know of anything in the camp that should not be there.

A week later we were invaded by the local Gestapo, who joined forces with the guards in the most thorough raid and search we ever experienced. Rooms were ransacked, floorboards ripped up and hiding places unearthed. They were jubilant as they captured maps, papers, compasses and clothing. During the raid one of the Gestapo men momentarily rested his briefcase on a table. When he turned around, it was gone, never to be seen again. From the briefcase we got new documents and a lot of useful information which consoled us on the loss of so much hard-earned equipment. More frantic Gestapo searches and threats of reprisals failed to unearth the bag or its contents.

Despite the loss of the briefcase, which they probably did not even report for fear of being shot by their superiors, the searchers departed happy. They had a good haul of escape equipment and if there had been a tunnel, they were sure they would have found it. The truth was that they had missed it as they inspected the laundry room and prodded the contents of a bubbling wash boiler loaded with clothes.

Those of us on the surface breathed a sigh of relief, but the next day, on the way to a shift at the 'coal face' of the tunnel, I was surprised to hear a faint grumble growing louder. Sometimes we heard the booming of the long-range Russian artillery on the eastern front, but this was more of a low, rolling rumble. Then there was a slight tremor and the grumble turned to a rumble and then a roar. Out from behind some buildings came one of the most eager ferrets, looking pleased with himself, and mounted on a huge steamroller that belched smoke as it trundled around the perimeter.

It transpired that the commandant was less convinced

than the Gestapo that no tunnel existed just because they had not found it. He was no doubt conscious that being a commandant of one of our camps, whether in Germany, Poland or Lithuania, was potentially a one-way ticket to the Russian front and the only way to avoid this fate was to keep us on the inside of the wire. So he had devised a novel way of deterring tunnelling, by driving a steam-roller back and forth over all the open ground under which a tunnel might lurk.

I held my breath and spared a thought for the crew who were underground digging as the vast machine rolled directly over the top of our tunnel route. When the coast had cleared, we hurriedly extinguished the boiler fire and were delighted to find not only our comrades unscathed but the tunnel roof holding solidly throughout. But the combination of the searches and the attempts to collapse all our months of hard work did have an effect. Our tunnel had already reached out beyond the perimeter fence, but was not yet at the line of trees that would give us shelter as we emerged. Half the tunnellers felt that we should risk breaking out into the open as soon as possible rather than wait for the next search to get lucky. The other half wanted to wait for the cover of the trees, even if it meant enduring the increasing possibility of the tunnel being discovered in the weeks it would take us to reach them.

The escape committee met to discuss the matter. Jock Alexander was strongly against the early break, while there were others equally passionate in its favour. I tended to lean towards those who wanted to dig the tunnel straight up now and get out as soon as possible. We argued back and forth long into the day and eventually we decided that we would recommend that the digging continue despite the risk of discovery, but that we would leave the decision to a vote by those who were on the escape. I was one of the few people who was on both the escape committee and the escape. Among the escapers, if anything the sense of urgency was greater. Again the arguments ranged back and forth on the growing risk of discovery against the chance that going off half-cocked would lead to disaster.

By now there was a real tension in the air, and one of my reasons for leaning towards an early breakout was that I now had enough experience to know that this increased the chances of discovery. It is hard to quantify, but somehow the tension prior to a jailbreak is like an invisible wave of static electricity that spreads through a camp, and somehow the ferrets often seemed to sense it, just as some people or animals can sense a storm coming long before the first cloud has appeared on the horizon.

We took a vote on it, and the majority was in favour of a breakout as soon as possible into the open ground on the other side of the wire. Immediately the decision was made, everyone, no matter how they had argued earlier, threw themselves completely into making the escape a success. Frantic work on clothing, maps and papers above ground was accompanied by energetic vertical digging down below. The NCO camp, from its election of a sergeant as leader to its determination to have a vote, even on escaping, was one of the most democratic structures I have ever been in.

The great length of our tunnel enabled us to get fifty men and all their kit along its length on the night of the breakout. Above ground, the camp was a hotbed of activity. In case there was a snap search, an elaborate series of ruses were devised to ensure that the guards did not notice fifty empty beds. Numerous papier-mâché dummies, adorned with real hair, were tucked into unoccupied bunks. They had been made by many prisoners under cover of the art classes that were meant to keep their minds off escaping. Some were more realistic than others, but all could pass for a dozing prisoner under a blanket in the dark. At the same time, holes were bashed in walls to allow people to be counted in one room and then slip away to another empty bed to be counted again. As the men in the huts waited and listened, part of them must have yearned to be one of the fifty in that tunnel, while another part of them thanked their stars they were not.

In the tunnel, I found myself once again at the front, but this time with the added apprehension that we would be breaking out into the open just a few yards from the wire on a regular patrol route. Our normal wonderful air conditioning thanks to the suction from the fire could not be used because the fire could not be lit at night when we were supposedly all locked up sleeping peacefully in our barracks. Soon the atmosphere in the tunnel was suffocating, and the closer one was to the tunnel face the worse the air got. One of the most claustrophobic feelings in the world is being in a 2-foot-square space, jammed up against a wall of earth and knowing that if there is a collapse there are fifty bodies lined head to toe behind you, who would take half an hour to reverse up the tunnel one at a time, by which time you would have long since suffocated.

On the other hand, as first man out I had the delight of digging through to the surface after so many months working underground and feeling that great first icy blast of air when we broke through. It rushed and whistled along the tunnel and I could hear the gasps of delight as the icy taste of potential freedom allowed them to breathe once again.

We had been pleased earlier at the signs that it was likely to be a windy, rainy night, during which we hoped the sentries would be less keen on prowling around than usual; and we had also made sure that our break was in the dark phase of the moon. By the time I poked my head above ground the rain had stopped, the wind had died down and everything seemed bright and still. I ducked down as the guard passed by, so close that I could hear each footstep. Then it was a quick, silent scramble to the surface and an endless, terrible crawl towards the cover of the trees. Each inch of those 10 yards in the open felt like a mile and I waited for the shout, gunshot or bayonet that would tell me I had been seen.

Amazingly, I made it to the trees undiscovered. I

waited for the next man and helped to get the escape chain going, with each person emerging after the guard had passed and making a dash for the trees, then I made my own escape, off and running through the darkness into the woods. This time I had decided to travel on my own. I had a home-made compass and some half-baked notion of heading east rather than west as expected, in order to hook up with the advancing Russians or maybe a group of partisans. Since the entire continent of occupied Europe lay between me and a good meal in London, the lure of heading towards Germany was not all that strong.

Minutes later, sirens wailed and searchlights flashed. I could hear the sound of gunfire coming from the direction of the tunnel. Seven of us had slipped out before the law of averages caught up with us. The eighth man out had bolted too early and the passing sentry had turned back to see him emerging from the tunnel entrance. The guard fired warning shots and the unfortunate escapee stood with his hands up, paralysed with fear. The soldiers swarmed over the escape area and fired down into the tunnel to discourage any further visitors from the under-world. Luckily, the steep angle of the rushed tunnel exit meant that most of the bullets dug harmlessly into the tunnel floor, though others helped to bring down part of the roof as the remaining forty or so would-be escapers did their best to reverse hastily towards the entrance chamber.

Suddenly the woods were alive with shouting pursuers

and snarling Alsatian guard dogs. I remember thinking about my childhood pet Alsatian Danny in Texas, whom I had grown up with from the age of five and who taught me anything I know about dignity. But these distant Teutonic cousins of Danny's were unlikely to be impressed by my previous alliance with a German Shepherd dog, and this time I knew the dogs were unlikely to be satisfied by a few handfuls of the Mixture. But just as I heard the barking and shouting getting closer, I came to the edge of a small river that encircled one side of the camp. I swam across the icy water and managed to lose the dogs, who continued to sniff and search on the far bank. I ran into the eerie luminous half light of a Lithuanian dawn and did not stop until I could no longer hear or see any trace of my pursuers.

Years later, I heard about what happened back in the camp as I was running across Lithuanian swampland, sucking in great, damp lungfuls of freedom. As the captured prisoners were marched off to the cooler, they managed to get word to those in the barracks without the guards overhearing that seven had escaped. Minutes later the host of guards, ferrets and officers descended on the barracks to make a head count. They were convinced that the man they had caught on the surface was the first one out and were jubilant that they had foiled such a spectacular escape attempt. As the guards went from hut to hut counting, they found numerous dummies slumbering peacefully in the beds. They added up the number of prisoners they had caught to those in the camp, and it came to the right total. The guards went to bed delighted.

While they slept, dreaming of medals for their good work, the men in the camp allowed themselves a quiet smile. They had removed all but seven dummies before the search. Consequently, with the camp satisfied that everyone was either tucked up or locked up, the outside world was not notified of the escape until the following day, by which time most of us were as far away as our spindly legs would carry us.

Next morning in the camp the Tally-Ho Club managed to ensure that the number counted tallied with the usual camp complement, with seven men engineering to be counted twice. All was well until one of the seven escapees was captured that morning and brought back to the cooler, which incidentally was now so crowded with those from the tunnel that the guards had to bring in double-decker bunks so that the prisoners could be kept in not very solitary confinement. Major Peschel stared in horror at the extra prisoner and immediately ordered a recount, but the mathematical wizards of the camp were one step ahead of them and on this second count they ensured that only six men were double-counted. The counters went away satisfied, though a little bemused at how they got it wrong the first time.

The following day another escapee was caught and returned, and once again the prisoners managed to rig the count, this time by five. By now the German officers were baffled. They always seemed to have the right number of prisoners, and yet more kept coming out of the woodwork from the outside world. A telephone call on the third day, announcing the capture of a third escaper more than 50 miles from the camp, caused the unfortunate Major Peschel to come close to bursting with rage, confusion and general apoplexy. He was going to check each man in the camp against his identity card, and he was not going to stop until he knew exactly who and where every prisoner was.

The guards, terrified of Peschel in a rage, marched meekly from their administration building carrying boxes of identity cards and set up shop, in orderly Germanic style, starting in A block at building A1. Peschel called his men around him in a huddle to give them exact orders on how to identify and count the prisoners, who seemed able to expand and contract their numbers at will. A box of the identity cards rested on a table behind them. In the two minutes that he took to brief his men, unseen hands lifted the box and passed it behind the backs of innocent-looking prisoners until it reached the stove at the end of the building. Up went the stove lid and in went 450 identity cards as a burnt offering. In other rooms smaller numbers were filched and the photos steamed off to use on forged documents in the future.

By this time the guards were so demoralized that they slunk off to form another plan. Soon the prisoners were all lined up on the parade ground. Count after count was made, right into the night, when the kriegies were illuminated by searchlight. As the guards' frustration turned to anger, and the risk of someone being shot for not knowing when to stop goon-baiting rose, Jimmy Deans was there to calm things down.

The commandant had a new plan. He had six guards bring three ladders and set them up as a sort of sheep crush of the type used to count penned animals. A chorus of bleating erupted from the ranks and prisoners shouted out random numbers in German as they were counted in the hope of putting the counters off. Despite their best efforts, the guards had forgotten to put a guard on the outside wings of the parade ground, so as some prisoners were counted they sneaked back to join the uncounted herd. When they had eventually counted everybody, the guards went into another huddle and declared that they had almost twice as many prisoners as they should have. Some optimistic characters urged them to let half of the prisoners go so that their numbers would add up, but instead they herded the men back to their huts. The next day, they finally managed to count properly, by which time most of the escapers had been recaptured, but I was still wandering around Lithuania.

The days that followed my escape in the autumn of 1943 remain closer to a dream than a waking reality in my mind. A combination of the poor rations, too many trips to the cooler on bread and water, then weeks of tough physical work on the tunnel, followed by the exertions of escape, swimming rivers and sleeping rough in wet clothes, had left me in pretty bad shape. I found myself dizzy and sometimes short of breath, wanting desperately to sleep, yet when sleep came finding myself startled awake by the strange noises of the countryside.

But that was only half the story. The other half was the strange almost supernatural landscape through which I was travelling. That part of Lithuania was like something out of a Grimms' fairy tale. Strange bayou-like marshes and swamplands rose up on all sides, interspersed with ancient woods of tall silver birches. Their narrow silver trunks and almost luminous green leaves seemed to glow from the inside in the perpetual twilight of dawn and dusk.

For a number of days I wandered in the countryside, using up my escape supplies and getting more tired and hungry by the day, but managing to avoid capture. This may partly have been because I was heading east, in the general direction of the Russian front, while any soldiers looking for me would have concentrated on the Baltic coast to the west, which is probably what I should have been doing too.

I waded through strange marshy meadows and bogs, avoiding quicksand by following the goat paths and places where I saw livestock grazing.

On the third night after my escape, I camped on the banks of a small lake of impenetrably dark water and fell into a fitful, feverish sleep. The water was so still it seemed like some huge dark mirror in a fairy tale and my dreams were filled with nightmarish faces staring back at me from the black depths of the water. When I awoke it was still dark, but the entire bank of the lake seemed to have been circled by silent German troops. I could not make them out but I could see the light from their flash lamps tracing the sky and dancing in reflection at the far side of the silent lake. Stranger still, their lights were all different colours – blue, red, orange and green. I shook my head, trying to get the vision to go away, but it just got worse. The silent soldiers now seemed to be throwing their torches in the air and these twisted and flickered upwards before they disappeared altogether.

Slowly my brain started to put facts together. There was no noise, and nothing to break the stillness of the night. There were no German soldiers. Their flash lamps were the strange natural phenomenon I have never seen before or since called swamp fires or ignis fatui – the real-life explanation for such superstitions as the will-o'-the-wisp. Gases were gradually leaching from the depths of the swamp and briefly ignited when they reached the surface, creating a small wall of flickering flames around the edge of the lake. Even with this rational explanation, it was an eerie place in the middle of the Lithuanian night for a sick, hungry runaway, and I broke camp and stumbled on in the darkness.

On the next night, bathed in that same eerie moonlight, I found myself circling around a large old mansion and cutting through its rambling grounds. I stood for a moment in the centre of a vast, beautifully kept Italianate garden, with manicured lawns and topiary hedges clipped in the shape of birds and animals. I stumbled along flag-stoned paths, past ornate fountains, and rested for a few minutes beside decaying statues of angels and cherubs.

All this in the middle of nowhere at the heart of a misty swamp.

Finally, too exhausted to go further, and feeling as if I was wandering around in someone else's dream, I found an outbuilding in a ramshackle farm and fell asleep on the straw. I was woken by being prodded with a pitchfork. A group of Lithuanian peasants crowded around me, staring distrustfully. The farm patriarch prodded me again and demanded in Lithuanian to know who I was.

At this point I knew I was probably in big trouble. The history of Lithuania is one of being rolled over by its larger neighbours. While some hated the Germans, others had sided with them to get rid of the Russians, whom they loathed. Others still had formed the core of several Baltic divisions of the SS. Many simply regarded anyone not from their village as some form of potential enemy. While those who hated the occupiers might offer help, in other areas an escaped prisoner was just as likely to be handed over or shot.

It took me and the farm patriarch some time to communicate, using smatterings of German and Russian – none of which either of us seemed to know. He asked me if I was Russian, I shook my head no. He spat on the ground and uttered what was probably a fairly heavy-duty curse, which I presumed indicated that he was not too fond of Russians.

The others crowded around and nodded belligerently. I nodded too, disloyally. Next he asked if I was Deutsch. I vehemently denied this, hoping that because they hated the Russians, they did not like the Germans by default. He spat again and came out with an even more bucolic Lithuanian oath against the Germans and all their works. His followers nodded and glared at me, just in case.

Was I British? No, I wasn't British, and I didn't fancy attempting to explain the vague relationship between America, Britain and the Royal Canadian Air Force. He seemed pleased that I was not British and turned to the others to make a gesture that implied that the British were all stuck-up aristocrats. The others smiled menacing gap-toothed grins and clutched their scythes and pitchforks even more threateningly.

Exasperated, he asked me a question I did not understand, but I guessed that it boiled down to 'Then just what the hell are you, and why are you in my barn?' I thought about saying I was American, but assumed they were no more fond of Americans than anyone else they had ever heard of, so I pointed at my chest proudly and explained that I was a Texan. The patriarch thought about this and chewed the word over in his mouth several times – 'Texan ... Texan. Hmmmm.' He turned to the others questioningly, but they all shrugged or looked blank. They had never heard of Texas either. The patriarch made up his mind. He extended a hand of welcome and pulled me to my feet. They did not have anything against Texans – yet – so I could stay. He shoved the pitchfork at me, luckily blunt end first this time. I took it and he pointed out into the fields.

That is how I found myself starting a new life as a

Lithuanian peasant. If a German patrol went by I would stop and gawp with the rest of the farm workers, then turn back to shovelling whatever was on the end of my pitchfork. It was harvest time and we worked from dawn to dusk, but at least I was getting fed and evading capture.

This went on for several days, but ultimately I could not see myself spending the rest of the war as a Lithuanian peasant, so I discussed my problem with the other farm workers, mostly in sign language. One explained, by drawing in the dirt with a stick, that on the shores of the Baltic there were what looked like boathouses. I might be able to break into them and steal a small boat to head across the Baltic Sea in the general direction of neutral Sweden.

The next day, I was back on the road, heading west this time, towards the coast. I bade farewell to my new farm friends and they seemed mildly sorry to see me go, loading me up with some vegetables for the road. I had not given them long enough to start disliking Texans.

After a few days of avoiding inhabited areas, often travelling at night or in the early morning, I reached the coast. There, spread out in front of me and shrouded in mist, was the whole Baltic Sea. I discovered a line of boathouses, just as described, containing small sailing vessels locked up for the duration of the war. I slid down a bank and approached them from behind. When the coast was clear, I broke a lock and examined the vessel inside. It was a small sailing boat, which it might be possible to sail single-handed, though I knew virtually nothing about boats, and my last experience of one had been being sick below decks on the huge troop ship on my way from Canada to England. But if I was going to make it to Sweden, I needed something that floated, and this seemed like the best bet.

The only problem was that there were several yards of beach and slipway between the good ship Ash and the water. I pulled at the boat, then tried hauling it with a rope and pushing it like a reluctant mule. But it would not budge. In my heart I knew that it would take four or five men to have any hope of shifting it. Though trusting strangers in Lithuania was a risky business, ultimately, if I wanted the boat to budge, I had no choice. I looked up and down the coastline and spotted several men in overalls digging in a field. I had managed to convince one group of peasants that Texans were really not all that bad, so I decided to give it a go again. I walked over and gave them a cheery greeting, but they just glanced up, then went back to tending their vegetables. I had been planning to give them some story about why I wanted my boat out of its house in the middle of the war, but since it sounded so improbable even to me, I decided that honesty was the best policy. I took a deep breath, and in my best Texan, supported by rather theatrical mime gestures, explained that I was an escaped American pilot, shot down by the Luftwaffe, and that I was trying to get the boat out to go to Sweden.

The diggers exchanged glances and then one wearily stopped digging and rested his hands on the top of his spade, eyeing me with something approaching pity. He spoke rather good if heavily accented English.

'Yes, we would love to help you, but we are soldiers of the German army, and you are standing on our cabbages.'

And that is how I quickly found myself handcuffed in the back of a big black car full of silent Germans, heading for the town of Hydekrug. Once I got there I was a bit dismayed when, instead of turning off in the direction of the POW camp, they dropped me off at a building in the town that boasted a large swastika over the entrance. It was the headquarters of the local Gestapo.

─✳─13─✳─

Gestapo Revisited

At Hydekrug Gestapo branch office, I gave my name, rank and serial number, still using my stage name of Don Fair. They fingerprinted me and threw me in a cell for a few days. When they came to get me out, I was very impressed by the size of my escort. I had started out from France a few years earlier with just two bored-looking guards. Now I was in the company of an officer and six armed soldiers. They marched me to the train station and got on a train with me. This meant that I would not be returning to the Hydekrug camp, which would have been a short drive away.

I assumed that they were taking me back to Stalag Luft III. Somewhere in their tidy minds they seemed to recognize that if I was recaptured and somehow had escaped being shot, that was the right place to deposit me, with orders that I should not pass Go, and should not collect

£200. Instead, I should miss at least six Gos while they put me in the cooler and threw away the key.

The train rumbled on and on, and my guards did not seem to feel much like chatting. I looked out of the windows at the devastation caused by war – a world of refugees from the east and bomber raids from the west. Some parts looked like lunar landscapes. Ragged children watched the train roll by from shells of burnt buildings. This was not a war that let anyone escape from its horrors.

After what seemed like an endless journey, the steam train started to pull into a big city heavily pockmarked with bomb-damaged buildings. As it hissed to a stop in the station and I saw the station nameplate, my blood froze. I was in Berlin.

I told my guards that they seemed to have taken the wrong train. One smiled grimly and said that it was certainly the wrong train for me. They marched me through the teeming central station. On either side I was flanked by huge pictures of Hitler and Himmler, so vast that they reached from the floor to the rooftops.

A black Gestapo car was waiting and as I rode in the back, heavily guarded, I felt a terrible sinking fear of what was to come. All my efforts, all the digging and starving, had come to this – back in the hands of the Gestapo, this time in Berlin, the heart of Hitler's darkness. I had been lucky once, but doubted I would be so lucky this time.

The car took me to a big dark building that looked like

either a prison or a court house and turned out to be both. There, I was interrogated yet again. I did my best to put on a brave face. A Gestapo man with small, clever eyes distorted through thick little glasses peered at the slim file of one Don Fair, who it seemed had behaved himself up until the point that he had developed a Texan accent and started a breakout spree in sleepy Lithuania. My interrogator then lifted the phone and called for another file. An assistant came in with a much more weighty volume. This turned out to be the correspondence relating to one William Ash, a serial escapologist who had gone somewhat quiet lately.

It turned out that the meticulous Gestapo had checked my fingerprints after my capture in Lithuania, and it did not take them long to gain my confirmation that I was indeed the prisoner formerly known as 'Tex' Ash – a nickname I had never really liked.

The Gestapo man was inquisitive. 'What do you think will happen to you?' he enquired. I recalled that the last time one of his Gestapo colleagues had asked me that question in Paris, the correct answer was judged to be that I would be shot forthwith, but I persisted in the illusion that all was well. I suggested that I was a prisoner of war and should be sent back to Stalag Luft III, which was clearly where I belonged, since they kept taking me back there.

Unfortunately the Gestapo man disagreed. During my spree of breakouts a paranoid subsection of the Gestapo had been plotting my movements across France,

Germany, Poland and Lithuania. Then came their realization that I was operating under an assumed identity. There was only one possible conclusion. I leaned in, intrigued to find out what I had been up to for the last few years.

The interrogator revealed his theory in triumph. Bill Ash – or whatever my real name happened to be – was not an ordinary prisoner of war but a professionally trained escapologist. I had been parachuted in with a cover story about crashing in the Pas de Calais before I was picked up in civilian clothes in Paris. Then I had fomented more than half-a-dozen escapes in Germany, Poland and Lithuania, some of which had tied up thousands of German troops for weeks. Having assumed a false identity I had moved from country to country training other eager POWs in the black arts of escapology.

I listened transfixed by this brilliantly woven story, and it seemed almost a shame to disagree, but I felt I had to set him straight. 'That's a splendid theory,' I observed. 'But didn't it ever strike you that I might just be very good at escaping, but terrible at getting away?'

He confided that he had not, and would not, consider such a preposterous theory. I was to be put on trial, and once it was confirmed that I was a professional escapologist sent to train others, I would no longer be protected by the Geneva Convention as a prisoner of war and could be shot with impunity. Without even trying to beat further secrets out of me, they threw me into a dungeon cell to await my fate.

It is a strange thing about the Nazi psychology that as they obliterated innocent lives over an entire continent they always liked to do so under the rule of law. If they did not have a law that said they could torture or execute you, they would rustle one up and put it on the statute books, so that they could kill you in a tidy manner.

My trial fitted in perfectly with that odd way of thinking. I was not allowed to attend myself, but each day a small glum German officer would come and tell me what had been going on, virtually none of which I understood. Then he would ask me a few perfunctory questions to prepare for the next day's hearing. He told me he was my defending officer, and I asked him what my chances were like. He said he was extremely confident. Unfortunately he meant that he was confident that my trial would run its course and I would be shot as planned, thus closing an untidy footnote in Gestapo history.

The trial went on for some weeks, and if the Third Reich had been in better health, I would no doubt have been duly convicted and shot. But at the close of 1943, things were not looking good for the Axis cause. They had been defeated by the Russians at the great tank battle of Kursk, they had been kicked out of north Africa, and their erstwhile friends in Italy had surrendered as the Allies fought their way towards Rome. Closer to home the Allies had intensified daylight bombing of German cities; in one day alone that winter they dropped 1,800 tons of bombs on Berlin.

Among the many buildings destroyed were records

| 1 | 2 | 3 | 4 | 5 | 6 | 7 | 8 | 9 | 10 | 11 | 12 | 13 | 14 | 15 | 16 | 17 | 18 | 19 | 20 | 21 | 22 | 23 | 24 | 25 |

Personalkarte I: Personelle Angaben

Beschreibung der Erkennungsmarke

Nr. *457*

Kriegsgefangenen-Stammlager: **Stalag Luft 3**

Lager: *Stalag Luft 2*

Des Kriegsgefangenen

Name: *Ash*	Staatsangehörigkeit: *USA*
Vorname: *William Franklin*	Dienstgrad: *P.O. 9/Lt*
Geburtstag und -ort: *30.1.17 Dallas, Texas*	Truppenteil: *RCAF* Kom. usw.:
Religion: *prot.*	Zivilberuf: *journalist* Berufs-Gr.:
	Matrikel Nr. (Stammrolle des Heimatstaates) *J-4787*
Vorname des Vaters: *William*	Gefangennahme (Ort und Datum): *Paris 19.5.42*
Familienname der Mutter: *Poizerrieid*	Ob gesund, krank, verwundet eingeliefert: *ges.*

Lichtbild

Größe	Haarfarbe	Nähere Personalbeschreibung
1.73	*braun*	Besondere Kennzeichen:

Fingerabdruck:

Name und Anschrift der zu benachrichtigenden Person in der Heimat des Kriegsgefangenen

1. Vater: Mr. W.F. Ash, 3340 Oliver st. Dallas Texas, USA.

2. c/o Lloyds Bank p Post Office London S.W.

Beschriftung der Erkennungsmarke Nr.   Lager: Name:

Bemerkungen:

Personalbeschreibung

Figur:	*schlank*	
Größe:	*1.7*	Lt. Feldpost vom Er
Alter:	*26 J*	*15.3.42* *um* mit Wirkung vom
Gesichtsform:	*schmal*	*23.7.43*
Gesichtsfarbe:	*gesund frisch*	*in*
Schädelform:	*rund*	Lager bis 19
Augen:	*blau*	
Gebiß:	*gut*	
Haare:	*braun*	
Bart:	—	
Gewicht:	*72* kg	
Besondere Merkmale:		
Deutsche Sprachkenntnisse:		

The cover of my prisoner of war file from Stalag Luft III, the 'Great Escape' camp.

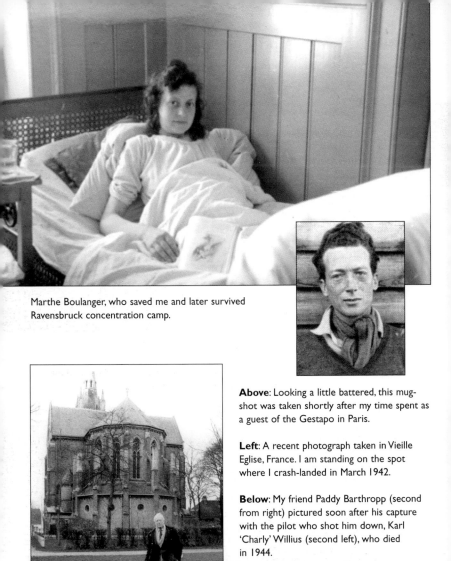

Marthe Boulanger, who saved me and later survived Ravensbruck concentration camp.

Above: Looking a little battered, this mug-shot was taken shortly after my time spent as a guest of the Gestapo in Paris.

Left: A recent photograph taken in Vieille Eglise, France. I am standing on the spot where I crash-landed in March 1942.

Below: My friend Paddy Barthropp (second from right) pictured soon after his capture with the pilot who shot him down, Karl 'Charly' Willius (second left), who died in 1944.

A guard post and exercise circuit, Stalag Luft III.

A typical escapers' tunnel. The width of most tunnels was dictated by the size of the bed boards that we used for shoring.

Above left: The entrance to Schubin camp in Poland. It was here that leading escape artists were sent late in 1942.

Above right: Eddy Asselin was my partner in the Schubin tunnel escape. The tunnel was named after him.

Left: 'Hetty' Hyde (left) and 'Wings' Day, senior escapologists at Schubin.

Below: John 'the Dodger' Dodge, captured while attempting to escape from the train on the way to Schubin.

Friends killed on the Great Escape: (from left) Ian Cross, Danny Kroll, Tom Kirby-Green, Roger Bushell.

Schubin comrades Jørgen Thalbitzer (left) and Jimmy Buckley (centre), killed on the tunnel escape. George Grimson (right) escaped Hydekrug but stayed locally to help others; missing, presumed shot.

Wire between the compounds at Stalag Luft III, which I was twice obliged to vault in daylight, once to change identity and once to swap escape plans with our neighbours.

Left: My friend the legless legend Douglas Bader, who was briefly incarcerated in Stalag Luft III before being sent to Colditz.

Above centre: Jimmy 'Dixie' Deans, who was elected leader of the NCO prisoners at Hydekrug.

Above: Fellow Luft III East compound Escape Committee member Joe Kayll.

Above: These specially trained guards ('ferrets') hunted for tunnels at Stalag Luft III.

Above: POWs at Schubin, 1942. Bill Stapleton and myself standing (with book under arm as usual), and Paddy Barthropp, front left. All three are still friends, sixty-five years later.

Left: The Sagan 'death march' took place in early 1945, as the Third Reich crumbled.

Stalag Luft III Commandant Von Lindeiner addressing his more unruly charges. I'm there, looking over his right shoulder at the camera.

Hilts, the 'cooler king' portrayed by Steve McQueen in the film *The Great Escape*, was an enjoyable but fictional character. Those of us who engaged in wartime escapes sadly had to do so without the aid of a motorcycle!

At a recent reunion with my friend and fellow escapee Paddy Barthropp.

offices and parts of the Nazi judiciary. Since I was locked in a dingy basement cell, I had little way of knowing if my RAF and USAAF friends had blown up any of my own records. All I could do in my dungeon was listen to the thuds and shudders as the buildings above me took yet another pounding from the Allied bombers. Fires raged in the streets, as they had in London a few years earlier. All I knew for sure was that the reports from my supposed defender became less and less regular, until one day he came in looking even more glum than usual. I feared the worst and asked him to give it to me straight.

'Terrible news,' he confided. 'The judges have decided that with things as they are your case must be postponed. Until we get a new trial date, you will be sent back to Stalag Luft III.'

I tried to look crestfallen at being robbed of the full majesty of Nazi justice and not tidily shot at the end of the proceedings.

'You do understand,' he tried to console me, 'that under present circumstances, your case could not have much priority?'

I told him I sympathized fully with their harrowing workload and urged them to take their time before getting back to little me.

Returning to Stalag Luft III by train, I continued to sprout ever more impressive detachments of guards as escorts. If only the war would go on long enough, I thought, I could probably solve the whole thing by having the entire German army shuttling with me from one camp to the next, leaving only a few Nazi boy scouts to defend France, Italy and the Russian front. If my spirits had plummeted as I fell back into the hands of the Gestapo, they soared like an eagle at the thought of getting back to Luft III. I knew it was a bit ironic to be so keen to get back to somewhere I had spent most of the last few years trying to get away from, but the threat of imminent death always gives an interesting perspective on less immediate problems.

I was greeted with a great homecoming. By early 1944 the camp had grown almost beyond belief, housing up to ten thousand prisoners, and my old east compound, where I was put back, had changed from being the main compound to being a relatively small one at the edge of a vast and sprawling complex. It and the other British camp, north compound, were heaving with shot-down humanity, and the American central and south compounds were full to bursting, mostly with fresh-faced bomber crews. While I was delighted to be back in east compound, I soon found out that this separated me from most of my old escaping comrades such as Paddy Barthropp, Tom Kirby-Green and Roger Bushell, all of whom had been moved to the bigger new north compound, where they were busy working on the tunnels Tom, Dick and Harry, that were to be used for the Great Escape.

But just as I was about to get used to being back in east compound, the authorities remembered that I had left camp by swapping identities and had made at least half-a-dozen escape attempts for their punishment to catch up with. I was thrown in the cooler.

Despite the isolation, it was good to be back. The Luft III regime, even in the cooler, was still more civilized than those I had experienced elsewhere, and considerably better than waiting to be shot in Berlin or flattened as collateral damage in the bombing raids there.

I was in the cooler for a long, long time.

Deprived of conversation, company and anything to read, I found that I had time to think. Never before or since have I had such a sustained period to think about myself, the world and the actions of those around me. I had seen heroism and treachery, selfless generosity and animal selfishness. The riot of experiences and the emotions they inspired kindled in me a lifelong interest in philosophy and politics, which are both the activities of tiny people in a world several sizes too big for them, struggling to make sense of it all. Politically, I came to conclusions that were to stay with me all my life, about the value of real democracy, the importance of people working together to improve life for everyone, and the necessity to stand up to bullies, exploiters or dictators as firmly as possible, and as early as possible.

The Germans used Russian pilot prisoners around the cooler for jobs like cleaning the latrines. I could occasionally snatch a conversation with them if I was allowed out for exercise, and I became friendly with one of them called Artum.

Artum and I swapped stories from earlier in the war.

He told me about possibly the most amazing escape from death in the entire conflict. A pilot friend of his was hit at thirty thousand feet over the eastern front and as his plane was engulfed in flames he baled out. He pulled frantically at the rip cord of his parachute, but nothing happened and it failed to open. He plummeted for what seemed like an eternity towards certain death, yet landed, in the depths of a Russian winter, on the side of a mountain in a huge drift of powdery snow perhaps a dozen feet deep. He crashed into the snow, making an impressive imprint, and descended a few yards as a giant human snowball, but the snow broke his fall without killing him. When he had finally stopped rolling, he clambered out of the drift with nothing more than severe bruising and was able to rejoin his unit.

The Germans treated Artum and his fellow Russians terribly and gave them the worst jobs and the worst rations. If they attempted an escape, they were shot out of hand. One day Artum and I were cleaning out latrines together – I think I was being punished for some minor infraction. A few months earlier the German Sixth army had been surrounded and destroyed at Stalingrad, blunting the Axis offensive in the east. Now the camp loudspeaker blared out even better news – Hitler's invincible Panzer army had been stopped quite literally in its tracks at the great Battle of Kursk. The tide really had turned. Artum translated for me and we both dropped our latrine cleaning mops and started dancing a jig of triumph, crowing 'Ruskis komen' to the world. Normally this activity would have got Artum shot and prolonged my spell in the cooler at least, but the guards just stood silently staring at us, so shocked were they by the news and the inevitable implication that would reach its conclusion in a Berlin bunker some two years later.

The Nazi treatment of their Russian prisoners is possibly the least known of all the atrocities of the war. Because I got to know Artum, I was able to get a sense of the enormity of these crimes. He was a big, blond Slav with a warm personality and the ability to smile and feel joy at any small victory, even in the heart of darkness into which we had fallen. But there were many Artums. Reliable estimates put the number of Russians taken prisoner in the course of the war at more than five million. Of these, more than three million are thought to have died in Nazi captivity – a death count that ranks alongside the unimaginable destruction of the Jews and Gypsies, but which attracted far less investigation or outrage in the west after the war, as the Cold War began almost immediately and our Allies were suddenly supposed to be our enemies. Two million of them died in prisoner-of-war or concentration camps, while another million died in unspecified German custody, many *en route* from their place of capture to the camps.

The death toll from starvation among Russian prisoners in the first years of the German offensive was greatly accelerated by the inhuman conditions suffered by the Russians in the camps. While we westerners were kept in cold, flea-infested huts, hundreds of thousands of

Russian prisoners were simply shoved into huge open barbed-wire corrals where they lived and died, exposed to the elements twenty-four hours a day. In the winter time when temperatures dropped far below zero they huddled together in the mud and ice. They died by the thousands from typhus.

While RAF officers were treated for most of the time according to the Geneva Convention, the Russians were dealt with as '*Untermenschen*' or subhumans throughout the war. Their rations were about a quarter of what we got, excluding the Red Cross parcels, which they did not get but which actually sustained us westerners far more than the official ration. The daily German diet for us was based on the minimum amount of nutrition needed to keep a person alive and the Nazis consciously fed the Russians on a quarter of this until they starved to death or succumbed to the diseases that follow starvation.

Back in Schubin camp, there had been a Russian compound beside ours. When we walked on circuits we could see the Russian prisoners, standing like skeletons, clothed in grey rags that had once been uniforms. We gave some of our rations to them via the guards, but they fed only those who worked. Those who were too sick or starved to work got even less. When a Russian prisoner died in one of the big overcrowded huts in which they were kept like animals, the others would keep his body, pretending he was still sick in order to keep getting his bread ration. The record for keeping a body was rumoured to be three weeks.

There were two distinct periods to the Nazi genocide of Russian prisoners. The first and worst came in the aftermath to Operation Barbarossa in 1941, in which Hitler's blitzkrieg swept across Russia, encircling vast numbers of Russian troops. Apologists for the death toll claim that their captors were overwhelmed by their own success and unable to cope with the volume of prisoners, but the Nazis' own documentation proves that they knew they were systematically starving their prisoners to death. More than two million Russian prisoners of war died in enemy hands in just eight months in 1941–2.

In the second period that followed, most of the Russian prisoners were used as forced labour. Thousands died as slaves in German mines and factories, but at least the death rate slowed down. At Hydekrug I had talked to British soldiers who had worked in some of the same mines. If a roof collapsed on a side seam leaving Russian prisoners trapped at the coal face, the guards would just seal it off, burying them alive rather than go to the time and expense of digging them out.

By the end of the war the Russian people had lost some 20 million of their number and after the remarkable defence of Stalingrad, the Wehrmacht knew that their days in the east were numbered. Their rout at Kursk marked the beginning of the end, and the guards knew it. They shuddered, knowing that when the Russians arrived on German soil the actions of their countrymen in Russia and in the camps would be neither forgiven nor forgotten.

When I emerged from my long spell in the cooler, the

other prisoners made a great fuss of me, and I discovered that in the year I had been away from Luft III, my requests to a Swiss organization which supplied books to prisoners had achieved remarkable results. It seemed that it supplied only what it regarded as 'good books' such as the classics and while I regretted the lack of cowboy novels, I was greeted by a veritable library that had arrived over the months. There were books by Descartes, Spinoza and Leibnitz, Pascal's *Pensées* and the complete works of Plato in French. Apparently the organization had a vast store of such books, but I was just about the only prisoner in the western hemisphere who had expressed any interest.

I was quietly glad of the chance to sit still and read. While I still burned to get out, I knew that the next time I fell into Gestapo hands would undoubtedly be my last, and after so much solitary confinement on iron rations, I was ready for a bit of a rest. I was very thin and had been living on my nerves for more than three years. To fill the time I would otherwise have spent escaping, I decided to write a novel. In order to gather enough paper on which to write, I used to save my chocolate ration and trade it for notebooks.

I don't remember much about the novel now, other than the slightly pretentious title *Happy in Ulabrae*, which was from one of Horace's *Odes* – no doubt another gift from my genteel new literary friends in Switzerland. Like the ode, it was about being content even when you have nothing very much to be content about. I worked on

it for some months, but missed the life of a serial escapologist. Finally, it was finished, a small neat pile of
notebooks which I kept in my locker beside my bunk.

I went out for a walk to celebrate, and as I passed close
to the main gates of the camp I saw a parked truck, waiting to go out with bits of broken engineering equipment
that were being replaced. A guard had just searched the
truck and was walking away with his back to me. For a
split second I hesitated. I felt I still had plenty of bad
novels in me, and was enjoying the relative peace and
stability of being back in Luft III, surrounded by familiar
faces. But there is something very deeply ingrained in me
that cannot resist a good escape. Perhaps a psychoanalyst
could some day test me for a previously unknown dis-
order called Houdini Syndrome.

Like someone who cannot resist peeking at the last
page of a book to see how it turns out, I jumped into the
back of the truck and it motored off.

I got all the way to the next set of gates, crouched in
the back, before being discovered. This was possibly my
shortest and most badly planned escape of them all. I
always envied the characters who spent years learning
fluent German, preparing immaculate forged papers,
Ausweis and first-class railway tickets, to enable them to
pretend to be Danish butter salesmen on the way home
from a successful business trip. My approach, on the
other hand, was more fundamental: get on the other side
of the wire and run like hell. As I was frogmarched back
to my barracks in order to pick up a few basics on my

way to the cooler, I pondered that the reality was that most of the would-be Danish butter salesmen also got caught, and that at least my style of escaping was based on quantity if not always quality.

While I collected my things from my room, the *Abwehr* or security head escorting me glanced around and his eye fell on the small stack of notebooks in my locker. He started to look at them suspiciously and I did my best to tell him that it was a story about people who lived a very long time ago, and any resemblance to the current world war or anyone in it was purely co-incidental. He lifted the first notebook and started to tear it very carefully into tiny pieces; then he did the same to the next and the next. By the time he had shredded the last one, there was an impressive pile of bits of paper beside his shiny jackboots. He ordered one of the guards to sweep it up and burn it, just in case some future generation should decide to painstakingly reconstruct my lost masterpiece from ten thousand tiny pieces.

As I lay alone in my cooler cell, I decided that rather than start another novel, perhaps I should get back to some more serious escaping. At least my work there seemed to be appreciated by both my fellow prisoners, and – admittedly in a more abstract way – by the Gestapo.

One of the highlights of that trip to the cooler was the sound of the sirens that announced the guards' realization that the largest prison breakout in the history of the war had just got under way in the nearby north compound. After nearly a year of planning and months of tunnelling, my old colleagues over there were up and off in all directions. The sirens wailed, as if bemoaning that so many had gone. The Great Escape had begun.

✳️ 14 ✳️

The Scent of Freedom

When I emerged from the cooler some weeks later in April 1944, I was terribly thin, but once again raring to go: full of plans involving tunnels, trucks, wire cutters, and employing cross-country escape tactics. As I attended my first *Appell* after my release, it felt strange to be in the middle of so many people again, after the seclusion of the cooler.

As we stood in neat rows, an ashen-faced Luftwaffe officer read out a list. Fifty of the air crew who had got out during the Great Escape from the neighbouring north compound had been 'shot while resisting arrest'. All fifty were dead and none wounded. A great gasp went up from all the men on *Appell*. Even by the standards of this dirty and vicious war, this was a brutal deed. Everyone knew that the escapers had been recaptured and then executed by the Gestapo. As the officer read out the names of the fifty, it read like a roll call of my old friends and comrades: Roger Bushell, Tom Kirby-Green, Ian Cross, Danny Krol. Others were still unaccounted for, including Wings Day and John Dodge.

My memory of the rest of that parade is hazy. I remember someone staggering forward out of the lines and guards' guns being raised, as if they feared a full-scale riot, but the truth is we were too stunned to even react. The guards too were appalled at the actions of the Gestapo. The senior German officer, looking ashamed, dismissed the parade. For a while we just stood there, frozen in shock, but gradually people drifted away. I remember being left on my own in the vastness of the parade area, feeling small and alone.

Yet that was exactly the feeling that my friends had set out to challenge. They knew the risks but were determined to act together. The Great Escape was one of the biggest, boldest and most brilliantly organized collective escape ventures of the war. Discussions about it had started before we left for Schubin. Jimmy Buckley had recognized Bushell's organizational genius and appointed him as his number two. We talked about the strategy of using mass escape to tie up vast amounts of enemy time and resources – making escape a weapon of war. We knew that only with a big, bold tunnel, supported by hundreds of people making civilian outfits and passes would we be able to make such a plan succeed. Then a great many of us, including Buckley, had been sent to Schubin, where we tried to put those plans into operation through the Asselin tunnel escape on which Buckley died, while those who stayed in Luft III, including Bushell, aimed to build another tunnel to be reckoned with.

It was Bushell's combination of implacable enmity to the Nazis and his great leadership skills that resulted in the unique plan behind the Great Escape. His aim was to lead an escape with 250 fully equipped escapees, fully trained and heading in every direction. They would tie the enemy in knots and make such a splash that their actions would be in every newspaper, both in Germany and at home. Instead of being passive victims, waiting for the war to end, the prisoners would take the war to the enemy in the heart of their homeland.

Roger Bushell's hatred for the Nazis had been sealed even before he reached Stalag Luft III when they executed an entire Czech family who had been hiding him while he was in Prague during a previous escape, following which he himself was tortured by the Gestapo. He had a scar beside one eye from a pre-war skiing accident and when he turned his tough face on any fellow prisoner, demanding the impossible in the interests of the escape, there never seemed any realistic response other than making it happen. He was one of the greatest natural leaders I ever met. Originally from South Africa, Roger had little time for any distinction between the more civilized Luftwaffe and the degenerate Gestapo. As far as he was concerned they were all 'the enemy' and his weapon was the tunnel.

As soon as he and some of the others were moved to the newly opened north compound, he ordered three tunnels to be started – Tom, Dick and Harry. They were to be the longest, most ambitious and best engineered of the war, thanks to a Canadian tunnel engineer, Wally Floody, whom I never met but who by all accounts was a remarkably hard-working and inventive individual. The entrances to two of the tunnels went straight through the concrete foundations below two huts and were concealed beneath wood-burning stoves. Digging in the soft sand of Sagan proved dangerous, and a great deal of shoring was needed. More than 4,000 bed boards were donated or requisitioned for this, leaving most of the compound sleeping on thin air and string.

The longer the tunnels got, the more people in the compound were required, not just for security and stooging operations, but to manufacture enough clothes and passes for a small army of escapees.

When Tom Kirby-Green was promoted within the Great Escape organization to the post of security officer, he worked alongside a remarkable American called George Harsh, who had the dubious distinction of having spent twelve years on a Georgia chain gang for murder before becoming a rear gunner in a bomber and ending up in a German POW camp. Together the two of them devised a security system that allowed the three vast tunnels to be dug under the very noses of the ferrets, with hundreds of tons of tunnel dirt being disposed of and almost daily searches being foiled for more than six months as tunnelling, tailoring, forging and escape catering continued apace on a grand scale.

Tom was the opposite of Roger in many ways, but just as brave and just as intelligent. He was a tall, suave and very well-educated young man who shared my love of books and also my allergy to bullies. Some people found him a bit eccentric, which may explain why we got on so well. We talked about politics and people around the world, from Africa to Latin America. In many ways he was a Bohemian, quite ahead of his time. He had been born of a colonial family in Malawi and had attempted to join up to fight the fascists in the Spanish Civil War, but had ended up fighting them in a world war instead. He became one of the youngest squadron leaders in RAF Bomber Command, at the ripe old age of twenty-three.

Anyone who thought of Kirby-Green as just a colourful character who brightened our drab lives with a love of salsa music and padded around in carpet slippers and a kaftan did not know much about his record either before or after being shot down. In the early days of the bomber war, anyone who managed more than ten raids was regarded as a rarity. Tom was shot down in October 1941 on his thirty-seventh raid. The Nazis regarded him as such a prize that his capture was announced on German propaganda radio by their chief announcer, Lord Haw-Haw, who was later hanged as a collaborator. As an escape artist, Tom was equally valuable. He also used his knowledge of Spain to help those who wanted to try reaching there or Gibraltar on their escapes.

Squadron Leader Ian Cross, or Crossie, was in charge of one of the two soil dispersal teams. Crossie had controlled a team of eighty men, including those known as 'penguins' who had clever cloth bags full of tunnel dirt hidden in their trousers with strings in their pockets that allowed them to release the soil to flood out around their ankles as they walked around the camp perimeter each day. To give just a glimpse of Crossie's achievement in ensuring that the tunnel soil was dispersed under the very noses of the guards without ever arousing suspicion, every 20 cubic feet the tunnels produced a ton of sand which had to disappear. The tunnelling usually progressed at the rate of about 3 feet a day and the most dirt that could be easily concealed by any one prisoner was 16 pounds. That meant that in the build-up to the Great Escape 18,000 individual journeys to get rid of sand went undetected. The record for the dispersal team run by Crossie and another Great Escaper called Jimmy James was getting rid of 3,600 pounds of sand in one hour.

One tunnel, Dick, was shut when the forest it was meant to surface in became a treeless area earmarked for yet another compound, but the other two pressed on. The abandoned tunnel was used as a handy hole to dispose of sand from the other two. The second tunnel, Tom, was almost at the wire in summer 1943, when its entrance was discovered by a keen-eyed ferret. The escapees turned all their energy to their one remaining hope, tunnel Harry. Eventually Harry stretched for 336 feet.

On the night of 24 March 1944, my friends made their

break for it. Because of an error in surveying, the tunnel came up short in the open and not far from a watchtower. Each escaper had to make it across the open ground to the cover of trees. Remarkably, some seventy-six out of more than 200 would-be escapers made it out before someone mistook a 'stay put' tug on a string signal cord set up between the tunnel and the trees for a 'go ahead' one. A prisoner popped up and was immediately spotted. Firing started, the sirens wailed, and the men inside the tunnel hastily tried to reverse.

So successful was this massive blitz out that a state of national alert was declared throughout the country and thousands of troops and home guard were tied up searching for them at a time when Germany needed every man it could get to shore up their failing, flailing war machine.

As I took in the news that so many had been murdered, my only relief came from learning that my friend Paddy Barthropp was safe – he had not yet emerged from the tunnel when the alarm was sounded and had managed to make it back to the hut. I also found out later that Wings Day and John Dodge managed to survive the Gestapo massacre but spent the rest of the war in Saxenhausen concentration camp.

Three of the seventy-four got all the way back to England. The fifty who were murdered were shot on the direct orders of Hitler as a warning to the rest of us. The remainder were either returned to the camp or sent to other prisons. Now, instead of fifty of those brave men digging through the unyielding earth, the soil of Germany was covering them for ever.

Yet I just could not think of Crossie and the others as dead. I pictured Crossie smiling as he was marched off to the cooler earlier in the war, in an incident that seemed to come from another lifetime. He had hidden in a truck full of pine-tree branches that was being driven out of the camp. A guard must have spotted him getting in and the truck was deliberately driven at high speed over the roughest possible ground for a long time, before one of the German officers stopped it and asked politely for Herr Cross to come out, assuring him that the walk to the cooler was much less bumpy.

One of the saddest things about the war was the loss of the remarkable contribution some of the men who died might have made had they got home. While the men in prison covered every shade of political opinion, there seemed to be an interesting connection between those of us who shared a fanatical desire to escape and a desire for a better world in the future than the one we had left behind. At one stage, alongside an international debating society, someone had set up a mock 'Parliament' to discuss the future after the war. Roger Bushell appointed himself Deputy Prime Minister of the Labour Party and announced the immediate nationalization of all major industries, to be operated for the public good rather than profit. Tom Kirby-Green proposed that there should be a new attitude to Britain's colonies, which recognized the rights of the black majority rather than treating them as servants or subjects. If these two had survived, the world would have been a more interesting place.

The aftermath of the Great Escape was serious for the Luftwaffe as well as for us. Commandant Von Lindeiner was relieved of duty and arrested, ironically becoming a prisoner himself, but escaping a firing squad. He had always tried to run the camp according to the principles of the Geneva Convention, and he generally had our respect, if rarely our obedience.

Things were to change after that. The Great Escape was recognized by the Gestapo as their chance to grab all prisoners including the pilots. Soon all the camps, including Stalag Luft III, came under Gestapo and SS jurisdiction, headed by Heinrich Himmler. Leaflets were printed and posted saying bluntly that anyone caught planning an escape or on one would be shot.

While our day-to-day existence within the camps did not change much with the change of administration, and the guards remained the same, there was no doubt that the repercussions if we were caught escaping would be very different.

Perhaps it was good that we did not know too much. SS General Berger, who was in direct charge of all POWs, claimed later that he was bawled out by Hitler at the Fuhrer's Wolf's Lair stronghold for not shooting more of us and for not destroying all Red Cross parcels. It is certain that Hitler and Goebbels toyed with the idea of shooting one of us for each civilian killed in the bombing of German cities, but were dissuaded by representatives of the army and navy.

Back in east compound, oblivious of such grand schemes, Aidan Crawley, Joe Kayll and I, along with one or two others, made up the escape committee. Joe was a quiet, gentle man of remarkable courage – one of the pioneers and only practitioners of the technique of chopping up an enemy plane with your propeller when out of ammo. He brought down a German bomber that way before he ended up in the bag. He was quite a fighter pilot, having downed nine enemy aircraft, and he won the Distinguished Service Order before the Battle of Britain had even started.

On his last sortie in June 1941 he had been flying a Hurricane as wing man for the ebullient Harry Broadhurst, who was in charge at Hornchurch. They ran into a high-level formation of more than twenty enemy aircraft, which started to peel off and dive down in an attempt to get behind the raiders and attack them from out of the sun. Every few minutes the pair had to turn back in to face an attack head on, firing short bursts in reply to save ammunition. This happened five or six times. Broady managed to finally get away over the Channel at sea level. Joe was not so lucky. As had happened to me in a Spitfire about a year later, Joe ended up with an engine full of holes, which he switched off to avoid fire. He hoped to glide as far across the Channel as possible before ditching, to increase his chances of being picked up by a British boat, but he was losing altitude so rapidly that he had to turn back and force-land in France, where he started a new career as a prisoner of war and a quiet but ardent escape artist.

Joe's record within the camps was equally impressive. He had been one of the organizers of the remarkable Wooden Horse escape at Luft III, in which three prisoners dug a blitz tunnel from under a wooden gymnastics horse while others, including my good friend Bill Stapleton, practised vaulting over it for hours on end. The Wooden Horse escapers made a home run, all the way to London, while Joe stayed to organize further escapes.

But there were not too many like Joe at this later stage in the war. The new threat of death upon capture and the shock waves from the murder of our fifty comrades had made escaping an even less attractive option for most prisoners. Then came news that was to make it definitely a minority pursuit.

In order to keep things going, we had been considering making a joint escape attempt with Americans in the compound next to us, and someone was needed to go and talk to them. I was chosen for this mission for several reasons. First, I had succeeded in the double-hurdle dash over the barbed-wire fences once before when I had swapped identity with Don Fair. An even more compelling reason for my new trip in the eyes of my colleagues was that I 'spoke American'. Most compelling of all was that I was the only one mad enough to want to go.

Once again, both compounds arranged distractions

for the machine gunners in the nearest towers, and I vaulted the fences in broad daylight, greeting another blurry figure who was hurtling in the opposite direction. He turned out to be the USAAF colonel with whom I was swapping places for a day or two, but there was not much time to salute.

While thoughts of escaping also appealed only to a minority in the American compound, the fact that many of the Americans had been 'in the bag' for a shorter period of time seemed to leave some of them at least with a continued, gutsy willingness to risk escape. The atmosphere in the American compound was also more boisterous, from horseplay to goon-baiting. They had annoyed some of my more stuffy English friends in the days before we were split up into different nationalities, but personally I found the Americans' energy very refreshing. My time with the Americans was made even more enjoyable by a surprise reunion with old friends from my schooldays in the Lone Star state. They even had good Texas names, such as Buck Wilson and Bulldog Macmillan. I enjoyed my strange reunion with these good-natured rumbustious guys in a place none of us ever thought we would end up.

When my friends went back to their nearby hut for the night, I stayed with some of the escape committee to go over plans. Later, as I dozed off in a strange bed, I heard an incredible row and racket coming from the nearby hut. It sounded like a fully fledged battle, but as the guards investigated, everything went quiet again.

Next morning, as I nervously prepared to do a repeat reverse performance of my high-wire act to get back to my own compound, I managed to snatch a few words with one of my pals from the hut next door. I asked him about the ruckus. He smiled sadly and told me it was just an argument about the war. I was incredulous. Here we all were, volunteers risking our lives in a battle between good and evil, all prisoners of that same enemy, and yet they were still arguing about the war. What the hell was there left to argue about? As I moved into position for my 100-yard dash over the death wire to the fence, my American friend called after me: 'Not *this* war. The Civil War!'

I was still smiling about this in an attempt to quell my terror when I stepped over the warning wire, climbed over the first fence, nodded at the American colonel hurtling in the opposite direction, then clambered back over our compound's barbed wire, across the danger zone and hopped the final warning wire to breathe a long sigh of relief as I strolled briskly away.

From a practical point of view our swap and intelligence gathering resulted in some general plans for joint action, but these were inconveniently overtaken by minor events in the outside world, such as the D-Day landings.

We had one or two wireless sets hidden about the camp, guarded like gold dust and moved when in danger. One day, one of the wireless operators came bursting out of whatever hut one of the sets was hidden in, whooping in delight, leaving others inside it to hastily hide the treasure. The D-Day landings in Normandy had started. By the look on some of the guards' faces, they knew that the end was fast approaching.

Word spread through the camp like wildfire, and the evil home-made hooch concocted from raisins saved from Red Cross parcels and the even more lethal brews distilled from potato peelings came out of hiding.

Even though we were by then in different compounds, I knew that my pal Paddy would be celebrating in style. He was an expert bootlegger and the skills of creating illicit alcohol and escaping had much in common. Ingenious methods had to be devised, materials prepared and ways found to stop the constant security searches from allowing the brews to fall into enemy mouths. Many of the stills were made from Klim milk tins, soldered together in much the same way as those made into air-pipes in the tunnels, but such stills were unwieldy and hard to hide. Pondering the magic combination of yeast, water and heat while shaving one morning, Paddy happened to glance up at the feeble 25-watt light bulb above him. In a slightly dangerous stroke of genius, he filled the casing with water, added the fermenting in-gredients, reassembled it all and switched on. From then on, he had a ready supply of alcohol and the satisfaction of knowing that the electricity providing the heat was being supplied unwittingly by his captors. But as the best television programmes say, don't try this one at home.

After D-Day, and for the first time since we had been

captured, we knew that sooner or later we would be going home. Escape attempts continued very occasionally after that, but it was recognized that the value of running around Germany tying up troops was weakened by the fact that virtually every able-bodied German had been shipped to one or other of the fronts. In this new situation, escapers were more likely to get knifed by a Nazi boy scout with a *jugend dirk* than to be chased by a truckload of soldiers. The scales of reason were weighing more and more heavily in favour of staying put.

Luckily, life is not always made up of safe, rational decisions. Those of us who thought that the only possible response to the Nazi threat of execution on capture was to make our escapes more daring and more successful continued to plot and plan. Speaking for myself, I had come into this war on my own terms and was very reluctant to sit meekly waiting for someone to tell me I had permission to leave it.

Even among the small number of hard-case escapologists, doubts were setting in, and we were being whittled away, losing would-be escapers as they tiptoed away one at a time, like jurors in a prison version of *Twelve Angry Men*, changing their verdict at the last minute. It was around this time that two of our dwindling number dug a blitz tunnel beside our perimeter fence. But the two men who had bravely done the dangerous work of digging the new tunnel were now starting to question the wisdom of using it themselves. This was a tunnel in need of escapees.

Perhaps it was my frugal upbringing in Depression-hit Texas coming out again, but I have never liked to see anything go to waste, be it inedible Klipfish or a perfectly good tunnel. A spectacularly mad but very brave New Zealander was also very keen and my fellow escape committee veteran Aidan Crawley was willing to give it a go. This was particularly plucky of Aidan, since he was determined by then to become a Member of Parliament when he got home, but the most likely outcome of this particular mission would be that he would have to be elected posthumously.

As we prepared to break out that night, some of the more timid prisoners became very indignant. They did not much mind us risking our own lives, but they were convinced that there would be reprisals on those still in the camp. I pointed out that if the brave ordinary French people who had risked their lives to help me and so many others had thought that way, they would all have collaborated meekly in return for a quiet life full of threats and hostages. Instead they chose to resist. We were soldiers, so there was even more reason for us to do so.

Undoubtedly there was truth on both sides of the argument. With the tactical objective of slowing down the enemy war machine diminished, at some point escaping became less a tactic and more a simple statement of defiance – an unwillingness to crawl in the face of oppression. The nervous prisoners took their worries to the commanding officer and he gently but firmly ordered us not to go. The mad New Zealander was outraged. Aidan Crawley was disappointed, and I pretended to be the same while breathing a large sigh of relief.

With nothing much left to do but wait for the Russians to reach us from the east, the British and Americans to reach us from the west, or the Gestapo to shoot us all if their negotiations did not work out, we settled down to sit it out. I could not be too angry at the more timid prisoners. Not only had all of them gone through some terrible, traumatic crash or parachute experience just to buy their tickets into Stalag Luft III, but after a few years the wire walls could seem strangely comforting in a sea of death and destruction, as well as suffocating and oppressive.

The lack of escapes left more time to think and talk, and perhaps the least discussed but most significant part of life inside the prisoner-of-war camps was that they were centres of learning and political debate to rival the best universities. Of course, they did have the drawback that if you broke the rules you were more likely to be sent to solitary than given another essay to write.

For many prisoners, this was the first and only chance in their lives not only to get more of an education but also to think about what sort of world they wanted after the war. Every camp I had been in had some sort of educational function, perhaps none more so than the NCOs' camp in Hydekrug. This may have been because there was a smaller percentage of graduates there and because the NCOs were mainly civilians who were keen to return to regular life outside the services as soon as possible. For whatever reason, the Hydekrug camp set up what was called the Barbed Wire University.

A guy called Eddie Alderton, who went on to become a professor at an American university, joined up with a group of men who had been lecturers before the war and used Eddie's experience of starting educational courses at Luft III to do the same at Hydekrug. These were not isolated teach-ins. At its height, the 'university' boasted 54 lecturers covering some 40 subjects with 1,000 regular students. They even had term times and faculties covering arts, science, medicine and law. Subjects studied, often with one eye to the future after the war, ranged from hotel management to local government.

When I wasn't trying to escape, I read or wrote, and the few pictures of myself as a prisoner I managed to keep all seem to show me with a hefty book tucked under my arm, usually one of the classics since cowboy novels were in short supply. Despite this and my love of education, I never really got anywhere with the courses. The few I started on tended to be interrupted by short periods of escape and then by long periods in the cooler. Still, escape was an excellent excuse for not doing homework.

Sometimes I wondered if much of the educational activity was a distraction from escaping, and there were certainly some prisoners who regarded escapes and the clampdowns that inevitably followed them as outrageous intrusions into their studying time, but most kriegies had a more balanced attitude. Active escaping was something of a minority pursuit, so the majority of prisoners had to find something else to do with their time. Some found it in sports, others in a remarkably well-developed theatrical community, who wrote and produced plays every few weeks in virtually every camp. It is true that the leading 'ladies' usually had five o'clock shadows, but apart from that, the performances were often remarkably good and served to keep up morale.

In the army prisoner-of-war non-officer camps, the men did not have this choice. They were forced to work for the German war effort in factories and mines, often in terrible conditions. But the Geneva Convention ensured that officer prisoners were not required to work. Consequently a vast sea of empty time loomed before every prisoner in our camps. These men could choose to lie on their bunks, moaning about their fate – and some did just that – or they could choose to do something about their lives. That choice often boiled down to doing something about it in the short term, which meant escaping, or possibly the cooler or an early grave, or planning something more long-term which usually involved thinking about or studying for the day when the war would be over.

All this study, debate and the occasional friction between restless escapers and those who wanted a quiet life contributed to some of the best political discussions I've ever heard. As prisoners, when not tunnelling or scrounging food, we had several years to ponder what sort of future we wanted, and what we were unwilling to return to. Most of our prison-camp debates centred on what sort of world we wanted to build after the war. We talked about what life had been like before the war, about mass unemployment and children going to bed hungry. We talked about democracy and how we could avoid being back in another war in twenty or sixty years' time that a future generation might have to fight. We argued the various merits of socialism and social democracy, and above all we planned for a better future.

The same sort of debates had been going on during the war back in Britain. Before I was shot down I had visited some aircraft factories on a morale-boosting mission with other pilots, and after the usual platitudes – for instance if it was a factory making propellers we were expected to tell the workers just how much better our planes flew if they had propellers – we would often talk about the future. This was no vague notion about 'a land fit for heroes' but a specific determination that if we were fighting and risking our lives, either at the front or on the equally dangerous home front, we were going to have a say in what followed.

This may help some people understand why Churchill, the greatest of all wartime leaders, whom we all respected as such, was rather promptly and soundly defeated at the ballot box immediately after the war, booted out of power and replaced with a more socially progressive government. During the war a major economic report back in Britain had proposed a new way forward. It was called the Beveridge Report and it basically outlined a strategy for full employment, the creation of a universal health service and publicly funded education as a right and not a privilege. In comparison to the pre-war years of stagnation, depression and forelock-tugging, it was a breath of fresh air and hugely popular with the public in Britain as well as with many of us prisoners of war.

While the war raged, Churchill effectively led a wartime coalition government of the mainstream parties, Labour, Conservative and Liberal, which agreed to shelve all such aspirational notions as the Beveridge Report until after the fighting was over. But the people continued their debate and our new generation who were risking their lives to stop an even worse world from becoming reality were not about to sit back and watch a better world put on the back burner until we were needed as cannon fodder for some other future war.

Looking at a copy of one of the prison-camp newspapers, the *Daily Recco*, produced by POWs first at Luft III, then at Hydekrug in the NCOs' camp, it is easy to see how much a part of this movement for progress some of us felt. The paper was a handwritten, one-page newssheet, produced under the toughest of conditions by a bunch of prisoners. It was eagerly awaited each day by a captive population starved of news apart from that gained by furtive listening to the BBC via a secret radio. The *Daily Recco* of Wednesday 8 March 1944 – 'head office Hut B9, branch office hut A3' – has a typical mix of news. One story reports that German radio claimed that 140 Allied planes were downed in bombing raids over Berlin; another story reports that the influx of new USAAF prisoners were settling in and getting used to the strange way the locals spoke. But one article sticks out. Under the biggest headline of the day is an article entitled 'The People's Government – it depends on you'. It goes on to say that the Beveridge Report and its call for economic and social security for everyone is too important to be shelved or denigrated by party political squabbles. The article exhorts kriegies to take part in the debate and to help change things when they get home. It ends 'It isn't a question of politics – a government of a country is elected to carry out the wishes of the people – make that wish felt, then perhaps we may get closer to government of the people, by the people, for the people.'

Since the circulation of the *Daily Recco* was somewhat limited by our imprisonment and the fact that only one copy was made each day, it is interesting to note that millions of other people were coming to the same conclusions at home – both those in uniform and civilians. In December 1944 Colonel McNamara, a Member of Parliament for the Conservative party, was killed in action. Normally the other parties in a coalition government would automatically have withdrawn in favour of a member of the same party, and indeed the main ones all did, including the Labour and Liberal parties. But so frustrated by the lack of movement on a post-war plan of social progress were some people that they found a voice through a small and previously unheard-of bunch called the Common Wealth party, whose one big idea was the immediate implementation of the Beveridge Report in full. Their candidate was an independent-minded RAF wing commander called Millington. The official candidate, a Conservative with the backing of the Labour and Liberal parties, was confident of seeing off the upstart. When the votes were counted the Common Wealth candidate romped home by 24,000 votes to 18,000, overturning a 6,000 Conservative majority from the previous election in 1935.

All the mainstream parties suddenly started paying a little more attention to the Beveridge Report and the idea that people wanted a better future. The report became the platform on which the Labour party was swept to power in a landslide result immediately after the war, including my friend and fellow escape artist Aidan Crawley, who was elected only months after getting back to Britain.

Somewhere along the line the politics of escaping and aspirations for a better world merged in my mind. For those of us who had known that tremendous feeling of being outside the wire, or who had at least tried to do so, the debate was about more than immediate pros and cons. Running for your life but knowing that it was your own decision to be there is the most liberating experience imaginable. Every step on the outside was a way of telling the world that freedom was the most important thing in the world, not just as some abstract notion, but personally, collectively, and even at risk of life itself.

The *Daily Recco* can claim a noble place in literature and politics, even if there was normally only one hand-written copy pinned up for all to see, but it is probably just as well that such a significant article did not appear on 2 April 1943. A notice for that day reads 'The Daily Recco – due to the bad weather conditions yesterday, Issue No. 40 was blown over the wire.'

✣ 15 ✣

The Death March

That winter of 1944–5 was one of the coldest in living memory. All but the most fanatical Nazis knew that the game was up, but none of them knew how to extricate themselves from the carnage they had helped to create. Like a Greek tragedy lumbering towards its inevitable conclusion, the war dragged on.

Some of the senior Nazis, including Goering and Himmler, still harboured hopes that a separate peace with Britain and America might yet be brokered, with a handy bargaining chip of 10,000 pilot officers who could be returned intact or in pieces, depending on the west's willingness to play ball on minor details such as overlooking war crimes.

For most of the winter we had been on half rations, each prisoner getting half a Red Cross parcel a week, but during January 1945 there was a substantial shipment and we were put back on full rations, which left us just hungry, rather than ravenous. In the chaos of a bombed-out Germany as the eastern winter began to bite, feeding and sheltering *Luftgangsters* was far from a high priority, and we clung to the hope of liberation as a source of inner warmth.

Each day we waited for news, but the front in the west had been bogged down by German counter-offensives and our premature optimism that D-Day would be rapidly followed by capitulation had given way for many to caution and doubt following the Allied defeat at Arnhem in September 1944.

But if progress in the west was slow, the red tide was sweeping in from the east at a phenomenal rate and we knew that Stalag Luft III was right in the path of the Russian advance. We listened to the German broadcasts and did our best to sift the reality from the propaganda. If they mentioned specific place names where there was fighting, we rushed from the loudspeakers from which the authorities made their announcements to the map in the library hut where people jostled for position to try to plot our Allies' progress.

We continued to listen to the BBC each day. This being wartime, we also took some of the BBC's more optimistic announcements with a pinch of salt, but between them, Lord Haw-Haw and our own horse sense, we had a good idea that the end could not now be too far away.

The camp's rumour mill went into overdrive. Every

few days there were contradictory rumours, always expounded with the absolute certainty that the teller's rumour was infinitely superior to others', and 'a sure thing' rather than 'duff gen'. First we were going to be evacuated. Next we were all going to be shot. Then we were going to be evacuated again. Next we were going to be abandoned in the camp to wait for the Russians. Those of us who had been active escapees started to try to get a little bit fit, thinking that we might have to either break out or possibly even fight our way out. Members of the escape committee started to make plans. If the SS decided to try mowing us down, we would make an attempt to storm their compound, grab guns and at least take some of them with us. In every compound men trained, in case they were called on for some last desperate defence or breakout.

By January 1945 we could hear the Russian guns booming, getting louder each day. Marshal Konev's Soviet forces had broken through in a spearhead and were reportedly less than fifty miles from the camp. On 21 January a group of Russian T-34 tanks had burst through the German lines and crossed the River Oder just north of Breslau. Even though they were forced to retreat by a German counter-attack, we knew that it was now just a matter of time until the camp was overrun.

Further north, the Russian advance swept over my former prison home at Schubin in Poland and we guessed they had overrun Hydekrug too. We heard rumours that the American prisoners who had replaced us at Schubin had been liberated. Yet strangely, despite the excitement, camp life went on much as before. People studied their lines for plays. Others played cricket. The hundred and one courses in everything from mathematics to law continued, though perhaps without very many attentive students. But the normality was an illusion. Just outside the gates of the camp a human tide of refugees was sweeping eastwards. The nearby little town was bursting under the strain of five times its normal population. The stress was beginning to show on our guards, who wanted to know if they could get their own families out of the area, but they were told no more than us prisoners.

The truth was that the German command structure was already starting to disintegrate. Lines of communication were being cut. The High Command would make one decision and a general on the ground would make another. Hitler, increasingly isolated and volatile in his Berlin bunker, would issue some insane order that contradicted their plans. Sometimes such orders were obeyed, since those who disobeyed could expect a bullet in the head from some fanatical SS man who had already burned all his bridges and was simply taking as many fainthearts with him as possible. But more often they were quietly lost amid a mountain of paperwork, much of which was being shovelled into fires to stop it falling into the hands of the Allies.

We prepared as best we could for the possibility of evacuation. The camp started to resemble some vast, disorganized workshop. Some prisoners were building sleds on which to carry their provisions and possessions. Others concentrated on repairing threadbare clothing for a march that promised to be long and cold. I did not do as much as I should have. For many of the men this would be their first venture outside the wire, but for me it seemed more like the continuation of a non-stop journey that had lasted three years. I was already wearing most of the clothes I owned to keep out the cold, and had a stash of the Mixture left. I was ready to go.

Each day we waited for the Russians to arrive, but in the end it was more German troops who swarmed in. An emphatic order for us to remain in the camp was countermanded later the same day. We were then given an hour or so to collect our few possessions though the evacuation eventually dragged on all night. The plan was to herd us out onto the road in a forced march back into Germany, to keep us out of the hands of the Russians. I found out later that the order to keep the pilots of Stalag Luft III as hostages came directly from Adolf Hitler at his 4.30 p.m. staff meeting in his Berlin bunker on 27 January 1945.

By that evening, the compounds were still operating normally but with liberation so close we could almost taste it. In the neighbouring south compound, which housed most of the Americans, those who believed that the show must go on at all costs were soldiering through the second act of a comedy called 'You Can't Take it With You' when there was a surprise extra actor on the stage. The senior US officer, Colonel Goodrich, who I believe may have been the same man who had vaulted the wires to swap places with me briefly some months earlier, gave a short but memorable performance. He told the audience that they had half an hour to pack and prepare for a forced march.

The same message was going out in our own compounds. We put on as many layers of clothing as we could in the hope of keeping out the worst of the snow and cold. We looked slightly comical, our thin hands and feet sticking out of puffed-up bodies that consisted of ten layers of clothing in all shapes and colours but not much else. At the same time, every stove in the camp was going full blast. We could only take what we could carry and every scrap of food, carefully hoarded for weeks or even years, was now being wolfed down. Wonderful cooking smells wafted around the camp. It was an insane scene. Things that were precious, from tins of food to boxes of cigarettes, were suddenly left on tables for others to help themselves, as their owners, cheeks bulging like hamsters and pockets bursting like nomadic misers, could accommodate no more. The stores were raided and I saw a group of prisoners staggering off with what looked like half a cow.

As people started to realize that they would barely be able to stagger out the gates with their heavy packs, never mind march for what might be hundreds of miles in the snow, they started to abandon cherished possessions. Suddenly wood was more important than food. Bed boards that would once have formed the roof of a tunnel were now requisitioned to make sleds. Our entire value system was turned upside down. Beloved books were thrown away – some estimates say that more than a million books were abandoned in the camp complex. Ornaments lovingly, painstakingly carved and kept for years as planned souvenirs were abandoned.

The American compounds left first at one o'clock in the morning of Sunday 28 January 1945. Our compound did not leave until some time nearer four in the morning. At the gates every man was given more to carry – Red Cross parcels. These, which had been so rare and so precious, were suddenly devalued. Every man could have as much as he could carry, and yet there would still be huge amounts left over. I heard afterwards that when we left there were still 23,000 Red Cross parcels left in the store, along with 2,500,000 cigarettes.

On our way out of the gate we found ourselves treading on half-opened and abandoned Red Cross parcels, from which only the lightest items such as chocolate had been looted. Looking at the ground, covered in wasted food, I thought about all the debates about commodity trading, and the value of key items such as cigarettes and chocolate. Suddenly they were worth only the remaining space in a pocket, even though we might be starving within a few days. With the German guards prodding us on, we joined a line of marching prisoners from the other compounds and the new reality was that the only thing that mattered now was a good pair of boots and the ability to put one foot in front of the other. By the time the last man left the camp, the column stretched for twenty miles.

As we marched past the food store in the east compound on the way out we were close to where the sixty or so Russian prisoners were kept. There were Artum and his comrades, lining the wire and waving us farewell. They were being left for their countrymen to discover. For the course of the war they had suffered more hunger and humiliations than any of the other nationalities of prisoner, but they now knew that liberation by their own people was close. They were half-starved, and several of us bent down to pick up some of the countless full cans strewn on the ground from the abandoned Red Cross packets. I grabbed a tin of Klim milk and lobbed it into their compound. Others did likewise and soon it was raining food on the delighted Russians. Cheese, butter and bully beef poured from the sky as the overladen guards tried to shove us along and the only casualty was a Russian who took an accidental direct hit from a tin of ham. Artum was a brave man, and as usual he was smiling. I never saw him again.

The abandoned cans and parcels were pounced upon by the ration-starved German civilian women who had worked in the camp, many of them censoring letters. They bent like gleaners in the fields, gathering what they could to feed their families, and then hurried back to their cellars, to wait with dread for the arrival of the Russians.

The column started by heading west, back into Germany and away from the advancing Russians. In the coming days we travelled west, south and north, with little apparent logic – any way but east. As we marched off to an uncertain destination and an even more uncertain fate, there was one bright spot on the bleak white horizon: all of the compounds were emptied out into one vast exodus, a giant, struggling, straggling mass of humanity, ten thousand in all.

On the first night my fellow travellers and I were almost dropping from exhaustion as we arrived in some small village, which I think might have been Friedwaldau, west of Sagan. We hoped for shelter in school halls or barns, but the village headman turned out to be a Nazi who did not seem to have noticed that the war was nearly over. He snarled and ranted at us, outraged at the thought of his village being contaminated by these *Luftgangsters*, and did his best to be unhelpful to us and to the guards who were trying to negotiate us a place to sleep. As they argued, the Russian guns rumbled like thunder in the background, as if attempting to remind everyone of the impending reality for the Third Reich. We stood for hours in the snow and some prisoners as well as a few of the guards started to develop frostbite in their feet, hands and faces – a problem that would get worse over the coming days.

Eventually, some people found billets in the village, while others of us were marched another few miles down the road to a hamlet, where we were crammed into a huge barn, too exhausted to do anything but find a few feet of ground between the bodies of our comrades on which to collapse and sleep.

The next morning as the sun thawed our bones and we wiped the grimy straw off our clothes, the guards attempted to make a count of the prisoners. Eventually they gave up and we just pulled out to continue to march to another small town, where we halted and haggled for food. As the journey wore on, it became clear that the German High Command, insofar as it still existed, had not made any plans to feed or house us. The supplies we had been able to carry dwindled and we grew more hungry and thirsty as the day wore on. All the marching in the snow took its toll and my mind started to wander back to that mountain of Red Cross food we had been forced to leave behind. At least we still had the more portable supplies such as chocolate and cigarettes and we started to barter with the villagers and farmers we passed. We cursed the fact that we had left so much coffee behind from the Canadian and American Red Cross parcels, as it was more valuable for trading even than cigarettes.

The mixing up of all the compounds on the march gave me the chance to be reunited for the first time in over a year with my old comrades from the other British compound. Soon, I found myself marching along beside Paddy Barthropp. It was wonderful to see him again and just like old times. The long line of troops made quite a spectacle – thin men looking fat because of a dozen layers of ragged clothing, bumping into old friends as we lurched along in almost a foot of snow that turned to icy mud with the churning of thousands of marching feet.

But the companionship of old friends could not keep

out the cold as we marched for hours, then days in the ice. The guards had been given orders to shoot anyone who got out of line, and at the back of the column was a line of vicious, snarling guard dogs ready to fall on anyone who lagged behind. Some of the guards were so dejected that they ignored any infractions as long as their officers were not looking. One elderly guard, plodding along miserably, was screamed at by an officer who discovered he was letting a prisoner carry his rifle because his shoulder hurt. Demoralized guards, numb prisoners and exhausted refugees all headed south and west, like debris floating on an incoming tide.

By the end of the war, even the dogs were confused. One small group of prisoners had fallen out because they had to repack their makeshift sled after the linen strips of bed sheet they were using in lieu of rope gave way. They were repacking their Red Cross food and trying to eat some of it rather than abandon it when one of the more vicious guards stormed up with two Alsatian guard dogs straining at the leash. He yelled at the prisoners to get going, but they continued to take their time, munching and packing, as if they were having a bizarre picnic at the edge of hell. The guard decided to unleash the hounds and, roaring a command for the dogs to do their worst, he set them on the prisoners. Despite their years of training, the dogs trotted up to the prisoners wagging their tails and begging for some food. They were rewarded for their disloyalty with corned beef and chocolate and settled in for a feast while their handler roared, yelled and hopped up and down to no avail. I like to think that maybe they were some of the guard dogs I had tried to bribe with a few handfuls of the Mixture over my years in the camps.

The entire march was broken up into numerous columns and the experiences of each one were quite different, depending on the nature of the guards in the immediate vicinity and what happened to them along the way. The Americans at the front of the column had been force marched for thirty miles on the first day, to make room for those coming along behind. The rest of us travelled shorter distances, but over more days, which gradually wore us down. Sometimes the snow stopped, and at others it whipped itself into a blizzard. Once I stopped to share a drink from a canteen with Paddy, and as I poured the water into a cup with a shivering hand, it froze solid before we had the chance to drink it. When the guards, laden down by full packs, became as exhausted as we were, an order was given to halt.

By now, every prisoner was wearing virtually every stitch of clothing he owned, and any semblance of an army had been replaced by an endless procession of people dressed in outlandish combinations of army, navy, air force and civilian gear from head to foot.

When our water ran out and the thirst got too much, we melted some snow to drink and tried to keep our spirits up in the bitter cold by telling bad jokes. At various times both Paddy and I were on our last legs from exhaustion and when one dropped in the snow, the other one would dissuade him from going to sleep. An icy slumber seemed to be an excellent idea, but would have meant never waking up again.

As we struggled westwards the column merged and separated with all the displaced humanity of the war. Proud Germans stood beside their houses looking at the elderly men and moon-faced boys who were all that seemed to be left of the Third Reich. Some cursed at us, but most just stared in amazement that it had come to this, or in terror at what would follow us from the east.

Yet ten minutes later we would be forced off the road by columns of trucks moving east, the way we had come. They were full of tough, experienced-looking soldiers heading for the front. In some places the SS were trying to prop up the crumbling morale of the people with die-hard Nazi zeal. They still had the power to threaten or intimidate the locals away from our column. Local children playing in the snow soon found out they could swap their sleds for more chocolate than they had ever seen, while their parents tried to barter basic foodstuffs for our more exotic fare.

At first the guards tried to stop us, but as the cold got to them they just ignored the transactions, only shooing us along if we stopped to haggle for too long and started to fall behind. They also got very zealous whenever a senior German officer was around. On one occasion a farmer, standing by the roadside watching the endless cavalcade of ragged humanity passing by, was attempting to negotiate with me over the swap of a circular loaf of bread for about forty cigarettes. Just as we were nearing agreement after a protracted haggle, a German officer strutted past and a guard who had been stumbling along dejectedly rushed over and shooed the farmer away. I was just starting to think of a few choice names to call him when he waited for the officer to disappear ahead and then he ran back, found the farmer and brought him back to me to complete the transaction. He accepted a hunk of bread for his role as middleman – a tiny gesture proving that the world we had all known was crumbling around us.

As a new economy developed, the camp currencies of cigarettes and chocolate started coming into their own once again. Prisoners grumbled if they were too far back in the column that those further ahead were offering too many cigarettes for a loaf and so were 'spoiling the market'. But not everyone was interested in buying and selling. One German couple fed a great huddle of us some thin, hot soup and would not take anything in return. Eventually the wife agreed to take some bars of soap, another of the simple everyday objects that takes on a real value in times of war. At that point a Prussian officer, who had not been able to get his head around the fact that all was lost, came up and shouted at the couple, pushing the prisoners onward on the march. The old man cowered but his wife stood up to the officer, saying that her son was a prisoner in England, and he had said in his letters that he was well treated, so she would do the same for us whether the officer liked it or not.

I remembered the letter my own mother had sent with

the same sentiments earlier in the war, and I was glad that even at this late hour, some feelings of humanity were creeping back into the open in Germany. A few years earlier such defiance might have cost the old lady her life, but now the officer just spluttered and kicked over the nearly empty soup bucket into the snow, where the contents melted the ice and formed a sad little puddle, like a miniature sea of humanity in a vast, frozen world. The officer shouted abuse at the couple, at us prisoners and then stormed off to find someone less difficult to bully.

By that evening many prisoners and some of the guards were suffering from severe frostbite and could not go on. Some were left with locals to await assistance from whoever came along next, but others were in too bad a way to wait. One German guard was close to death from frostbite and gangrene. His only hope was to have his foot amputated. This operation was done with no proper instruments or anaesthetic by a prisoner called Digby Young, who had to rely on some medical training as a student before the war. All he had to work with was some alcohol and a few kitchen knives. It was a terrible thing but he managed to save the man's life.

Days and nights merged into a nightmare of frozen travel, in which we huddled, bartered, shivered and stumbled ever on. At times on the march it fell to minus ten and we sought what little shelter we could find along the way. Staggering with exhaustion, we reached a little town called Muskau. Although the temperatures made it seem more like Moscow, Muskau felt like an oasis. It was normally a picturesque little town, wrapped around a stately home belonging to the Arnhim family, one of whom had been a German general in North Africa. The locals were old-fashioned and had never been overly keen on Hitler, so they treated us relatively well. Some of the luckier prisoners were put up in the stables of the stately home where they had hot and cold running water and as much hay as they could eat. Previously the stables had been one of Europe's best stud farms and it seems that the horses had had a better time over the last few years than we had.

Soon we were on the march again and the weather seemed more bitter than ever as we marched straight into the teeth of a biting wind, heads bent, backs arched, pulling sleds or helping those too sick to go on alone. Paddy and I staggered along, talking nonsense when we had the energy, to keep us from slipping into icy oblivion. As we walked, the temperature dropped below zero again and the snow swirled around us once more.

I tried to concentrate on what Paddy was saying as he stumbled along beside me. He was outlining his latest plan to escape from the column. As far as I could tell over the noise of our chattering teeth, his plan was simple and elegant. 'We just keep walking along as we are now,' he confided. I leant in to catch his words. 'Then, when we have lulled them into a false sense of security, all of a sudden and without any warning, we die on them.' I agreed with him that this was one foolproof way to escape from the people who had held us prisoner for so long, but suggested we might save the last part of the plan for a little later.

Paddy and I ended up with dozens of others huddled in a vast glass and brick factory. The place used French slave labour but by the time we arrived in the evening it was deserted. Luckily, the furnaces had to be kept at white heat all the time and we went into the vast central hall of the works with as much delight as if we were tourists in a cathedral. I put my sodden prison-issue boots next to a furnace to dry out, and we huddled around the ovens, basking in the warmth.

Just as I was nodding off, a rumour circulated that there was food to be had. We dragged ourselves up, while leaving a few comrades to guard our precious place by the boiler. The French prisoners and some of the local women had started a soup kitchen, working with infinite patience to fill a thousand tin cups and billy cans held in our outstretched hands. Teeth chattered and frostbitten fingers curled around cups as we tasted the first warmth in what felt like a lifetime. Back by the boilers there was more cooking going on, with every kind of Red Cross tin being arranged around the furnaces, warming nicely. As I fell asleep, I hoped we might be able to stay here for ever, or at least until the Russians arrived.

In a corner office, some of the radio operators who had kept us informed through their secret receivers in the camp were setting up shop. They had lovingly carried their home-made contraptions with them and they strung up a wire aerial, then hunched over with their headphones and listened to the BBC telling us that the war was almost over. There was little concrete news, and the truth was that few people, whether Russian or German, prisoner or civilian, had very much idea what was happening, other than the unavoidable observation that Germany was getting smaller by the day. As my comrades discussed the latest news and rumours, I fell into a deep sleep, warm for the first time in days.

When I woke, stiff but snug, the factory was a seething mass of activity. We were pulling out, and I hurried to get ready. When I went to put my nice warm boots on, I found that they had been a bit too close to the oven and were cooked to perfection. As I pulled them on, the soles came away from the crumbling tops. I wrapped what was left of them in rags and when the order came to march on I continued forward like a shambling wild man as the cold seeped in through the cloth to my feet and threatened frostbite.

But the weather seemed to have broken. Sleet was replaced by rain and the wind was a little less biting than it had been in the days before. While we were grateful not to be frozen to death, we started worrying about drowning in mud. The hundreds of wooden sleds which had saved our lives by allowing us to carry enough supplies to survive were now almost useless, bumping along on the mud and rocks. Just as we were leaving, some of the men had managed to persuade the French factory prisoners to operate one of the giant lathes in the glass factory and a helpful engineer turned out several pairs of little wooden wheels, turning some of our sleds into wagons.

For another two days we staggered on, heading west and north further into the dying heart of Germany, with only the food and water we carried or what we could get by bartering. At one point an Allied plane swooped low over another part of the endless column and some men dived to either side of the road, fearing we would be strafed. A few trigger-happy guards thought it was a mass breakout and started firing. Several wounded men, so close to freedom, was the result.

As we trudged along we sometimes passed other groups of prisoners being marched for no apparent reason in the opposite direction. When we passed a column of Russian prisoners we saw how comparatively well off we were. They were all skeleton-thin, their brave, sunken eyes burning out of skull-like faces covered in full, ragged beards. Their fanatical SS guards treated them like animals, herding them along with whips and rifle butts.

We could do very little, but one of us threw over some cigarettes. Then somebody else threw some chocolate. Soon there was a small, silent bombardment going on. The Russians smiled and clutched at this act as much for its humanity as for the much-needed food. One pack of cigarettes fell short and a Russian prisoner reached out for it. As he did so, one of the SS guards lifted his rifle and smashed it into him. When the man fell under the blow the SS man screamed at him and continued to smash him in the face and kick him like a dog. A collective roar went up from our side of the road and several hundred Allied prisoners stopped and moved a few dangerous inches towards the Russian column.

The SS man turned around and looked astonished, as if it had never occurred to him that anyone might object to his actions. Other SS guards fingered their weapons nervously, not knowing whether to turn their backs on the Russians or on us. It was a very dangerous moment. Some of our guards, seeing what had happened, ran over to the SS guard and shoved him on. His grateful colleagues were glad to move on rather than face a riot in which they might have killed a lot of us but we would have ensured that a few of them were torn to pieces along the way. The battered Russian managed to get back in line, and even managed a smile through the blood as he picked up the packet of cigarettes. The Russians knew that the Red Army was coming and they would neither forgive nor forget.

When our column reached the town of Spremberg, we huddled in the railway yards and were eventually loaded into cattle cars, much as so many innocent Jewish people were sent to their doom. At the time, we had no idea of our destination and wondered if we were moving closer to safety or closer to a bullet in the last act of Hitler's demented rule. Possibly the worst thing about the march was not the cold, nor the sickness, nor the thirst, but the simple lack of a destination. Rumours that we were to be shot rippled up and down the lines every day and when we saw the empty cattle cars waiting to take us to destinations unknown there were few of us who did not wonder if it would be our last journey.

The cattle cars were so crowded that it was impossible to sit down, and those who managed it, or fell down, found that the floors were covered in cattle dung. Many of the men were throwing up, suffering from a dozen different illnesses. Even before the train pulled out, conditions were almost unbearable. By the time we had been rolling along for the best part of a day, it was like being in hell.

We were starting to suffocate and were desperate for a drink of water. The guards refused to stop and eventually after we had shared what little water we had, we looked for another solution. Some bright spark noticed that we were sharing our journey with one of the padres. We suggested that it was time to liberate his bottle of holy water. At first he was not very keen on the idea, but when it became apparent that not only was it the right thing to do but that if he didn't he was probably going to be a good candidate for instant martyrdom, he reluctantly agreed. We passed the water and got a sip each. Later, some other smart thinker thought to drain one of the steam engine cisterns, so we got another mouthful of muddy warm water to keep us going.

The cattle cars rolled on and stopped somewhere between Bremen and Hamburg. By now, with a worsening case of jaundice and having spent so much time in punishment cells over the previous three years – maybe six months if you added it all up – I was close to dropping. A medic took one look at me and ordered me to remain, along with other prisoners who were too sick to travel. Most were in an even worse state than I was, some suffering from frostbite, others with dysentery.

I bade a quick farewell to Paddy and my other mates. It was a war of unexpected reunions and sudden partings. Chance meetings, determined by which door you knocked on in a French village or which pilot was shoved into a cell beside you, had shaped my life. Perhaps I was lucky that the people I met were the bravest, funniest souls you could hope to have as friends. But maybe behind almost every door there lurks someone with the potential to be remarkable. I thought of all the hurried farewells – the smile and wink from Jimmy Buckley as he scooted out of that tunnel back in Schubin, never to be seen again; the simple goodnight I had said to Josef and Giselle in a Paris apartment hours before the Gestapo had burst in and taken us in opposite directions for ever. These and a hundred other farewells crowded my increasingly ill brain, but as usual I and my friends just laughed, and arranged to meet up in some warm London pub, not too far from Piccadilly, some day.

A minute later they were all gone, continuing the gruelling journey that lasted thirty-six hours on that hell-train to a *Marlag* or navy prison camp farther north, where the conditions were even worse in terms of overcrowding and starvation. Paddy and many of my other friends were liberated near the end of the war, and in true Paddy style he travelled home part of the way in a stolen fire engine. He is still my friend and comrade, sixty years later.

Incredible as it may seem, those of us coming from Stalag Luft III had it easier than the men from some of the other eastern camps such as Schubin, Hydekrug and Stalag Luft II, all of which were being similarly evacuated away from the advancing Russians. They were marched in ragged columns like ours for up to six weeks, east and west, first one way and then doubling back in the opposite direction as the front lines twisted and turned in the death throes of Hitler's war. Many had even less warning of their departure than we did and had little rest, food or water along the way. Day after day, their guards tried to avoid capture first by the Russians, then by the Americans. My old sergeant friends from Hydekrug had a terrible time, marched more than a hundred miles to no-one knew where for weeks, but they were fortunate to be still under the leadership of that quiet tough man Jimmy 'Dixie' Deans.

Dixie had managed to purloin a bicycle and rode up and down the lines, negotiating with the guards and helping his men, who were strung out in different columns. He was ever-present, organizing barns in which to sleep, getting medical attention for the sick and helping his men to avoid the SS detachments which were then roaming the country looking for anyone, Allied or German, whom they could find an excuse to shoot. On one occasion, cycling in full British uniform, he was caught alone between two columns of his men. An angry German officer wanted to shoot him on the spot, but Dixie just told him off in his excellent German and cycled off, hoping he would not get a bullet in the back of the head.

But there were some things even Dixie could do nothing about. One day, from out of the white winter sky, four RAF Typhoons mistook the ragged columns of prisoners for retreating German soldiers. So-called 'friendly fire', possibly the biggest euphemism ever coined, was a problem in this war just as much as in more recent ones. As the planes fired rockets and strafed the column, bullets chewed up the ground and men dived for cover but thirty were killed, just weeks from liberation.

Dixie then did something truly remarkable. He went to the German commander and asked for permission to cross through the battle lines to tell the Allies that the marching columns were prisoners from their own side, not enemy soldiers. The German officers by now knew that, sergeant or not, he was a remarkable leader and they agreed, either out of honour or to preserve themselves in the trials that they knew would take place after the war.

So Dixie made the incredibly dangerous journey through the German defences and then through the Allied battle lines, where bullets whizzed over his tattered white flag. He debriefed a senior British commander to ensure that his men would not be attacked again. The commander was a bit bemused at a mere sergeant being in such a senior position and even more amazed when

Dixie refused to be evacuated back to Britain. Instead he retraced his dangerous journey across the battle front to rejoin his men. He may have been 'only' a sergeant, but in the eyes of any of us who knew him, James 'Dixie' Deans was a five-star general.

Back in my own particular road to ruin, now far to the west from our starting point, I was taken with the other sick prisoners to an encampment somewhere outside Bremen. It was a crude hospital camp with no facilities, teeming with men suffering from dysentery, gangrene, malnutrition, frostbite or, like me, from jaundice. That ailment by this stage pretty neatly summed up my feelings about the Third Reich as it went through its long overdue demise. As the days turned into weeks and still the war dragged on, I just hoped that my own end would not coincide with that of the Reich.

I felt so sick that I could barely move as I lay in an overcrowded compound dotted with tents, waiting to be liberated and thoroughly disgusted with myself for not escaping under my own steam. All the efforts, all the adventures had come to this – a bone-thin creature lying in a sick bed waiting to be shot or saved. I felt one last burst of outrage burn up inside me, like the last flaring and flickering of a candle before it goes out. Then I heard the rumble of mechanized infantry and self-propelled guns. I got a new lease of life and stood up, wobbly on my feet, to greet the Allies. At least I was alive. At least . . .

But it wasn't the Allies. Row upon row of white-clad German soldiers from a crack mountain division poured into the camp and started setting up their self-propelled guns. Behind them, some well-camouflaged Tiger tanks rumbled into the compound and were strategically placed. These were tough troops who had been through five years of victory and defeats, and they were digging in for one last stand on their home turf.

Their commanding officer had chosen the camp with some idea that the Allies would not shell their own prisoners, but as the first shells from the advancing British forces whistled in from the west, both I and the German soldiers knew that this battlefield was not going to be safe for any of us. The alpine troops put up a fierce resistance with small arms fire, as the boom of their self-propelled guns was joined by the roar of the cannon on the Tiger tanks.

Rockets screamed over our heads, shells burst around us and shrapnel showered down like rain. I did not feel particularly afraid, but my body seemed to disagree: my knees began to shake so violently that I had trouble staying standing. Then there was a cry for help. The shelling at the top of the camp had become so intense that we either had to watch those in the camp hospital die in a hail of shells and ragged shrapnel or else evacuate them to somewhere less immediately dangerous. All of a sudden my legs decided they were working again. All they needed was something to do. I and some other prisoners who were still well enough to walk started to evacuate the sick bay. Those too ill to walk we carried on our thin backs to a less dangerous corner of the camp.

If anything, the shell fire, both incoming and outgoing, intensified. These battle-hardened German soldiers had nowhere left to run and they were making a real fight of it. Like the English during the Battle of Britain, these men were fighting for their home soil and the rights and wrongs of the war were forgotten in one last fierce, senseless battle.

I knew that the hundreds of sick prisoners were continuing to get the worst of it, unable to move to safety, and I thought here at last was something I could do to make myself useful in the war. I would stage one last escape and try to reach the Allied troops. I drew a mental map of the locations of the prisoners, the enemy guns and the concealed Tiger tanks, and then I slipped out of the compound and across the desolation of the battlefield.

I should not make out that my motives were altogether heroic. I wanted to help my fellow prisoners, and as always found myself on the side of the underdog, attempting to protect those who were unable to protect themselves. But I also had simpler, more human motives. One was pride – I had come into this war on my own terms and I was going to leave it that way. I would rather risk a bullet in the back than cower under a hail of shells, wondering if the next incoming round would finish me off or liberate me. Lastly, I still had the old ticking clock, deep within me, that simply saw the chance for one last escape. It would not be a Great Escape, like that of my fifty friends and comrades who died on that magnificent breakout less than a year earlier and who were now at rest under the cold clay, but it would be a great escape for me. After a wartime of escaping and being recaptured, this time I was going all the way. This time for better or worse, life or death, would be my last escape: my home run.

As I dived and dodged through the wire, then through craters and around perimeter defences, with tracer fire zipping around and the air thick with shrapnel, I had that old feeling again. I was eight years old, back in Texas, off and running with ten cents in my pocket and a world to explore.

The chaos of the battle seemed to fade, and in my mind I was running through the green fields of France, looking for and finding a friendly face to hide me. Next I was struggling through the mud of Poland; then I was swimming the black, deep rivers of Lithuania. And finally I was back at the edge of a field in western Germany with the battle raging behind me. I dived through a hedge and found myself on a small road. I ran down it, running as if half the guard dogs in Germany were snapping at my heels. Or maybe it was just Danny, my beloved Alsatian in Texas, running beside a fiddle-footed five-year-old to make sure he did not fall down.

Ahead of me I could see a tank and some raised guns. I slowed down, but I kept moving forward. Rifles clicked at the ready. 'Don't shoot!' someone shouted. 'He's British!'

I replied, 'Actually I'm American. And Canadian. And British. It's a long story.'

But the story would have to wait. I passed on the position of the enemy tanks and guns, and my new acquaintances, the Guards Armoured Division, were able to direct their fire at the key enemy positions and away from the prisoners as best they could. After another intense exchange of fire the Allied armour advanced and the white-clad warriors finally threw down their weapons and surrendered.

My new friends in the Guards made a great fuss of their unexpected American catch, getting me to a medic while attempting to ply me with cigarettes, chocolate and field rations. One week later I was on a plane from Luneberg Heath, soon to be the scene of Germany's formal surrender, heading back to an airfield near London, and from there to a hotel on the south coast where a man could eat his fill and still know where his next meal was coming from.

Victory in Europe, VE Day, was approaching. I had entered the war on my own, crossing over from the Depression and the Hungry Man diner in Detroit on a bridge that led to a lot more than Canada. I was ending the journey in the company of strangers, several thousand miles from home, yet I felt this was where I belonged.

Europe lay in ruins. Under the rubble, or at peace in country churchyards, lay about twenty men and women whom I was lucky enough to call friends. Their faces tumbled over each other in my mind, from the young recruit unable to escape his blazing Spitfire, to Victor Beamish, winking as he set off on yet another sortie over the sea; from brave French men and women whom I loved but whose names I never even knew, to men such as Jimmy Buckley, George Grimson and Roger Bushell, quietly determined as they emerged from the darkness of yet another tunnel. All gone, along with sixty million other people who had families, hopes and dreams like the rest of us. Too many names and too many faces, heaped up in a mental monument to the waste of war, but also to courage and shared humanity.

Yet I was back in England and on solid ground – the same ground I had flown over and fought for just a few years and what felt like a lifetime earlier. From up there in the cockpit of a Spitfire with the sun at my back, the land below had all looked peaceful, permanent and still, whether the timeless curves of the River Thames, the medieval spires of Lincoln Cathedral or the ancient monolithic circles at Stonehenge. It was a rich prize, and worth fighting for, but the real prize had been the people, an entire generation from all parts of the globe who had taken quiet, personal decisions that had shaped their future and sometimes cost their lives. Together they had decided that the world deserves better than fear, stupidity and greed. People can soar as well as any Spitfire.

William Ash
London, 2005

Postscript

One of the best things about the publication of the hardback edition of *Under The Wire*, apart from all the great free food at the book launches which almost made up for my days on bread and water in the Cooler, was that research during and after the book appeared produced new answers to old questions and a few great surprises.

When I was shot down over the Pas de Calais in Spring 1942, I had little time to think about the man attempting to fill my beloved Spitfire with holes. I had been too busy trying to do the same to him and his colleagues. Aerial Dogfights are fast, messy encounters at the best of times, with planes diving and dodging, one minute getting off a short burst in the general direction of a foe, the next minute diving for your life to escape another enemy on your tail. In such circumstances no-one blows a half-time whistle and makes a note of the score, so it is very difficult to tell who shot down whom. Add to that the fact that some of the combat reports on the German side went up in smoke and that even back in Britain most of us were too busy thinking about living and having fun before the next life-threatening encounter to bother too much about filling in forms, so it is easy to see why putting a face to a passing enemy pilot is not easy.

Despite that, combat records on both sides did survive and the most likely candidate for the man who ended my spell in the sky and inadvertently started my new career as an escapologist has emerged as Luftwaffe Major 'Gerd' Schöpfel.

Gerhard Schöpfel was born in a little town called Erfurt, about half way between Frankfurt and Berlin. He was a policeman who transferred to the Luftwaffe in 1936, posted to JG 26, a unit that would later be described as the top guns of the German air force. He saw a lot of action in the early days of the war, shooting down his first Hurricane in 1940 during the Battle of France and shooting down four Hurricanes in one day during the Battle of Britain. By the end of 1940 he had shot down 20 of our planes and been awarded the Knight's Cross. One year later he was appointed leader of JG 26 when the previous commander, Germany's most celebrated World War II fighter pilot Adolf Galland, was promoted to General.

By the time Gerd and his colleagues were taking pot-shots at my stricken Spitfire above the Pas de Calais at the end of March 1942, he had chalked up 36 aerial victories and as I tried my best not to demolish the church in Vielle

Eglise, I became number 37. His unit was the first to be equipped with the then new Focke-Wulf 190s, a process which was apparently completed in the last week of March 1942, just in time for me to join in the celebrations. As I scrambled out of the wreckage, one of the FW 190s zoomed down to see if I had survived. I hid in some under-growth near the smoking ruins of my Spitfire. Perhaps it was Schöpfel, taking a closer look, since his combat report for the day read: *17:00, Pas de Calais, Spitfire of 411 Squadron*. I suppose if you have to be shot down, at least it might as well be by someone who is rather good at it.

Schöpfel's own luck ran out in August 1944, when, after reaching a tally of 45 victories and 700 sorties, he was shot down over Germany and baled out wounded. He ended up in ever-more senior non-flying posts in charge of ever-decreasing numbers of functioning aircraft and pilots as the Luftwaffe and the Third Reich crumbled. He then had to follow in my footsteps and spent nearly five years as a prisoner of war, in his case in the Soviet Union.

After his release around 1950 he became a chauffeur, though ferrying fat-cats around the streets of post-war Germany must have seemed rather dull to such a fine pilot, and he eventually returned to aviation as a sales executive. He lived to a ripe old age and I'm very sorry I never got to meet him under slightly less hostile circumstances.

While I did not dwell at the time on who I had faced in the air above Vielle Eglise, I have always been interested to find out more about the remarkable French men and women who risked their lives to help me.

The fragmented nature of the underground railroad that spirited airmen out of France and the high casualty rates caused by its infiltration by spies and betrayals by either petty criminals or by brave participants tortured beyond endurance, make it difficult to say who did what with any degree of certainty. Until now, I have never managed to find out the true identity of the man who collected me from my hiding place in the Pas de Calais and brought me safely by train to Lille, then through the streets of occupied Paris to another safe house. I only ever knew him as Monsieur Jean, and for obvious reasons we tried to find out as little as possible about each other. As it turned out, my lack of knowledge was a great advantage when being beaten by the Gestapo.

A flurry of helpful research after the publication of the hardback edition of this book brought to light a new name as the most likely candidate for the man who risked his life to help save mine – Jean de La Olla.

What became known as the Pat O'Leary Line was a chain of operatives and safe houses stretching from northern France where I was shot down, all the way south to Spain, with allied airmen moved from house to house until they could be guided across the Pyrenees and eventually back to England.

By the time I was shot down in March 1942, the escape network in the north of France was in chaos, caused by the betrayals of a double agent called Sergeant Harold Cole. Cole was a petty criminal and deserter who had conned his way into a key position in the resistance before betraying dozens of allied agents and airmen into the hands of the Gestapo. Cole, once dubbed 'the worst traitor of the war' by Scotland Yard worked for the British, then the Germans, then the American intelligence services, in reality only ever working for himself until his past caught up with him in a gun fight above a Paris bar in 1946 that ended with him shot dead by a French detective.

In the aftermath of the 1942 betrayal by Cole, the leading agent code-named Pat O'Leary sent Jean de La Olla north to rebuild the escape line from a base in Lille. The chaos following Cole's treachery meant that I remained in hiding in Quercamps for several weeks until Monsieur Jean came to collect me. He brought me first to Lille, then Paris, dropping me at the door of the couple I knew only as Josef and Giselle, in whose apartment I was eventually captured. Monsieur Jean did not even come in, but turned and hurried away. That was the last I ever saw of him. My efforts to trace him and the couple who were arrested sheltering me in Paris came to nothing in the chaos following the war.

Jean de La Olla continued his resistance work until he himself was betrayed in 1943. He was tortured in Fresnes prison by the Gestapo and sent to a series of concentration camps, but managed to survive the war. The Parisian couple who were arrested at the same time as me were even harder to trace, but there is an intriguing mention in a French memoir written by one of the leaders of the Pat O'Leary escape line that may provide a clue.

Louis Nouveau, who ran the line in Marseilles while

de La Olla worked in the north, describes in passing how an allied flyer was hidden in Paris around May 1942, sheltering with a man known as Miquet and his girl-friend. There was no opportunity to move the airman on and he remained there for many weeks before all three were captured after a raid on their apartment and taken to Gestapo headquarters.

Some months later Nouveau and de La Olla were also both captured and imprisoned in Fresnes. Nouveau recounts how the character known only as Miquet, despite being sentenced to death for sheltering the air-man, would call out to the other prisoners from a hole in the window of his condemned cell, encouraging them to resist and keeping their morale high. Jean de La Olla later confirmed to Nouveau that Miquet was saved from the firing squad when his girlfriend came forward to claim that she and she alone was guilty of sheltering the allied airman. Miquet's death sentence was commuted to imprisonment and his girlfriend was sent to Ravensbruck concentration camp, but both of them somehow survived the war. I have no way of knowing for sure if this was the couple that sheltered me, but the circumstances, their remarkable courage and their devotion to each other all seem to fit the bill. I owe them my life.

While all this was going on, I had been battered by the Gestapo, rescued by the Luftwaffe and sent to Stalag Luft III. Ever since I vaulted the wire between compounds in that camp for the first time in 1943, in order to buy my ticket to the NCO camp at Hydekrug in Lithuania, I have wondered what happened to the blurred shape, hurtling in the opposite direction over the wire to take my place. We passed each other and swapped identities in a matter of seconds as the guards in the machine gun posts dozed or watched a variety of side-show distractions we had cooked up. That was the last time I remember seeing Don Fair, though for the best part of a year he pretended to be me and I pretended to be him in various corners of the Third Reich.

My efforts after the war to find out what happened to the real Don Fair never resulted in contact. I heard that he had survived the war and returned to his native New Zealand. A bit of digging around the time of publication of the hardback of *Under the Wire* resulted in the news that Don Fair had settled in London after the war, had lived less than a mile from my home in West London, had married and had a family, as well as a very successful career as an economist.

Even before his wire-climbing swap with me in Luft III, Don Fair was already one of the fraternity of keen escapologists. The first camp he was in included French and British soldiers who were taken out on work parties. Don and two colleagues swapped places with three Frenchmen, then hid out in some woods before hitching a ride on a train they hoped would bring them to Spain. Instead they were marooned in train marshalling yards at Frankfurt. They managed to sneak out of the yard and made their way along quiet country lanes until captured by a truckload of German troops.

When Don ended up in Stalag Luft III, he was in the compound for NCO Sergeant pilots next door to mine, separated by two tall wire fences and assorted machine gun posts. Don had a friend called John who was in my compound and John helped to arrange the identity swap between myself and Don. I would get one step closer to escaping as the sergeants were shipped out to a new camp in Lithuania, while Don would get to be reunited with his friend John in the slightly more convivial surroundings of the Officer's compound, where he apparently spent an enjoyable six months as the new, improved William Franklin Ash with a temporary promotion.

Meanwhile, under my new identity as Don Fair, I was shipped out to Lithuania, helped to dig the tunnel from there and ended up back in the hands of the Gestapo after a fleeting tour of various eastern European swamps. When I admitted my own identity, since there seemed little benefit in hiding it, I was shipped off to Berlin for further investigation and trial. But back in Stalag Luft III the tidy German authorities now found they had one William Ash too many. The real Don Fair was duly shipped off to rejoin his NCO colleagues in Hydekrug with the promise of a month of solitary confinement in the Cooler waiting for him at his destination.

Luckily for Don, when he arrived at Hydekrug, the camp cooler was already booked solid like a popular theatre, thanks to the recapture of all my fellow tunnel escapees. Don was by all accounts a very friendly and sociable guy, so he was not much looking forward to a month of solitude, but luckily not everyone in the camp regarded isolation as a bad thing. Everyday camp life was noisy, crowded and often irritating as it was impossible to escape the close proximity of several hundred fellow inmates within close range at any moment of the day or night. Hank Hunter, a journalist before he was shot down, decided that he would use his time behind barbed wire to read the entire canon of British poetry, from ancient to modern. The only trouble was he could not hear himself think in the jostling atmosphere of everyday camp life. So, for the princely sum of ten cigarettes per day, he agreed to do a new identity swap with Don Fair. Don was apparently an excellent bridge player and had amassed a small fortune in cigarettes, enough to keep Hunter happy and himself out of the cooler for an entire month.

When a guard came some time later, hollering for Prisoner Fair and announcing it was 'Time for the Clink,' Hank Hunter, clutching a mighty pile of poetry books and a prodigious supply of cigarettes, was marched off for a very peaceful month in the cooler, while Don decided to pursue the excellent educational opportunities at that camp that I described earlier. He heard that there was an exam for the Institute of Bankers one afternoon and sat it to pass the time. Six months later he got word he had passed. By the time of D-Day in early summer of 1944 he progressed to the intermediate exam in Economics of the London School of Economics, but still had not heard if he had passed by the time the war ended and he was back in London. Undaunted, he sat the exam again in London before the first set of results rolled in and he became probably the only person to pass the exam in two successive years. He went on to have a distinguished career as an economist. Sadly, despite being a near neighbour in London for all those years, I only found out all this a few years after Don had passed away. Still, I was delighted to be joined at the launch of *Under The Wire* by his widow and his son, thus closing a circle that had had begun with a mad gallop across a warning wire into no man's land some sixty years earlier.

So, in a strange way, this book reunited me with three people who had helped to shape my life even though we barely met each other. Sometimes when I sit opposite some young person on the tube train in London and see them casting a furtive glance at the ancient character facing them, I wonder about such fleeting meetings and just how important a chance collision with a stranger can be. From the days when I sat as a small boy in the New Mexico sunshine listening to a man who had rode with Billy the Kid, to the present day when I was able to stand in the Imperial War Museum in London at the exit of an exact replica of one of our wartime tunnels as a small boy, born in the 21st century, tried my tunnel out for size. Maybe he will think back in another eighty or ninety years, after a lifetime of his own adventures, to the strange old guy who shook his hand as he emerged and congratulated him on his first escape.

Revisiting my own wartime wanderings made me think about just what united a group of young strangers in prison camps and beyond. We came from Britain, Canada, France, Australia, New Zealand, Czechoslovakia, Denmark, Poland, Russia and South Africa and a dozen countries besides. Yet the differences between us were celebrated – the cheek and determination of the Aussies, the deadpan understatement of the Brits and the sheer joy of life and fearlessness of those eastern Europeans fighting to free their homelands. Fighter pilots and bomber crews kidded each other about being 'bus drivers' or 'little friends' but we were always on the same side. British aristocrats and American hobos joined forces to soar in the sky or escape from deep underground.

In peacetime we only tend to see the differences, not realizing that what united us then is still there now, like a tunneler approaching the surface, waiting to pull down that first handful of earth that is topped with a tuft of grass; waiting for the first breath of cold night air that will bring us to freedom.

William Ash
London, 2006

Acknowledgements

Most of the events in this book took place between sixty and seventy years ago, so I hope readers will forgive Brendan and me if we have tried to capture the spirit of the time, rather than the letter of it.

While I retreat behind the splendid excuse of old age, which I've been using since I turned seven, Brendan, with only the flimsy pretext that he wasn't born at the time, has had the unenviable task of proving that some of the people I remembered really did exist, including me.

To everyone who helped us with recollections and photos, our sincere thanks, and apologies if the following list leaves anyone out. Special thanks to two good friends who shared some of these adventures and are still around – the ever-helpful Bill Stapleton and the irrepressible Paddy Barthropp. We also want to thank the Haley Memorial Library for the photo of outlaw George Coe;

George Frame and his grandson Chris for the picture of the good ship *Georgic*; John Asmussen for the photo of the *Scharnhorst*; the always generous Richard Smith for a photo of Wilfred Duncan Smith, who saved my life with good advice; Nicole Asselin in Canada for the picture of my Schubin tunnel partner, her flamboyant father Eddy; Charles Rollings and Penny Cooper for photos of the brave, elusive Jimmy Buckley who died on the Schubin escape along with Jørgen Thalbitzer whose life story was translated from Danish for us by Pernille Schulz; fellow Hydekrug inmates Alfred Jenner and Cal Younger for photos of James 'Dixie' Deans; Ron Richardson for the RCAF 411 Squadron photos; William Newmiller of the US Air Force Academy and the staff of the Imperial War Museum for pictures of the camps.

We were also blessed with wonderful editors – Simon Taylor at Transworld in London and Sean Desmond of St Martin's Press in New York, plus Robert Kirby at PFD and Jasper Smith of General Public Entertainment, who both helped to make it all happen.

On the home front, Brendan's thanks to Shelly and mine to Ranjana for their constant love, friendship and support.

William Ash MBE

Index

Berlin Gestapo and trial
300–5
march westwards to
freedom 340–67
Asselin, Edmund ('Eddy') 208–9,
217, 219, 222–3, 229–30, 255

Bader, Douglas 101, 151, 157–8,
160–2
Baltic Sea 297–8
bank work 38
Barber, Anthony 219
barrage balloons 53–4
barter on final march 352–3, 358
Barthropp, Paddy 58, 147–8,
152, 153, 160, 170, 225
account of first escape 232–4
celebrates D-Day landings
329
on final march westwards
349, 355–6
survives Great Escape 322
tunnel in Luft III 257
Battle of Britain 43, 52, 60
Beamish, Victor 59, 60, 73–5,
76–7, 82–3
Beaufort bombers 71, 73, 79–80
bed-boards in tunnels 215, 278
bedbugs 186
beer *see* alcohol, illicit
Berger, SS General 324
Berlin 270–1, 301–5
Beveridge Report 336, 337
Biggin Hill airfield 92
Bismarck battleship 79
blankets for civilian clothing 198
Blatchford, 'Cowboy' 105–7
blind spots in escape technique 30

Blitz *see* London, view during
Blitz
'Blond Beast' camp guard
202–3, 205, 244–5
boilers, hot-water 277, 283
Bomber Command 71–2
books in camp 259, 312, 333,
346
Boomer, Flight Lieutenant 102
Boulanger family (Pas de Calais
area) 118–25
Brest (France) 71–2, 78
Broadhurst, Harry 59, 325–6
Browning machine guns 47
Buckingham Palace Christmas
card 200–1
Buckley, Lieutenant-Commander
Jimmy 164, 170, 217, 219, 224
escape with Thalbitzer
238–44
Burden, Paul 42, 45, 47, 48
Bushell, Roger 239, 306,
317–18, 323
'Butcher Boy' camp guard 246

Cam, Pauline 113–15
camps, hobo 34–6
Catley, Jack 277
cattle truck train 359–61
Cernay, Otto 224, 238
Chamberlain, Gordie 104
Churchill, Sir Winston 78, 82,
240, 256, 335–6
Cilliax, Otto (German Fleet
Commander) 76, 81
Civil War, Spanish 36
claustrophobia 213
clogs 114, 186–7

INDEX

Picture Acknowledgements

Photographs for the picture section and the jacket have kindly been supplied by William Ash, except for the following:

First section
George Coe: Haley Memorial Library; Charles Lindbergh's parade, 1927: Yale University Library, Lindbergh Collection, image no 5719. The *Georgic*: courtesy George R. Frame; Stan Turner: courtesy 411 Squadron, Ron Richardson and Serge Holoduke. The dual-control Magister: courtesy 411 Squadron. The *Scharnhorst*: courtesy John Asmussen; Wilfred Duncan Smith: courtesy Richard C Smith.

Second section
Stalag Luft III guard post: McDermott Library, US Air Force Academy; typical escapers' tunnel: Imperial War Museum, London HU21234. Entrance to Schubin camp:

Imperial War Museum, London HU212022; Eddy Asselin: courtesy Nicole Asselin; John Dodge captured: Imperial War Museum, London HU1607; Lt. Cdr. James Buckley RN: courtesy the Buckley family and Penny Cooper; wire fencing at Stalag Luft III: McDermott Library, US Air Force Academy. Douglas Bader: Hulton Getty; Jimmy 'Dixie' Deans: courtesy Cal Younger; 'ferret' guards at Stalag Luft III: McDermott Library, US Air Force Academy; Sagan 'death march': McDermott Library, US Air Force Academy; Commandant Von Lindeiner: Imperial War Museum, London HU21063. Steve McQueen in *The Great Escape*: British Film Institute.

Every effort has been made to trace copyright holders and any who have not been contacted are invited to get in touch with the publishers.

ONE FOURTEENTH OF AN ELEPHANT
A memoir of life and death
on the Burma-Thailand Railway
Ian Denys Peek

In February 1942, following the fall of Singapore, Denys Peek was one among tens of thousands of British and Commonwealth soldiers taken prisoner by the Japanese. This extraordinary book is his account of the three years he spent as a POW, working on the infamous Burma-Thailand Railway. It stands as a haunting testimony to those who lived and died there – and a salutary reminder of man's potential for inhumanity to his fellow man . . .

'WRITTEN IN THE PRESENT TENSE, LIKE A LOOSE-LIMBED DIARY, HIS ACCOUNT OF WHAT HE SAW AND SUFFERED . . . IS TOUCHING, VIVID, ANGRY AND UTTERLY COMPELLING. IT IS ALSO EXCEPTIONALLY WELL WRITTEN'
Sunday Times

'WITH THE STEELY COURAGE HE DISPLAYED AS A CAPTIVE . . . HE TELLS HIS STORY WITH DELICATE OUTRAGE AND BONE-CHILLING HUMILITY. READERS ARE LEFT ONLY TO QUESTION THE PATH OUR WORLD TOOK TO ARRIVE AT SUCH BRUTALITY'
Good Book Guide

'PEEK DREW ME IN WITH HIS DETAIL, HIS LACK OF SENTIMENTALITY AND HIS DOWNBEAT ACCOUNT OF KINDNESS, COMRADESHIP, BRUTALITY AND COWARDICE'
Guardian

'HARROWING AND MOVING . . . A DEPTH OF INTENSITY WHICH HISTORICAL RECORDS CAN ONLY HINT AT'
Yorkshire Post

'A HORRIFYING AND EXTRAORDINARY BOOK'
Allan Massie, *Literary Review*

'ONE OF THE MOST COMPELLING ACCOUNTS OF LIFE ON THE BURMA-THAILAND RAILWAY . . . A VALUABLE RECORD'
Spectator

'POWERFUL, EVOCATIVE AND IMMEDIATE'
Soldier magazine

0 553 81657 8

BANTAM BOOKS

**WITNESS TO WAR: DIARIES OF THE
SECOND WORLD WAR IN EUROPE
Everyday accounts by the men, women
and children who lived through it
Richard J. Aldrich**

From the moments of unbearable tension as Europe waited for the
coming conflict in 1938 to its tragic dying embers in 1945, the Second
World War changed millions of peoples' lives. It was the greatest tidal
wave of destruction and displacement the world had ever seen.
For ordinary men and women, it was a cataclysm they could have
never before imagined. Here is their extraordinary collective testimony,
an alternative history of a world in motion.

Most of these diaries involved a degree of danger and secrecy.
In occupied Europe a captured diary could betray friends and relatives
to the enemy. Some were downright illegal, such as those kept by
soldiers on the front line. Here, rare material from figures such as
Joseph Goebbels, Jean-Paul Sartre, Evelyn Waugh and Noël Coward
has been unearthed along with the insights of those close to
Winston Churchill and Adolf Hitler.

Witness to War is the innermost thoughts of people from
every walk of life. Their daily terrors, their fears and feelings, scribbled
down and secreted away, are revealed for the first time. Previously
undiscovered diaries have been brought to light to reveal an eye-opening,
immediate and intimate glimpse of a different kind of war.

'STANDS HEAD AND SHOULDERS ABOVE ALL THE
OTHER [WWII] BOOKS FLOODING OUT TO MEET THE
60TH ANNIVERSARY. [ALDRICH] GIVES AN EXCELLENT
PICTURE OF A WORLD IN AGONY'
Spectator (Books of the Year)

0 552 15108 4

CORGI BOOKS